# RECENT READER TESTIMONIALS

"The new edition of the best-selling job-hunting book *What Color is Your Parachute?*, in addition to the tried-and-true advice for job seekers Dick Bolles has provided for close to 40 years, has new information on job-search productivity, job clubs, and how to organize and manage your job search. *What Color is Your Parachute?* is deservedly the world's most popular job hunting book with over 10 million copies sold in 26 languages.

This 2011 edition is as relevant today as when it was first published. Dick Bolles insightfully stays on the cutting edge of job-searching and the book is full of new and updated suggestions, along with the classic advice that continues to hold true today."
—Alison Doyle, About.com Guide

"I graduated college in 2008, wallowed hopelessly in career frustration and later received the best career advice of my life . . . which was to read your book *What Color Is Your Parachute?* Today, I am happily employed in [a] job that is the envy of my peers. I'm living proof of the power of your book and I recommend it to everyone I meet. It will eternally be the gift I give to recent graduates. Thank you for writing your book! I cannot begin to describe how much I have enjoyed it."
—Whitney Moore

"Anyone looking for career direction advice or solid information about how to find the job that's right for them should begin their search with Richard Bolles's classic book, *What Color Is Your Parachute?* It's been named one of the most influential books of all time for a reason—it has probably changed the course of more people's lives than almost any book except the Bible. Richard updates the book every year so it is always relevant."
—Eric Wentworth

"Dick Bolles is effectively the 'inventor' of career management as we know it today."
—Tom O'Neil

"If you go into the bookstore and find the section on jobs, careers or networking— the reason that section even exists is because of Dick Bolles. His book, *What Color Is Your Parachute?*, has helped many people find their true passion at work. Plus he is a great man."
—G.L. Hoffman, JobDig

"Dick Bolles is the last person on earth who needs my recommendation. Everyone knows his value to the world of career development. My recommendation/gratitude is for his friendship. He's a wonderful human being, joyful, resilient, and generous."
    —Ellen Jackson

"Dick Bolles is clever, and witty and has some superb ideas. . . ."
    —Karen Elizabeth Davies

"I want to recommend Dick for the hard work he has put in both as an author and as a coach. The amount of influence Mr. Bolles has had on the people in career transition, such as myself when the Dot-Com bubble burst, is immeasurable. . . . His sage wisdom has forever changed my life and I insist that all future employees read the parachute book."
    —Devin Hedge

"I just wanted to tell you how grateful I am to you and your book, *What Color Is Your Parachute?*. I graduated from a 4-year university in May, and I had no clue what I wanted to do, or how to look for a job. Like any kid, I thought I knew the best way to do things and that I didn't need anyone's advice, but after a few months of unemployment I realized that this wasn't true. My dad had given me a copy of your book, but after a few months of nothing, not even an interview, I really read it, did the exercises, and trusted in what you were saying. I didn't believe that I would find MY job, the perfect job for me. But I did, at a nonprofit that does cleft lip and palate surgery missions to China and Africa. This job has literally every single attribute that I listed, and I wouldn't have known what attributes I needed in a job unless I had done your exercises. I'm sure you get probably hundreds of emails a week saying the same thing, so I'll keep it short—I just wanted to say that I owe my happiness in my job to you and my dad. I recommend your book to EVERYONE, including strangers."
    —Heather Smith

"How can any of us in the career and employment industry not only recommend Dick, but . . . thank him (and the Good Lord) for single-handedly creating the industry we love and cherish? I know, for sure, I would not be where I am today if Dick and his parachute hadn't led the way. No, *What Color is Your Parachute?* is not the Bible. But it may be a distant second. :-) I know I speak for every single person who works in the career/employment industry when I say . . . 'THANK YOU, DICK' for all you've done. You are one of those very few people who truly are 'a legend in your own time.'"
    —Jay Block

# WHAT COLOR IS YOUR
# PARACHUTE?

"I DON'T HAVE A PARACHUTE OF ANY COLOR."

# WHAT COLOR IS YOUR PARACHUTE?

## 2012

### *40th Anniversary Edition*

## RICHARD N. BOLLES

**TEN SPEED PRESS**
**Berkeley**

This is an annual. That is to say, it is revised each year, often substantially, with the new edition appearing in the early fall. Counselors and others wishing to submit additions, corrections, or suggestions for the 2013 edition must submit them prior to February 1, 2012, using the form provided in the back of this book, or by e-mail (dickbolles40@gmail.com). Forms reaching us after that date will, unfortunately, have to wait for the 2014 edition.

**PUBLISHER'S NOTE**

This publication is designed to provide accurate and authoritative information in regard to the subject matter covered. It is sold with the understanding that the publisher is not engaged in rendering professional career services. If expert assistance is required, the service of the appropriate professional should be sought.

Copyright © 2012, 2011, 2010, 2009, 2008, 2007, 2006, 2005, 2004, 2003, 2002, 2001, 2000, 1999, 1998, 1997, 1996, 1995, 1994, 1993, 1992, 1991, 1990, 1989, 1988, 1987, 1986, 1985, 1984, 1983, 1982, 1981, 1980, 1979, 1978, 1977, 1976, 1975, 1972, 1970 by Richard Nelson Bolles.

All rights reserved.

Published in the United States by Ten Speed Press, an imprint of the Crown Publishing Group, a division of Random House, Inc., New York.
www.crownpublishing.com
www.tenspeed.com

Ten Speed Press and the Ten Speed Press colophon are registered trademarks of Random House, Inc.

Jacket people illustrations (upper left to lower right) copyright © Shutterstock.com/sculpies; iStockphoto.com/enjoynz; iStockphoto.com/4x6; iStockphoto.com/Illustrious.

Photo of Phil Wood by R. Philip Hanes, courtesy of Mrs. Charlotte Hanes.

The drawings on pages vi-vii, 37, 230, and 258–59 are by Steven M. Johnson, author of *What the World Needs Now.*

Illustration on page 72 by Beverly Anderson.

ISBN: 978-1-60774-010-0 (paper)
ISBN: 978-1-60774-011-7 (cloth)

ISSN: 8755-4658

Printed in the United States of America on recycled paper (20% PCW)

Front cover design by Patty Benson of Goodsite Web Solutions, Santa Cruz, CA
Back cover design by Colleen Cain

Interior design by Betsy Stromberg and Colleen Cain

10 9 8 7 6 5 4 3 2 1

Revised Edition

The wonderful actress
Anne Bancroft (1931–2005) was once
loosely quoted as saying
about her husband, Mel Brooks,
*My heart flutters whenever I hear his key*
*turning in the door, and I think to myself,*
*Oh goody, the party is about to begin.*

That is exactly how I feel
about my wife,
Marci Garcia Mendoza Bolles,
God's angel from the Philippines,
whom I fell deeply in love with, and married
on August 22, 2004.

What an enchanted marriage this is!

# The 2012
# Table of Contents

## III. ADVANCED JOB-*CREATION* TECHNIQUES

## IV. INVENTORY OF WHAT YOU HAVE TO OFFER THE WORLD

WHAT skills do you most enjoy using?

WHERE do you want to use those skills?

HOW do you find the name of that kind of job (or jobs)?

## V. EACH ONE TEACH ONE

## THE PINK PAGES

    BOOKS
    WORKSHOPS
    ONLINE COURSE

# Preface: The 40<sup>th</sup> Anniversary Edition of This Book

*June 13, 2011*

In the midst of these annual revisions, it's time to pause for a moment and celebrate. Forty years! Yes. For forty years, so far, I've been writing, updating, and revising this book, every year. Well, I did miss one year—1975. But otherwise, every year.

It's been more of a journal, than a book. A journal kept so far for forty years. New entries, new ideas, new events, every year. I often joke with people, when they ask how many books I've written over the years. The correct answer is ten. But, thinking only of *Parachute,* I say, "Forty—all with the same title, though different inside."

The basic core *has* stayed the same since the beginning: *Where do you go from here with your life?* The answer to that has always boiled down to answering just three questions, and they have remained the same these forty years: WHAT, WHERE, and HOW. (*WHAT* are your favorite transferable skills? *WHERE* would you most like to be able to use those skills? And *HOW* do you find the name or names of that job, and the places that have such jobs, and the people with the power to hire you?) But around that core have spun dozens of new developments, year after year, like planets in orbit around the sun.

A writer's dilemma is easily stated: how much is too much information? How much is too little? I think there is too much information floating around out there—particularly on the Internet—and if you try to include it all, the book turns into hundreds of pages. So my responsibility is to sift it down, and talk only about the most essential truths. But (a big "but") I think it is my responsibility to gather as much of the information as possible here on my desk, before I sift it down to what seem to me to be the essentials.

In other words, I define the writer's task to be that of a fisherman: cast a wide net, haul in a large catch, but then pick out only the best fish from all those taken in the net.

So, throughout the year, I cast my net. I accumulate vast files on all the stuff that has an effect on our jobs and our ability to feed ourselves and our families: the catastrophic triple disaster in Japan; the surging demonstrations by armies of unemployed youths and others, throughout the Middle East; the devastating earthquakes in Haiti, New Zealand, and elsewhere; the BP oil spill in the Gulf of Mexico; BRIC (the emerging economies of Brazil, Russia, India and China, and their ravishing appetites for energy and everything else); the stubborn unemployment rates all around the world; the soaring national debt of countries all around the world; the adoption of stringent budget cuts, all around the world; the crippling numbers of foreclosures on homes; the loss of equity in homes; the loss of jobs in particular industries; the credit crunch; the rising costs of gasoline; the rising food prices and shortages; pandemics; famous businesses going belly-up; diminishing pensions; longer working lives; free trade; outsourcing; the iPhone 4, the iPad 2, Android, Web 2.0, social media, Facebook, Twitter, blogs, texting, clouds, LinkedIn, LinkUp, Checkster, Workblast (video resumes), and omnibus search engines devoted exclusively to job openings, such as Indeed or SimplyHired; changing job-hunting techniques; soft skills; social networks; portfolios; behavioral interviews; counselors' associations; and individual job-hunters' stories. Plus, four times a year I do nothing but interact with job-hunters and career-changers, gathered in my home, for five days at a time. By such personal interaction, I stay very up-to-date on the current problems men and women are running into, out there in the World of Unemployment.

But then, having cast the widest net possible all year long, when it comes time to write my annual update of this book, I haul in my nets, sort out the fishes, and try to pick only the best. Now my job is not to know, or write about, too much. Now it is my job to write simply, and distill the mountains of information down to the basics. My job is to find the ideas that give the reader hope. For this is, in the end, a Book of Hope, masquerading as a job-finding manual.

Incidentally, I didn't get here, alone. I do not stay here, alone. I am not inspired, alone. I am not able to write, alone. So, I am filled with gratitude. First of all, I am enchanted by every moment of my life with such a wondrous woman as my wife, Marci. I am so grateful for her. My especial thanks to Marci for playing hostess to the Five-Day Workshops we conduct every three months, in our home in the San Francisco Bay Area. It is a rare woman who will let twenty-one strangers come be guests in her home for five days at a time, cooking breakfast and lunch for them all, while radiating grace and individual concern for each, throughout. *(For details, write to fivedayworkshop@aol.com.)*

I'm grateful for my only sister, Ann, who died on May 11th, this year. She was a dear. I shall miss her voice, and her wisdom.

I'm grateful for my four grown children and their families: Stephen, Mark, Gary, and Sharon, plus their most-loving mother, my former wife, Jan, who shares in all our family gatherings; and my former stepdaughter, Dr. Serena Brewer, whom I helped raise for twenty years, who now shares her natural-born compassion with the people of Butte, Montana. I'm grateful, too, for Marci's grown children, Janice and Adlai, with their families. I love them all dearly, dearly, dearly.

In addition, I want to express my gratitude to my dearest friend (*besides Marci*), Daniel Porot of Geneva, Switzerland—we taught together two weeks every summer, for nineteen years; then there is Dave Swanson, ditto; plus my international friends, Brian McIvor of Ireland; John Webb and Madeleine Leitner of Germany; Yves Lermusi, of Checkster fame, who came from Belgium; Pete Hawkins of Liverpool, England; Debra Angel MacDougall of Scotland; Byung Ju Cho of South Korea; Tom O'Neil of New Zealand; and, in this country, Howard Figler, beloved friend and co-author of our manual for career counselors; Marty Nemko; Joel Garfinkle; Richard Leider; Dick Knowdell; Rich Feller; Dick Gaither; Warren Farrell; and the folks over at Ten Speed Press in Berkeley, California, now an imprint of the Crown Publishing Group of Random House, and Crown's head, Maya Mavjee, who has been very kind to me.

Last December we buried Phil Wood, founder of Ten Speed Press and my friend for forty years. He was a dear man, and I owe him more than

I can say for helping *Parachute* find its audience, and for letting me have great control over the annual editions. *Parachute* would never have sold ten million copies, were it not for him.

**Phil Wood at Bohemian Grove**

I much appreciate my current friends over at Ten Speed: Aaron Wehner, publisher, George Young, Kara Van de Water, Lisa Westmoreland, and Colleen Cain.

My especial thanks to my readers—all ten million of you—for buying my books, trusting my counsel, and following your dream. I have never met so many wonderful souls. I am so thankful for you all.

In closing, I cannot fail to mention my profound thanks to our Great Creator, Who all my life I have known through my Lord Jesus Christ, as real to me as breathing, and the Rock of my life through every trial and tragedy, most especially the assassination of my only brother, Don Bolles, with a car bomb, in downtown Phoenix, Arizona, back in 1976—now memorialized in one of the rooms at the Newseum, in Washington, D.C.

I am very quiet about my faith; it's just . . . there. But it is the source of whatever grace, wisdom, or compassion I have ever found, or shared with others. I am grateful beyond measure for such a life, and such a mission as Our Creator has given me: to help people make their lives really count, here on this spaceship Earth.

Dick Bolles
RNB25@aol.com
www.jobhuntersbible.com

# GRAMMAR AND LANGUAGE NOTE

I want to explain four points of grammar, in this book of mine: pronouns, commas, italics, and spelling. My unorthodox use of them invariably offends unemployed English teachers so much that instead of finishing the exercises, they immediately write to apply for a job as my editor.

To save us unnecessary correspondence, let me explain. Throughout this book, I often use the apparently plural pronouns "they," "them," and "their" after *singular* antecedents—such as, "You must approach *someone* for a job and tell *them* what you can do." This sounds strange and even wrong to those who know English well. To be sure, we all know there is another pronoun—"you"—that may be either singular or plural, but few of us realize that the pronouns "they," "them," and "their" were also once treated as both plural and singular in the English language. This changed, at a time in English history when agreement in *number* became more important than agreement as to sexual *gender*. Today, however, our priorities have shifted once again. Now, the distinguishing of sexual *gender* is considered by many to be more important than agreement in *number*.

The common artifices used for this new priority, such as "s/he," or "he and she," are—to my mind—tortured and inelegant. Casey Miller and Kate Swift, in their classic, *The Handbook of Nonsexist Writing*, agree, and argue that it is time to bring back the earlier usage of "they," "them," and "their" as both singular and plural—just as "you" is/are. They further argue that this return to the earlier historical usage has already become quite common *out on the street*—witness a typical sign by the ocean that reads, "*Anyone* using this beach after 5 p.m. does so at *their* own risk." I have followed Casey and Kate's wise recommendations in all of this.

As for my commas, they are deliberately used according to my own rules—rather than according to the rules of historic grammar (which I did learn—I hastily add, to reassure my old Harvard professors, who despaired of me weekly, during English class). In spite of those rules, I follow my own, which are: to write conversationally, and put in a comma wherever I would normally stop for a breath, were I *speaking* the same line.

The same conversational rule applies to my use of *italics*. I use *italics* wherever, were I speaking the sentence, I would *emphasize* that word or phrase. I also use italics where there is a digression of thought, and I want to maintain the main flow of the sentence. All in all, I write as I speak. Hence the dashes (—) to indicate a break in my thought.

Finally, some of my spelling (and capitalization) is *weird*. (You say "weird"; I say "playful.") I happen to like writing it "e-mail," for example, instead of "email." Most of the time. Fortunately, since this is my own book, I get to play by my own peculiar interpretations; I'm just grateful that ten million readers have *gone along*. Nothing delights a child (at heart) more, than being allowed to play.

P.S. Speaking of "playful," over the last forty years a few critics (*very* few) have claimed that *Parachute* is not serious enough (they object to the cartoons, here, which poke fun at almost *everything*). On the other hand, a few have complained that the book is *too* serious, and too complicated in its vocabulary and grammar for anyone except a college graduate. Two readers, however, have written me with a different view.

The first one, from England, said there is an index that analyzes a book to tell you what grade in school you must have finished, in order to be able to understand it. My book's index, he said, turned out to be 6.1, which means you need only have finished sixth grade in a U.S. school in order to understand it.

Here in the U.S., a college instructor came up with a similar finding. He phoned me to tell me that my book was rejected by the authorities as a proposed text for the college course he was teaching, because (they said) the book's language/grammar was not up to college level. "What level was it?" I asked. "Well," he replied, "when they analyzed it, it turned out to be written on an eighth grade level."

Sixth or eighth grade—that seems just about right to me. Why make job-hunting complicated, when it can be expressed so simply even a child could understand it?

R.N.B.

# INTRODUCTION

*It was the best of times,*
*It was the worst of times,*
*It was the age of wisdom,*
*It was the age of foolishness,*
*It was the epoch of belief,*
*It was the epoch of incredulity,*
*It was the season of light,*
*It was the season of darkness,*
*It was the spring of hope,*
*It was the winter of despair,*
*We had everything before us,*
*We had nothing before us,*
*We were all going direct to heaven,*
*We were all going direct the other way . . .*

CHARLES DICKENS (1812–1870)
*A TALE OF TWO CITIES*

# Chapter 1. How to Find Hope

If we had such a thing as a national bumper-sticker for our cars, the bumper-sticker of the year would be: "I'm out of work, I can't find a job, and I've tried everything."

Of course not everyone would display it; some 139,000,000 people in the U.S. have jobs, after all. But some 15,000,000 do not. And 6,000,000 of them would display it for longer than twenty-seven months. That's how many have currently been out of work that long. Just here in the U.S. Beyond these shores, well, tragically high unemployment is a world-wide problem, as we have seen throughout the Middle East this year, and other restless nations of the world.

Everywhere we go, these days, we hear this cry: "I've been out of work forever, and I can't find a job, no matter how hard I try." And we do try hard. Often in vain. We are thrown out of work, we go looking for work the way we always used to, but this time we come up empty. This is a brand new experience for many of us. And one that we didn't see coming. Nothing works. Unemployment drags on.

This shakes us emotionally to our core, and often leads to a plunge in our self-esteem. Those twins, depression and despair, frequently follow hard on its heels. Life feels like it is never going to get any better. This feels like *forever*. (I know. Like any normal American, I've been thrown out of work twice in my life. It was not fun.)

What do we need?

Well, we desperately need a job. Of course.

But more than that, while we are out of work we desperately, desperately, need Hope.

# THE KEY TO FINDING HOPE

Experts have discovered, over the years, what is the key to Hope. And it is just this: Hope requires that, in every situation, we have at least two alternatives.

Not just one way to describe ourselves, but two ways, at least.

Not just one way to hunt for a job, but two ways, at least.

Not just one kind of job to hunt for, but two kinds of jobs, at least.

Not just one size company to go after, but two sizes, at least.

Not just one place we really would like to work at, but two places, at least.

And so on. And so forth.

In order to have Hope while you are out of work, you have to make sure that in every situation you find yourself, you're not putting all your eggs in just one basket.

To have only one plan, one option, is a sure recipe for despair. I'll give you a simple example. In a study of 100 job-hunters who were using only one method to hunt for a job, typically 51 abandoned their search by the second month. That's more than half of them. They lost Hope. On the other hand, of 100 job-hunters who were using *two or more* different ways of hunting for a job, typically only 31 of them abandoned their search by the second month. That's less than one-third of them.

The latter kept going because they had Hope. And so this truth should always be on your mind:

> If you are to hold on to Hope you must determine to always have at least two alternatives, in everything that you are doing while looking for work.

# A LIST OF JOB-FINDING ALTERNATIVES

Just to be sure we're "choosing cards from a full deck," let's rehearse what *are* the alternative options we have, when we're out of work. There are eighteen different ways of looking for work. You probably know many of them, but just for the sake of completeness, let's list them all. They are:

1. Self-Inventory. You do a thorough self-inventory of the transferable skills and knowledges that you most enjoy using, so you can define to yourself just exactly what it is you have to offer the world, and *exactly what job(s)* you would most like to find.

2. The Internet. 82 percent of Americans now go online, for an average of nineteen hours *per week* apiece. If you're among them, and your goal is to work for someone else, you use the Internet to post your resume and/or to look for employers' "job-postings" (vacancies) on the employer's own website or elsewhere (with omnibus job-search sites such as Indeed or SimplyHired, and of course specific "job-boards" such as CareerBuilder, Yahoo/Hot Jobs, Monster, LinkUp, Hound, "niche sites" for particular industries [*see www.internetinc.com/job-search-websites for a directory*], and non-job sites such as LinkedIn, Facebook, Twitter, or the immensely popular Craigslist). If, on the contrary, you're considering working for yourself, you use the Internet to learn how to do this, how to establish your brand, and how to get the word out to a wider audience as to just what you have to offer.

3. Networking. You ask friends, family, or people in the community for "job-leads" (*rhymes with "Bob reads"*). There are two ways of doing this, one sort of *blah*, one really useful. In the first case, you use the lame "I lost my job; if you hear of anything, let me know," which leaves your network completely baffled as to what you're looking for, unless it's same old same old of what you've always done. Far better way: after using method #1 above, you tell them in specific detail what you mean by "anything." And then see how close they can come to *that*.

4. School. School means high school, trade schools, online schools, community colleges, four-year colleges, or universities. You ask a former professor or teacher or your career/alumni office at schools that you attended if they have any job-leads.

5. The Feds. You go to your local federal/state unemployment service office, or to their OneStop career centers (directory at www.careeronestop.org) to get instruction on how to better job-hunt, and also to find job-leads.

6. **Private employment agencies.** You go to the private analog to the federal/state agencies (directory of such agencies can be found at www.usa.gov/Agencies/State_and_Territories.shtml).

7. **Civil Service.** You take a civil service exam to compete for a government job (http://federaljobs.net/exams.htm and/or http://tinyurl.com/9vyfqe).

8. **Newspapers.** You answer local "want-ads" (in newspapers, assuming your city or town still has a newspaper, online or in print, or both). The Sunday editions usually prove most useful. See http://tinyurl.com/d58l8z for how to use them; for a directory of their online versions, see www.newslink.org. There is also a site that lets you see current news about any industry that is of interest to you *(where vacancies have just opened up??)*, at http://www.congoo.com/Industry.

9. **Journals.** You look at professional journals in your profession or field, and answer any ads there that intrigue you (directory at http://tinyurl.com/dlfsdz).

10. **Temp Agencies.** You go to temp agencies (agencies that get you short-term contracts in places that need your time and skills temporarily) and see if the agency/agencies can place you, in one place after another, until some place that you really like says, "Could you stay on, permanently?" At the very least you'll pick up experience that you can later cite on your resume (directory of such agencies, and people's ratings of them, at www.rateatemp .com/temp-agency-list).

11. **Day Laborers.** You go to places where employers pick up day workers: well-known street corners in your town (ask around), or union halls, etc., in order for you to get short-term work, for now, which may lead to more permanent work, eventually. It may initially be yard work, or work that requires you to use your hands; but no job should be "beneath you" when you're desperate.

12. **Job Clubs.** You join or form a "support group" or "job club," where you meet weekly for job-leads and emotional support. Check with your local chamber of commerce, and local churches, mosques, or synagogues, to find out if such groups exist in your community.

There is an excellent directory at Susan Joyce's job-hunt.org (http://tinyurl.com/7a9xbb).

13. Resumes. You mail out resumes blindly to anyone and everyone, blanketing the area. Or you target particular places that interest you, and send them both digital and snail-mail copies of your resume, targeted specifically to them. Ah, but you already knew this method, didn't you?

14. Choose Places That Interest You. You knock on doors of any employer, factory, store, organization, or office that interests you, whether they are known to have a vacancy or not. This works best, as you might have guessed, with smaller employers (those having 25 or fewer employees; then, if nothing turns up there, those places that have 50 or fewer employees; or, if nothing turns up there, then those with 100 or fewer employees, etc.).

15. The Phone Book. You use the index to your phone book's Yellow Pages, to identify five to ten *entries* or *categories* (subjects, fields, or industries) that intrigue you—that are located in the city or town where you are, or want to be—and then phone or, better yet, visit the individual organizations listed under these headings *(again, smaller is better)* whether they are known to have a vacancy or not. Incidentally, the Personnel Manager (http://tinyurl.com/3jnjewo) or Human Resources office there—*if* they have one—is that employer's friend, not yours. Their basic function is to screen you out, so avoid them if possible. Sometimes, to be sure, you will stumble across an HR person who likes you and is willing to become your advocate, there. If so, you're one lucky woman (or man).

16. Volunteering. If you're okay financially for a while, but can't find work, you volunteer to work for nothing, short-term, at a place that has a "cause" or mission that interests you (directory of such places can be found at www.volunteermatch.org). Your goal is not only to feel useful, even while you haven't yet found a job, but your hope is also that down the line maybe they'll want to actually hire you for pay. The odds of that happening in these hard times aren't great, so don't count on it and don't push it; but sometimes you'll be surprised that they ask you to stay, for pay.

17. **Work for Yourself.** You start your own small business, trade, or service, after first carefully observing what service or product your community lacks but really needs (see http://tinyurl.com/3rwxmka; also http://tinyurl.com/3syrmq7).

18. **Retraining.** You go back to school and get retrained for some other kind of occupation than the one you've been doing. Especially important if you don't know computers at all.

## LIES, DAMN LIES, AND STATISTICS

That's how some wag once *declined* the word "lies." I mention this here, because Alternatives do give you Hope, but statistics can take that Hope away, if you give them undue weight.

Much of it depends on what statistics you pay attention to. The media, the Internet, blogs, tweets, twenty-four-hour news channels on TV, newspapers, and magazines, all love statistics. *But they generally are in love with a very particular kind of statistics, namely those that convey bad news.* Discouraging news. Doom and gloom.

Why is this so? I dunno. But it is. Example? With regard to the labor market in the U.S., there are always two sets of statistics floating around *for each month.* First set of statistics: let's take the month of February 2009, the height of the recent Recession. As reported on a website called JOLT (*Job Openings & Labor Turnover*)[1] 4,360,000 people in the U.S. found jobs that month. Yes, you read that correctly. And at the end of that month, 3,006,000 additional vacancies remained unfilled and available. Good news, right? 7,366,000 vacancies were available or filled, that month alone. At the height of the Recession.

Ah, but every month there is a second set of statistics, reported on the first Friday of each month by the Bureau of Labor Statistics, called the Current Population Survey.[2] It is typically called *The Unemployment Statistic,* though it is more accurate to think of it as *"the monthly measure of the size of the work force in America."* Anyway, the CPS said that during that same month, February 2009, the size of the total labor force in the U.S. shrank by 726,000 jobs. And so, the unemployment rate rose from 7.6 percent to 8.1. Bad news, to be sure.

---

1. www.bls.gov/jlt
2. www.bls.gov/cps

Okay, there you have it: two sets of statistics, one good news, one bad news. Now, which of these two sets do you think the media pounced on? Yep, you guessed it: *the bad news* set. "726,000 workers lose their jobs," commentators and news analysts shrieked. "Unemployment rises to 8.1 percent." Along with that, they threw in, "There are six unemployed workers now for every vacancy." All in all, it was enough to take the heart out of even the most optimistic job-hunter that month. Or any month.

## HELPFUL STATISTICS

We have to always watch which statistics we are paying the most attention to.

For, surely, statistics can sometimes help us, and not merely depress us. Let's post a few guideposts here about how statistics can help you:

1. *Statistics can save you from wasting your energy.* For example, when considering job-hunting methods, it can be helpful to know what the odds are that a particular method will richly repay you for the time spent on it, or what the odds are that a particular method will likely be a complete waste of your time. We will see this, when we discuss the five *best* ways to hunt for work, and the five *worst* ways (comparatively speaking).

2. *Statistics can guide you toward particular targets.* They can tell you when a particular company is having the kind of challenges you would love to help solve, and when a company has more problems than you would ever want to deal with, because they're about to tank.

3. *Statistics can encourage you*, if you know how to read them. Consider, for example, this set of encouraging statistics just published, as I write (by *CBS News Report*[3]):

   a. Laid-off workers thirty-four and under have a 36 percent chance of landing a job in a year

   b. Laid-off workers in their fifties have a 24 percent chance of landing a job in a year

---

3. http://tinyurl.com/3ex7ryz

c. Laid-off workers over sixty-two years of age have an 18 percent chance of landing a job in a year

Encouraging? Sure. Look at it again. It says that if you're under 34 years of age, 36 out of every 100 are going to find a job this year; and even if you're over 62 years of age, 18 out of every 100 are going to find a job this year. So the only question is: why shouldn't you be among them?

After all, the above statistics summarize the experience of all job-hunters, most of whom typically choose only one method of job search. You, however, know enough to choose two or more methods, and thus increase the odds that you will indeed find meaningful work.

## CONCLUSION

Hope can give you wings, persistence, and energy. If you're out of work, and want to stay upbeat, then greet the sunrise, go for a walk, count your blessings, listen to beautiful music, drink more water than usual, eat simpler, exercise more, laugh with your family and friends, watch cartoons, take naps in the daytime if you can't sleep well at night, but for heaven's sakes, don't obsess about depressing statistics. Just determine to find alternatives for everything you are doing about your job-hunt and your life. You want to be the exception to whatever the odds are, about anything. Hold on to Hope, and you can beat those odds.

### Discussion

*Job-hunter: Well, there may be all those vacancies out there that you claim, but I go on the Internet every morning, and I can't find any of them in my area or specialty.*

Career-counselor: Searching the Internet is only one way of hunting for those jobs that are out there. What's your second way of searching for jobs?

*Job-hunter: I only have the Internet.*

Career-counselor: Well, there are at least 17 other ways of looking for those jobs that are out there. Read them, then choose and use three other alternatives to "just the Internet."

*Job-hunter: I'm a construction worker. I see there are lots of job vacancies, but none in construction that I can find.*

Career-counselor: How else would you describe yourself besides "construction worker"?

*Job-hunter: I've always been a construction worker.*

Career-counselor: Well, that's a "job-title." There are other ways to describe yourself besides a job-title.

*Job-hunter: Like what, for example?*

Career-counselor: Like: "I am a person . . . who . . . "

*Job-hunter: Who what?*

Career-counselor: "I am a person . . . who has *these* skills, and *these* knowledges, and *this* experience." Take the job-title off yourself; find a more fundamental way to describe yourself to yourself. And to others. Once you have at least two alternative ways of describing yourself, you increase the range of jobs you can apply for, and thus keep Hope alive.

*Do not let us speak of darker days;*
*Let us speak rather of sterner days.*
*These are not dark days; these are great days—*
*The greatest days our country has ever lived;*
*And we must all thank God that we have been*
*allowed . . .*
*To play a part in making these days memorable*
*In the history of our race.*

WINSTON CHURCHILL (1874–1965)

# Chapter 2. Survival Skills You Most Need in Today's World

Maybe you're not unemployed. Maybe you're just adrift, or bored, or puzzled about where to go next, with your life. You're at some cross-roads in your life: you can't stand your job anymore, or you have a new handicap you're trying to adjust to, or you're just out of the military, or just out of prison, or just out of college, or just out of a divorce, or you've just lost an important person in your life. Or you've just found the most important person in your life, and you're ready to look for some deeper purpose for your remaining time here on Earth.

Well, that's why this isn't just a book about job-hunting.

It's about something larger, which we may call life/work planning, or (as I think is much more realistic) life/work designing.

*Designing* is more appropriate because you can't possibly predict what is going to happen to you, even next week, much less plan for it. *Planning your life* is becoming increasingly unreliable in today's world. On the other hand, when you design something, it's like setting out on a journey: you assemble all the elements necessary, even if you aren't sure which particular elements you will actually need, when the time comes. You pack with all conceivable scenarios in mind. You may need *this* or *that*. You may not. That's *designing*.

Now, the fact that *"work"* was written as a subscript, above, is also significant. It conveys the point that our general subject is *life planning* or *life designing*, but there is a doorway into the whole subject, which it is important for us to use. As the subscript suggests, that doorway is our *work*. Or, to be more specific, our *survival* in the world of work. It's the doorway, because it is the most difficult to solve; therefore, you begin with that. The other parts of life, learning, and leisure, are relatively easy to figure out, once you've solved the arena of work.

Okay, so that's the major subject of this manual. Of course, you may say that survival in the world of work isn't *your* big issue right now. You're working on one of the other three great issues in the Pyramid of Life[1]—figuring out what's going on, or what your mission on this Earth is, or how well you're achieving it:

Well, that's great! But stop for a moment. Think.

Imagine your life here on Earth as being like a journey in a boat down a long and winding river. For now, the journey may be going smoothly. But you are wise, and you think ahead; so you knew enough, before launching, to put certain supplies in that boat. One of which, I'll bet, was a life jacket or life preserver.

You know you'll probably never need it, but on the other hand, what if you do? What if you run into some huge rocks, or capsize, or develop a leak in the bottom of the boat, or head into a heavy storm that swamps your boat? You'll need that life preserver or life jacket.

The moral of this allegory? *Designing! A survival skill!* You've got to always assemble ahead of time what you might need, to survive, should outrageous and unanticipated circumstances suddenly arise.

---

1. Described at length in my 1978 paperback book, *The Three Boxes of Life and How to Get Out of Them: An Introduction to Life/Work Planning*, now out of print, but available online, used, for as little as $4.00 U.S., at sites such as Amazon.com.

# ESSENTIAL SURVIVAL SKILLS

Okay, so what do we need to assemble ahead of time in order to survive? What skills must we learn and master?

A human's first necessary survival skill: *the skill to communicate with others, and form a community.* We need to be able to tell others what we need, and learn to hear what they need. Left alone, we would perish early; every baby knows that. From the beginning of our life, we need care, help in time of need, and of course, love. Others will need this also from us.

A human's second necessary survival skill: *the skill to protect ourselves,* either as an individual or as a community, from anything out there that might hurt or kill us.

A human's third necessary survival skill: *the skill to keep ourselves healthy.* We can be attacked from within as well as from without, by a virus, bacteria, or disease. We need healing skills, as well as the healing skills of others, to maintain a strong immune system.

A human's fourth necessary survival skill: *the skill to find shelter.* Even if we are by nature nomads, we still need some kind of shelter, portable or not, to protect us against the elements. We must build or fashion it ourselves, or buy it from someone.

A human's fifth necessary survival skill: *the skill to clothe ourselves.* Either we must know how to make it ourselves, or else know where to buy it from others.

A human's sixth necessary survival skill: *the skill to find food.* Again we must either grow it, or fish it, or slay it, ourselves, or else buy it from others.

Those were the traditional six survival skills that we as humans need. But now a seventh has been added, due to this time in which we now live. And that is *job-hunting and job-creation skills.*

Oh, those skills have been around for a long time, but for many they were kind of optional, since many of us never had any particular difficulty in finding work. Only recently has job-hunting become elevated to the rank of a survival skill, right up there with the other six.

In part, this is because the national imperative for nation after nation is increasingly going to be: enact reforms, cut spending, take wage cuts, cut benefits too, endure austerity, reform the tax system, produce revenue, require people to work longer and retire later—as more than one expert has been predicting.[2]

As a consequence of all this, more and more people are in danger of losing their jobs, and becoming what the media are prematurely calling "a lost generation": *people out of work, and unable to find any.* In Britain, for example, it is predicted that 300,000 will lose their jobs as a consequence of current budget-cutting there.[3] A similar fate potentially awaits other nations around the world, and some are already in trouble financially, such as Iceland, Greece, Ireland, Portugal, and yes, even the United States.

Therefore, the maxim of this twenty-first century is: it's up to you; you're not likely to be rescued by someone else, anymore. You've got to become better at hunting for a job, now, yourself, or perish! Job-hunting has become a survival skill; else, if you're out of work for any great length of time, you are in danger of becoming a member of what economists are calling "the lost generation."

## ASSUME OUR JOB-HUNTING SKILLS ARE NOW OUTDATED IN THESE NEW HARD TIMES

In light of the peculiar challenges that we face this decade *(2011–2020),* we must start with fresh thinking. Fresh thinking, and fresh honesty.

Let's start with honesty: it is fair to say that many if not most of us have job-hunting skills that are comparatively elementary.

Elementary? Yes, because in job-training program after job-training program, in support groups, and even in books, we have only been taught three most basic job-hunting skills: *how to write a resume, how to search for vacancies on the Internet using social media,* and *how to conduct a job interview.*

What's wrong with these elementary job-hunting skills? Well, nothing. And everything. It all works rather well . . . if times are good. It's only when times turn hard, like now, that our elementary job-hunting skills suddenly don't work. What a shock! They turn up *nothing* in spite of

---

2. Floyd Norris, "Resentment Is Rising in Euro Zone," *New York Times,* April 15, 2011, page B1.
3. Ibid., page A3.

the fact that there are millions of vacancies every month, in good times and bad, as we have seen.

> It's tempting to blame it on the economy, but it is wise to preserve the possibility in the back of our mind that maybe the techniques we are using work well in good times but don't work well in hard times.

Therefore, times such as these require that we upgrade our job-hunting skills. We must learn what *advanced job-hunting skills* look like, and then master them in practice, in our own life. This is necessary to guarantee our survival, economically, physically, mentally, and spiritually, in times like these. Job-hunting has become essential to our survival.

*Survival job-hunting* has five essential parts; here they are, with the reason why we need them:

> *Sometimes the thing that is holding us back is we are approaching our crisis with the wrong attitudes. So, the first essential part of Survival Job-Hunting is to work on our:*

1. Attitudes. Attitude is everything. But periodically attitudes need to be re-examined, and rethought. In this case, we must learn what attitudes are necessary for survival in this new world. Basically, they are: learning that what got you here, won't necessarily get you there; learning to focus on what is within your power, not what is not; learning to always seek alternatives, for everything you do; learning to pay more attention to the world around you and the world within you; learning to be inventive even in everyday tasks; learning to seek out a supportive community while job-hunting; and learning there is meaning to everything.

> *Sometimes there are job vacancies out there that we would want to apply for, if we could find them; but we can't, because we're using the wrong methods. So, the second essential part of Survival Job-Hunting is we need to master more:*

2. Advanced job-finding techniques. As we have seen, there are always job vacancies out there. *Maybe* it will turn out that, even so, there are no jobs in our specialty or at the salary we need, in our geographic area; but we need to be sure of that, before we move on to the next step in survival job-hunting. There are more effective and advanced ways to find vacancies than we are commonly taught. We must move beyond relying just on resumes, job-postings, agencies, and the Internet. If they turn up nothing, then it's time to discover new and more advanced ways to find those vacancies that are out there.

*Sometimes there simply are no job vacancies that appeal to us, so we must know how to create jobs. Therefore, the third essential part of Survival Job-Hunting is we need to master:*

3. Advanced job-creation techniques. Yes, suppose we can't find any job vacancies in our area, in our specialty, then what? Well, if we can't find any vacancies, then we must learn how to create jobs; learning not only how to found our own business, but also how to speed up the job-creation process as done by employers around the country. And we must learn how to make a career-change, when we are puzzled about where to go from here with our life; and we hate our old job, or are simply bored, and want to do something new and different with our lives, or we want to find some deeper sense of mission or purpose for our life. It is worth noting that when we create new work for ourselves, we often help create new jobs for others.[4]

*Sometimes the problem is we do not realize all the richness of what we have to offer to the World. So, the fourth essential part of Survival Job-Hunting is:*

4. Inventory. We must go back and inventory what we have to offer the world: what transferable skills, what knowledges, what experience, what values. The purpose of this research is to discover *alternative ways* of describing who you are. You can no longer restrict

---

4. "Briefing on the Economy," *Time*, April 11, 2011.

your definition of yourself to just your old job-title. No longer: "I am a construction worker (or whatever)," but "I am a person who . . ." Maybe, after all this, you will decide you can put together a new career with what you already know. Or maybe you'll want to go train for a whole new career. *Maybe.* But first, you should inventory what you already have. It's broader, deeper, richer, than you think.

*These new tools should be taught to everyone, but we don't have enough teachers or trainers to do that. Therefore, an essential part of Survival Job-Hunting is that once we have learned these life-saving skills for ourselves, we turn outward from ourselves and share what we have with the rest of the world; each one of us must commit to go teach at least one other person. So, the fifth (and final) essential part of Survival Job-Hunting is:*

5. Each one teach one. It would be nice if we had enough trainers to teach this to the whole world, in time. But we don't. The famous literacy pioneer, Frank Laubach, said that when you don't have enough trainers to train everyone who needs it, the fastest way to spread a survival skill is to mandate that each person, once trained, makes a commitment to go teach at least one other person. We cannot let millions suffer because they do not know what to do in this new economy. If we gain the knowledge, it is our responsibility to turn around and share it.

## CONCLUSION

Our pathway from here, is clear: we will proceed, step by step, through these five essential parts of Survival Job-Hunting, in the following order:

I. Attitudes

II. Job-finding

III. Job-creation and career change

IV. Inventory of what we each have to offer to the world

V. Teaching others through *"each one teach one"*

## Discussion

*Job-hunter: It doesn't feel to me like we're in a survival mode in this country. Plenty of people have jobs. I think this country is still very prosperous.*

Career-counselor: Well, you're right. To be exact, 139 million people have jobs in this country. But any of us can be thrown out of work any time, without warning. And we aren't spending time thinking about that possibility ahead of time, are we?

*Job-hunter: No, we aren't. I mean, I can't speak for others, but it never occurred to me that I might be unemployed. And unemployed for this long.*

Career-counselor: Well, that's why we call this a survival mode, in this country; and in other countries around the world. Let me give you an analogy. You see a swimmer in danger of drowning. Can't swim very well. Has no life jacket. Is about to go under the water for the third time. His arms are flailing the water desperately. Get the picture?

*Job-hunter: Sure. He's in trouble.*

Career-counselor: Yes, but he's in trouble because he didn't put on a life jacket before he ever went out into the water. If he knew he might have trouble surviving out there, he would have put on that life jacket.

*Job-hunter: So, you're saying . . .*

Career-counselor: I'm saying, you prepare now, if you want to survive later.

# THE FIVE PARTS OF JOB-HUNTING AS A SURVIVAL SKILL:

# I.

# ATTITUDES NECESSARY FOR SURVIVAL

*Ask not for tasks equal to your powers;*
*Rather, ask for powers equal to your tasks.*

PHILLIPS BROOKS (1835–1893)

# Chapter 3. The Three Attitudes Necessary for Survival

Show me two job-hunters. Both are essentially the same age. Both have the same background. Both have the same intelligence and history. Both have been out of work for the same amount of time. It's been many months, now. Both are struggling, financially. They get by on what little they've saved, what occasionally they can sell, plus help from family and friends, the occasional brief odd job, that sort of thing.

But there the similarities end.

The one is quietly smoldering with anger, barely suppressed. He is mad at the universe, and in no particular order, his former employer, his former co-workers, the government, his profession, his college, friends, and God. He is very quiet, doesn't talk much, and when he does talk, it is to complain about how his life has turned out. He is sullen, gloomy about his future, feels he has been declared disposable, and that his life as he knew it is essentially over.

The other is just as depressed about how his life has turned out, but he wakes up each morning glad to see the sun, puts on beautiful music, walks a great deal, counts his blessings, is in a job-support group, focuses on other people's troubles, not just his own, is a great listener, spends each new day trying to be a better person than he was the day before, remains active in his job-hunt, tries to learn or study something new each day, essentially sees life as an adventure, and is willing to wait patiently for the next chapter to unfold.

Yes, show me two job-hunters, and I will show you how important *attitude* is. Which one of those two do you think is more likely to find a job, first?

*In whatever circumstances we may find ourselves in life, attitude is everything.*

When we are out of work, and desperately trying to survive, we don't just need to master more advanced job-hunting *techniques*, but we must also pay strict attention to our *attitudes*. Job-hunting most always involves competing with others for the job, sad to say, and it is often our attitude that gives us the advantage. Here are three attitudes to adopt.

## FIRST IMPORTANT ATTITUDE FOR SURVIVAL WHILE OUT OF WORK

Some years ago, when I was doing a lot of counseling, not just about careers, a friend of mine asked me if I would be willing to see someone he knew. Her name was Mary. She had been diagnosed with multiple sclerosis, or MS. She had been to a wide range of medical specialists: neurologist, psychologist, internist, you name it. They all had declared there was nothing they could do to help her with the disease. My friend said, "Would you see her?" "Sure," I said, "but I'm not sure there's anything I can do."

The next day my friend brought her over. She walked very stiffly up the front sidewalk, came in, sat down, and after exchanging a few pleasantries, I got down to business. "Mary," I said, "what is multiple sclerosis?" "I don't know," she said, in a dull voice. "Well, then," I said, "that makes us even; because I don't know, either. But here's what I propose. I'm sure that a huge proportion of whatever MS is, is out of your control. There's nothing you can do about it. But that proportion can't be 100 percent. There's got to be some proportion—let's say it's even just 2 percent—that is within your control. We could work on that. Do you want to begin that journey?" She said yes. Over the next few weeks she improved, and finally was free of all symptoms (typical of the disease, for a spell, but this lasted for a very long time), and now—free of all stiffness—she became a model on 57th Street in New York City.

This story about Mary illustrates an important *attitude*: in any situation we may ever find ourselves, no matter how much we feel we are at the mercy of vast immutable forces that are totally beyond our control, we can always find something that is within our control, however small, and work on *that*. Sometimes that may only change a little, sometimes it may change a lot. You just never know. But what we do know is that by working on even that 2 percent, it saves us from a feeling of complete powerlessness.

This certainly applies to any time we are unemployed, particularly if it drags on and on. To paraphrase the above, addressing it to job-hunters: *I'm sure that a huge proportion of the situation you are facing, is out of your control. There's nothing you can do about it. But that proportion can't be 100 percent. There's got to be some proportion—let's say it's even just 2 percent—that is within your control. You can work on that. Who knows what a difference that may make!*

So this brings us to our

> First Important Attitude for Survival While Out of Work: While you are out of work, and feel you are up against large forces that you are powerless to change, determine to find something that is within your power to change, even if it's just 5 percent or only 2 percent of the total; find it, and throw your energies into it.

Some examples of what is within your control when you're out of work: getting more sleep; drinking more water (we almost always need more water than we think we do, but that's water, not just fluids); walking more; reading the book 14,000 *Things to Be Happy About*[1]; doing more studying about advanced job-survival skills (reading *this* manual, more than once); getting into a supportive community with other job-hunters, if you haven't already; doing a detailed inventory of yourself, using the Flower exercise in chapter 13; learning to become more observant of the world around you; listening harder to other people; and talking more to successful job-hunters, to quiz them about what they did, step by step, to find work.

*In whatever circumstances we may find ourselves in life, attitude is everything. We must never ever give up.*[2] *There is always something we can work on.*

---

1. By Barbara Ann Kipfer. Workman Publishing, 2007, revised and updated.
2. Winston Churchill (1874–1965). It was also he who said, "If you are going through hell, keep going."

# SECOND IMPORTANT ATTITUDE
# FOR SURVIVAL WHILE JOB-HUNTING

There is a book out there with a clever title: *What Got You Here Won't Get You There.*[3] When we are unemployed during hard times, and for long times, that's an important thought to remember.

Some people think that any suggestion that there may be something that a job-hunter is doing wrong, is essentially "blaming the victim" for the situation they are in. This is nuts. Self-introspection is the way to improve any company, any marriage, any nation. And any job-hunt.

Looking forward and not backward, asking, "Is there something *I* could be doing better?" is often the pathway to saving that company, marriage, nation, and job-hunt!

When unemployment is dragging on and on, everything should be on the table for examination. We need to question all assumptions. Assume we are in a new world. Rethink all our strategies. Revisit everything we think we know for sure, and ask if in fact things have changed. Think whether there is something new we need to learn, remembering always that before we can learn we sometimes need to unlearn (some things).

So this brings us to our

> Second Important Attitude for Survival While Out of Work: We need to assume that nothing that worked before will necessarily work now. We need to reexamine every job-hunting method there is (*next chapter*), and reconsider whether there is a better way that we could be going about this.

*In whatever circumstances we may find ourselves in life, attitude is everything. We must never shrink from doing the hard work of rethinking our whole strategy.*

---

3. By Marshall Goldsmith, with Mark Reiter. Hyperion, 2007.

## THIRD IMPORTANT ATTITUDE
## FOR SURVIVAL WHILE JOB-HUNTING

I recall a talk I heard many years ago, that made a deep, lasting impression on me. It was a doctor speaking; a doctor turned researcher, as it happened. He was reporting on a study that some colleagues had made of healing, at the hospital where he worked in New York City. They had long known that some people healed faster than others, but now they wanted to find out why.

So, as I recall, they searched through their records of recent patients to find matched pairs: essentially two people of the same age, with the same background, the same basic health record, who had undergone the same procedure or operation in that hospital. One member of each pair healed faster than the other, often by far. The doctors therefore questioned each pair at length to find out what was different about the person who healed faster. The common explanations that would occur to any thoughtful layperson proved to have no correlation with the rate of healing. Was the one who healed faster more optimistic than the other? No. Well, then, was it their habits: eating, sleeping, exercising? No. Was it their family history? No. Was it their status as single or married? No. Was it a belief in God? No. Well, then, what was it?

It turned out that those who healed faster believed that everything that happened to them had meaning, even if they didn't know what the meaning was, at the time. They believed that nothing meaningless ever happened to them. The ones who healed slowly did not believe this. This was independent of whether they believed in God or not.

The reason this talk made such an impression on me was because it demonstrated that what we are *thinking* actually can influence the body. It seemed to follow that it could influence our minds and spirits also.

I was also struck by a part of his report that said, ". . . even if they didn't know what the meaning was." Apparently, just to believe that nothing about our life is meaningless is a powerful idea.

So, here we have it:

Third Important Attitude for Survival While Out of Work: We need to assume that nothing that happens to us is just senseless and meaningless, including being out of work for a long time. In the context of our total life, it will eventually turn out to have meaning, even if that meaning is the forging of our soul to make it stronger and more compassionate toward the needs of others worse off than we are.

Interesting! *In whatever circumstances we may find ourselves in life, attitude is everything. When we are out of work, we must never shrink from doing the hard work of rethinking our whole strategy.*

## SURVIVAL JOB-HUNTING IS NOT JUST ABOUT BETTER TECHNIQUES

Certainly, after observing the job-hunting and career-changing scene for forty years, I am convinced that those who feel that no period in their life is meaningless, have a definite advantage over other job-hunters or career-changers. And a by-product of that attitude is that they do not despair. *For those who do despair, and feel depressed, I refer you to Appendix B at the back of this manual, for some suggestions of fourteen things you can do about that.*

But what do we mean when anyone says, "This time in my life has meaning, but I don't know what that meaning is, right now." *Why* don't we know it right now?

I think one reason may be that the period of time we are talking about, is only Act I in a two-act play. One time when I had been fired without warning, I had an appointment that very afternoon with my dentist. He was an old man and upon hearing my news, he waved his finger at me, and said, "You won't believe a word of what I'm saying right now, but this will turn out to be the best thing that ever happened to you. I've seen it happen too many times to doubt it."

Well, he was right; it led eventually to my writing this book to try to help a bunch of really desperate people; and that changed my whole life.

The first Act, being fired, seemed meaningless to me, until the second Act, the writing of this book, came along to give the first Act meaning.

So, if this long time of unemployment seems pointless and meaningless to you, you would do well to wait for the second Act that follows, whatever that may turn out to be, to find out what the meaning of this first Act was.

## WHAT IS *THIS TIME* FOR?

I do think we can hurry that up, *sometimes*. We can give meaning to this period of unemployment now, rather than just waiting for that meaning to unfold by itself somewhere further down the road. There are ways we can define, at least to ourselves, what the meaning of this period of unemployment is, *now*.

One way to get at that definition is to ask ourselves, "What is *this time* for?"

Say we are out of work. Say it's been twenty months. Naturally, we are tempted to answer that question as, "*This time* is for finding work." And since we haven't (so far), then this whole time of unemployment seems dangerously close to meaningless.

But suppose we come up with a different answer to the question "What is *this time* for?" That could give these twenty months meaning, right here and now.

Different answers? What kind of different answers? Well, I think there are five. Here they are, in order:

1. "These months have meaning because I am making this a Time for Thinking."

   *This time* is our chance to rethink our whole philosophy about what is important to us, in life, and what is not. We have time to think through, and write out, what we think about all the elements in a *Philosophy of life*. You can choose from:

   Beauty: which beauty stirs us, what its function is in the world
   Behavior: how we should behave in this world
   Beliefs: what our strongest beliefs are
   Celebration: how we like to play or celebrate, in life
   Choice: what its nature and importance is
   Community: what our concept is about belonging to each other; what we think our responsibility is to each other

Compassion: what we think about its importance and use

Confusion: how we live with it, and deal with it

Death: what we think about it and what we think happens after it

Events: what we think makes things happen, how we explain why they happen

Free will: whether we are "predetermined" or have free will

God: see Supreme Being

Happiness: what makes for the truest human happiness

Heroes and heroines: who ours are, and why

Human: what we think is important about being human, what we think is our function

Love: what we think about its nature and importance, along with all its related words: compassion, forgiveness, grace

Moral issues: which we believe are the most important for us to pay attention to, wrestle with, help solve

Paradox: what our attitude is toward its presence in life

Purpose: why we are here, what life is all about

Reality: what we think is its nature, and components

Self: deciding whether physical self is the limit of your being, deciding what trust in self means

Spirituality: what its place is in human life, how we should treat it

Stewardship: what we should do with life's gifts to us

Supreme Being: our concept of, or what we think holds the universe together

Truth: what we think about it, which truths are most important

Uniqueness: what we think makes each of us unique

Values: what we think about ourselves, what we think about the world, prioritized as to what matters most (to us)

2. "These months have meaning because I am making this a Time for Learning."

There must be *something* you've always wanted to learn more about, but never could seem to find the time. Well, now you have the time. Not a clue as to what you want to learn about? Then start with a fantasy game, to flex your mental muscles. Imagine, if you will, a Dream School: you can study anything, your teacher can be anyone, and the place can be anywhere. So, in this fantasy, what do you want to learn?

Here is an example or two:

| I Want to Learn | I Want My Teacher to Be | I want to Learn This In |
|---|---|---|
| How to fly | Superman | Tahiti |
| How to write music | Mozart | Vienna |

Make a complete list of anything that comes to mind—the wilder the better. Then go back and see if any subject popped up that you would seriously like to learn more about.

You have a rich library on the Internet of *free* videos on almost any subject you can think of. Here is a sampler:

www.brightstorm.com: math and science, free videos

www.freesciencelectures.com: astronomy, biology, chemistry, technology, you name it, free videos

http://openculture.com/freeonlinecourses: 350 from top universities, free

www.learnerstv.com: thousands of free downloadable video lectures

http://ocw.mit.edu/courses/audio-visual-courses: from MIT, of course

Incidentally, go to YouTube, type in the name of your favorite college or university (like: Stanford), and see if they have a channel on YouTube. Try the same thing with iTunesU (like: UC Berkeley), though some of those courses may cost ya. Try the same thing with Google. Type in the name of your favorite college or university plus the words "free video lectures" and see what turns up.

There are also a tremendous number of online courses, from online universities like Capella, where you can even get a degree, if you wish. Of course, they charge for this. Anyway, those can be found at http://oedb.org.

3. "These months have meaning because I am making this a Time for Repairing."

   "*Repairing*" can be taken in several ways. The most obvious ones are, of course, fixin' up stuff that has needed fixin' for ages, but you just never got around to it. Walls, appliances, cars, furniture, you name it. You probably have a long list in your head, that you filed under *Procrastination*. Now is a great time to tackle that list.

   But "*repairing*" can also mean relationships. The family or friends who you neglected because you were just too busy. The ones who just need a thoughtful letter, or phone call, a visit, or a hug. Maybe a sitdown, where you let them talk about themselves, rather than it being all about You.

   Even *Facebook* hasn't abolished the need for old-fashioned ways of getting in touch. As John Naisbitt famously warned us ages ago, "High tech needs to be complemented by high touch."

4. "These months have meaning because I am making this time a Time for Growing."

   The old model of our lives was that personal growth was essentially a matter for the young. That model has now been turned on

## Traditional View of Life

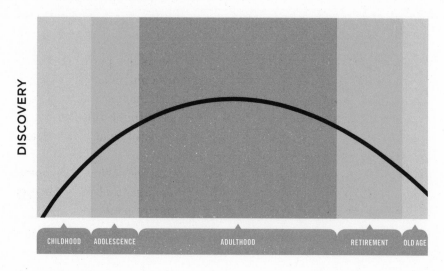

DISCOVERY

CHILDHOOD ADOLESCENCE       ADULTHOOD       RETIREMENT OLD AGE

its head, by *life*—as many think tanks, including the American Association for Retired Persons, have increasingly come to emphasize. The AARP, for one, now highlights how important growth is throughout our life, as shown by its increasing emphasis on life/work planning, illustrated dramatically in this fashion:

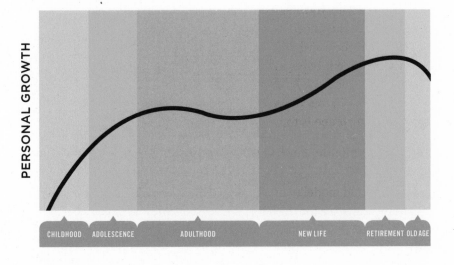

**New View of Life**

PERSONAL GROWTH

CHILDHOOD  ADOLESCENCE  ADULTHOOD  NEW LIFE  RETIREMENT OLD AGE

These graphs are courtesy of Emilio Pardo, Executive Vice-President and Chief Brand Officer, AARP. Copyright © 2011, Emilio Pardo.

Long periods of unemployment occur even as our personal growth is still climbing higher and higher. These difficult times give us more time to grow in courage, to develop stronger character, to increase our empathy for others who are suffering through difficult times, too. It is our chance to join a job support group, to make new friends, and to learn the value of community.

"Personal growth" eventually stumbles across the subject of competition. Competition is a part of life. Competition *to get a job* often mirrors how much competition we often run into, *after we get the job*.

But personal growth demands a different attitude toward competition. It stresses that our primary competition shouldn't be between ourselves and others, but rather between the man or woman I am *today*, versus the man or woman I *used to be*. That's what growth is all about. A period of unemployment can be an excellent time to work on *that*.

And, finally:

5. "These months have meaning because I am making this a Time for Helping."

    There may be someone right in your building, or someone right on your street, who needs some kind of help. The elderly, the infirm or handicapped, the people whose luck has run out. Open your eyes and look around.

    Also think of what kinds of volunteer work you might be doing with your spare time, while you're waiting for the job-market to turn upward in your field and specialty. There's no telling how much good you can do with this downtime that life has given you, here.

## SUMMARY

As these times in which we live become more challenging, as we realize job-hunting has turned into a survival skill, it is not merely necessary for us to go and learn more advanced job-hunting and job-creation *techniques*. We must learn, and teach, how important *attitudes* are, also, if we are to survive. In job-hunting, as in life, when it comes right down to it, *attitude is everything.*

### Discussion

*Job-hunter: I've always wanted a chance to study famous painters a little more. Do you think that's a good thing for me to be doing with my time, when I'm out of work for quite a spell?*

Career-counselor: Well, why wouldn't it be?

*Job-hunter: I was just thinking that if a prospective employer found out this is how I'm spending my time, they'd think I was a little frivolous, and not serious about my job-hunt.*

Career-counselor: Well, this should be a supplement to one serious job-hunt on your part, not a replacement for that job-hunt.

*Job-hunter: Oh, a supplement!*

Career-counselor: Yes, your time should have two goals: job-hunting and learning, not just one. Never slack up on devoting a lot of time, each week, to your job-hunt or career-change. Learning about art is what you do, after it's time for you to rest from your job-hunting labors: namely, evenings or weekends.

*God, grant me the serenity
to accept the things I cannot change,
the courage to change the things I can,
and the wisdom to know the difference.*

REINHOLD NIEBUHR (1892–1971)

# Chapter 4. How to Deal with Handicaps

Survival, as we saw in the previous chapter, begins with paying attention to our attitudes. And the one that counts the most is our attitude toward ourselves.

When we go job-hunting many of us think that we have some special handicap (hidden or obvious) that is going to keep us from getting a job. Our attitude is, I probably won't be able to find a job because:

> I have a physical handicap *or*
> I have a mental handicap *or*
> I never graduated from high school *or*
> I never graduated from college *or*
> I am just graduating *or*

I just graduated two years ago and am still unemployed *or*
I graduated way too long ago *or*
I am too beautiful or handsome *or*
I am too ugly *or*
I am too fat *or*
I am too thin *or*
I am too old *or*
I am too young *or*
I have only had one employer in life *or*
I have hopped from job to job way too often *or*
I am too near retirement *or*
I am too inexperienced *or*
I have a prison record *or*
I have a psychiatric history *or*
I have not had enough education and am underqualified *or*
I have too much education and am overqualified *or*
I am Hispanic *or*
I am Black *or*
I am Asian *or*
My English is not very good *or*
I speak heavily accented English *or*
I am too much of a specialist *or*
I am too much of a generalist *or*
I am ex-clergy *or*
I am ex-military *or*
I am too assertive *or*
I am too shy *or*
I have only worked for volunteer organizations *or*
I have only worked for small organizations *or*
I have only worked for a large organization *or*
I have only worked for the government *or*
I come from a very different culture or background *or*
I come from another industry *or*
I come from another planet.

In other words, our attitude toward ourselves in some cases basically boils down to acting as if there are only three weeks in our life, when we are employable!

Okay, fine! But if you think you have a handicap that will keep employers from hiring you, take heart! No matter what handicap you have, or think you have, it cannot possibly keep you from getting hired. It can only keep you from getting hired *at some places*.

## ATTITUDE: YOU IN RELATION TO THE EMPLOYER

So, let's look at some *good* attitudes toward yourself. When you are unemployed, this begins, not surprisingly, with how you think of yourself in relation to employers. The first thing to keep in mind is this:

> There is no such thing as "employers." They are not all the same tribe. Each of them is an individual. But as far as you are concerned, there are basically only two kinds of employers *out there*: **employers who are interested in hiring you** for what you *can* do; and **employers who are not.** With the latter you should thank them for their time, and ask if they know of any other employers who might be interested in someone with your skills. Then, gently take your leave. And write and mail them a thank-you note that very night. Then keep going until you find that other kind of employer: the one who only looks at what you *can* do, not at what you can't.

The second thing you want to keep in mind, is that "handicap" is a loose term, referring to either job-hunters' *disabilities* or employers' *prejudices*. There is a difference, and you need to remember that.

Suppose you cannot hear. If you are considering a job that requires acute hearing, then that is a disability: it means there are certain skills you don't have, that are essential, at least for *that* job.

But now let us suppose you can hear perfectly, but you are way overweight. If you are applying for that same job, this is not a disability unless it interferes with your ability to do that work. Nonetheless, a particular employer may be prejudiced against overweight people, and simply won't hire you.

So, here's the distinction: a disability is something within *you*. A prejudice is something within *the employer*.

Both may appear as handicaps that keep you from getting hired, but it is important to understand that *a real handicap* is a disability you have— you cannot do some important task required in that particular job. On the other hand, a prejudice is *a phantom handicap*. It may raise its ugly head in one particular interview or more, but if you keep on going, find the right employer, then poof!—the so-called handicap vanishes.

You must just be sure you don't share some employers' prejudices. That is, don't look at yourself through their eyes. Look at yourself through your own eyes.

## DETAILED STRATEGIES FOR DEALING WITH YOUR ATTITUDE TOWARD AGING

One handicap, or employer prejudice, that is getting increased attention in the days ahead is age. Millions of baby boomers (*the 76 million people born 1946–1964*) are beginning to enter the so-called "retirement years." (Ha!) A lot of them are not finding pensions waiting, but are going to have to keep working long after they thought they would have to. What are they running into?

Well, let's say it's you who is getting older. It happens. Let's say you're in your fifties—or maybe you're already in your sixties, or seventies, or even eighties. What are employers going to think about you? Well you know what they're going to think, at least some of them. They will think you're too old for them to hire. Why? Well, in some cases they just think so. *Prejudice!*

But in other cases, their concern is their bottom line. Their reasoning is that you will cost too much. Given all your years of experience, you might easily expect a high salary—*but* they could hire two inexperienced workers in their twenties for what it would cost them to hire just you. You would cost them too much. Also, you would cost them too much if they're a company that still has a generous pension plan—though that is increasingly a vanishing breed these days. Or you will cost them too much, they think, if age means more medical problems, and they are mandated to have a medical plan.

Still, there are some employers out there who *will* hire you, regardless of age, if . . . (and here we have quite a list of *ifs*—all of which lie within your control, thank heaven, depending on your attitude).

They *will* hire you:

*If* they are a small company and they don't have to put you late into a pension plan; and

*If* you come with a positive attitude toward your aging. To assist in this, it is helpful to think of your life not in terms of work but in terms of music—particularly a symphony. A symphony, traditionally, has four parts to it—four movements, as they're called. So does Life. There is the first movement, infancy; then the second movement, the time of learning; the long third movement follows, the time of working; and finally, this fourth movement, traditionally called "retirement," though now that is an increasingly complex concept. It is much better to think of it as the Fourth Movement, a triumphant, powerful ending to the symphony of our life here on earth.

Onward with our ifs: and

*If* you convey energy, even in this period of your life. Ask any employer what they are looking for, when they interview a job candidate who is fifty years or older, and they will tell you: *energy.* Okay, but where shall we find energy, after fifty? When we were younger, energy came from the *physical* side of our nature. We were "feeling our oats," as they say. We could go all day, and all night. "My, where do you get all your energy?" our grandmother would ask us. We were a dynamo . . . of *physical* energy. But after fifty, physical energy may be harder to come by, despite workouts, exercise, and marathons. Increasingly, our energy must spring not from our muscles but from our excitement about Life; there are inevitably *some* employers dying to have that excitement in their organization; and

*If* you have done some life/work planning, and you know alternative ways to describe who you are and what you can do, because you did the self-inventory in chapter 13; and

*If* you have learned what it is you especially can contribute *because of* your age. You have learned, above all else, a precious skill: namely, how to handle interruptions. Martin Luther King Jr. said it best, just before his death:

*"The major problem of life is learning how to handle the costly interruptions—the door that slams shut, the plan that got side-tracked, the marriage that failed, or that lovely poem that didn't get written because someone knocked on the door."*

Many employers prize this attribute in any employee, because interruptions are the bane of their existence; and

*If* you keep going on interviews until you encounter an employer or two or three who share this understanding of age. What do I mean by *keep going?* Well, here is an actual job-hunter's records (the "process" she is referring to, is the PIE method, to be described in chapter 7):

*"Here are the figures you wanted: In the course of my surveying, September through November, I was referred to 120+ people. Of these I contacted 84 and actually met with 50. I met most people at their offices, a few for lunch, a couple for dinner, and one for breakfast! The process worked so well for me, I am really excited about my new prospects."*

Having the right attitude toward yourself often means this kind of persistence, keeping at it, working at your job-hunt far longer and far harder than the average job-hunter would ever dream of doing. And why? Because you know your own worth and you know you will be valuable to any organization that is able to see you clearly, and without prejudice about your age.

## ATTITUDE: YOU IN RELATION TO OTHER JOB-HUNTERS

I said earlier that a good attitude toward yourself depends, in part, on how you think of yourself in relation to employers. It also depends on how you think of yourself in relation to other job-hunters. Especially if you think that you are handicapped, while they are not.

Maybe this is the point where I need to remind you that everyone looking for work is handicapped. *What?!*

Well, sure. As we have seen, a real handicap means there are some things that a person cannot do. To see what that means here, let's start with how many skills there are, in the whole world. Nobody knows the number, so let's make one up. Let's say there are 4,341 skills in the world.

How many of those 4,341 do you think the average person has? Nobody knows that number either, so again let's make one up. Let's say the average person has 1,341 skills. That's a lot. That would be 1,341 things the average person can do.

But 4,341 skills in all the world minus 1,341 that the average person can do, leaves 3,000 things the average person *can't* do. Of course, what those 3,000 are, will vary from person to person. But, in the end, *everybody* is handicapped. Everybody. In each of our cases, there is a lot we can't do.

So when you go job-hunting, if you have a real handicap, what's so special about *your* handicap, compared with others'? The answer is *nothing*.

Unless—*unless*—you are so disheartened by the fact that you are handicapped, and so focused on what you *can't* do, that you have forgotten all the things you *can* do.

Unless you're thinking of all the reasons why employers might not hire you, instead of all the reasons why employers would be lucky to get you.

Unless you're going about your job-hunt feeling like *a job beggar*, rather than standing tall to offer yourself as *a helpful resource* for this employer.

## What You Can Do, What You Can't

To focus our attention on what we can do, not what we can't, here's a useful exercise. Take a piece of paper and divide it into two columns:

| I have this skill: | I don't have this skill: |
| --- | --- |
|  |  |

# A LIST OF 246 SKILLS AS VERBS

| | | | | |
|---|---|---|---|---|
| achieving | acting | adapting | addressing | administering |
| advising | analyzing | anticipating | arbitrating | arranging |
| ascertaining | assembling | assessing | attaining | auditing |
| budgeting | building | calculating | charting | checking |
| classifying | coaching | collecting | communicating | compiling |
| completing | composing | computing | conceptualizing | conducting |
| conserving | consolidating | constructing | controlling | coordinating |
| coping | counseling | creating | deciding | defining |
| delivering | designing | detailing | detecting | determining |
| developing | devising | diagnosing | digging | directing |
| discovering | dispensing | displaying | disproving | dissecting |
| distributing | diverting | dramatizing | drawing | driving |
| editing | eliminating | empathizing | enforcing | establishing |
| estimating | evaluating | examining | expanding | experimenting |
| explaining | expressing | extracting | filing | financing |
| fixing | following | formulating | founding | gathering |
| generating | getting | giving | guiding | handling |
| having responsibility | heading | helping | hypothesizing | identifying |
| illustrating | imagining | implementing | improving | improvising |
| increasing | influencing | informing | initiating | innovating |
| inspecting | inspiring | installing | instituting | instructing |
| integrating | interpreting | interviewing | intuiting | inventing |
| inventorying | investigating | judging | keeping | leading |
| learning | lecturing | lifting | listening | logging |
| maintaining | making | managing | manipulating | mediating |
| meeting | memorizing | mentoring | modeling | monitoring |
| motivating | navigating | negotiating | observing | obtaining |
| offering | operating | ordering | organizing | originating |
| overseeing | painting | perceiving | performing | persuading |
| photographing | piloting | planning | playing | predicting |
| preparing | prescribing | presenting | printing | problem solving |
| processing | producing | programming | projecting | promoting |
| proofreading | protecting | providing | publicizing | purchasing |
| questioning | raising | reading | realizing | reasoning |
| receiving | recommending | reconciling | recording | recruiting |
| reducing | referring | rehabilitating | relating | remembering |
| rendering | repairing | reporting | representing | researching |
| resolving | responding | restoring | retrieving | reviewing |
| risking | scheduling | selecting | selling | sensing |
| separating | serving | setting | setting-up | sewing |
| shaping | sharing | showing | singing | sketching |
| solving | sorting | speaking | studying | summarizing |
| supervising | supplying | symbolizing | synergizing | synthesizing |
| systematizing | taking instructions | talking | teaching | team-building |
| telling | tending | testing & proving | training | transcribing |
| translating | traveling | treating | trouble-shooting | tutoring |
| typing | umpiring | understanding | understudying | undertaking |
| unifying | uniting | upgrading | using | utilizing |
| verbalizing | washing | weighing | winning | working |
| writing | | | | |

*Chapter 4*

Then, look at the (*transferable/functional*) skills list on the opposite page, and copy as many skills as you choose onto that piece of paper, putting each skill in the proper column, depending on whether you *can* do the skill, or *cannot*. (*Or not yet, anyway.*) Use additional sheets, as needed.

When you are done with these two lists, pick out your favorite five things that you *can* do, and *love* to do; and write out some examples of how you actually demonstrated that, sometime in your recent past.

Incidentally, if you want a longer list, for any reason, Canadian career expert Martin Buckland has a free list of 2,010 action verbs at Elite Resumes (http://aneliteresume.com).

## HOW TO DEAL WITH "NO CAN DO, BUT WANT TO DO"

What about a real *disability:* something you *can't* do, but really want to be able to do? Maybe someone has invented a technology or simple strategy that helps you get around that disability. You never know. There are some very clever people out there. So, if your particular disability has a name, look it up on the Internet. Put its name into a search engine like Google, and see what turns up. Look particularly on the list it gives you for any professional association that deals with your disability. Contact them, and ask them what information they have.

An alternative way of dealing with this is to search for *related* jobs. Example: one career counselor in Europe was working with a young teenager who wanted to be a pilot. Problem: his eyesight was too poor. So the counselor sent him out to the large airport nearby, with a pad of yellow paper and a pen, and told him to spend the day listing every different kind of occupation that he saw or heard about, there at the airport—besides pilot. The next day he showed his list to his counselor. It was very long. When asked if he'd come across any occupation that interested him, he said, "Yes. I love the idea of making the seats that they put inside new airplanes." So, that's the job he pursued. He ended up in the airline industry, even though he couldn't be a pilot.

As for employer *prejudices*, you may have to cast a wider net in your search, than just the Internet. The kind of things you won't find there: the detailed help for ex-offenders that Dick Gaither offers. So let me tell you about him. He is head of Job Search Training Systems in Indiana, and has worked with ex-offenders a lot over the years. Ex-offenders, regardless of their past history, and their counselors will find lots of help if you e-mail Dick at workwizard@aol.com. He will send you 126 pages of helpful information and guidance. It's free. A great public service, from a tremendous human being.

## ATTITUDE: FINALLY, YOU IN RELATION TO YOURSELF

As most of us know, the proper attitude toward ourselves is called "good self-esteem." But self-esteem is an art. An art of balance. A balance between thinking too little of ourselves, and thinking too much of ourselves.

The name for thinking too much of ourselves is "egotism." We have all run into that, at some point in our lives, so we know what it looks like. Some of us have even caught a passing glimpse of it in the mirror.

In our culture and others, we are taught to recoil from this in horror. We even have mythologies warning us against it; the story of Narcissus comes to mind. Poor guy! (*See http://tinyurl.com/a3a33 if you are unfamiliar with the myth.*)

In order to avoid egotism, a lot of us go way overboard in the other direction. We shrink from ever declaring that we have any virtue, any excellency, any special gifts, lest we be accused of boasting. And so we fall into that opposite pit from egotism, namely, ingratitude. We appear ungrateful for the gifts that life, the universe, God—you name it—has already given us.

So, how do we adopt the proper attitude toward our gifts—speaking of them honestly, humbly, gratefully—without sounding egotistical? Just this: the more you see your own gifts clearly, the more you must pay attention to the gifts that others have. The more sensitive you become to how unusual you are, the more you must become sensitive to how unusual those around you are. The more you pay attention to yourself, the more you must pay attention to others. The more you ponder the mystery of You, the more you must ponder the mystery of all those you encounter, every loved one, every friend, every acquaintance, every stranger.

Self-esteem is an art. It is the art of balance. A balance between thinking too little of ourselves, and thinking too much of ourselves. But we can only think too much of ourselves if we lose sight of others. Look at yourself, but equally look at them—with wonder.

That is the proper attitude we all should set as our goal.

## Discussion

*Job-hunter: I never thought of egotism this way. I always thought that if you talked about yourself being good at something, that was boasting. I'd heard about "the tall poppy" theory of life, with its implication that you shouldn't stand taller than others in your field.*

Career-counselor: Well, I think that's true. But you make yourself equal to others not by lowering yourself but by raising them up. I ask you, what are the favorite skills of your best friend or mate? Do you know? Are you sure? Have you asked them what they think? Have you complimented them on these skills, during the past week?

*Job-hunter: I've got to go now; I think I have work to do.*

Career-counselor: No longer worried about being egotistical, eh?

*Job-hunter: No, I'm just worried about them. I want them to know how excellent they are.*

Career-counselor: Just remember, it's no sin to praise yourself as long as that heightens your awareness of what there is to praise in them.

# THE FIVE PARTS OF JOB-HUNTING AS A SURVIVAL SKILL:

# II.

# ADVANCED JOB-FINDING TECHNIQUES

*It is common sense to take a method and try it. If it fails, admit it frankly and try another. But, above all, try something.*

FRANKLIN D. ROOSEVELT (1882–1945)

# Chapter 5. The Best and Worst Ways to Look for Those Job Vacancies That *Are* Out There

Number of people in the U.S. who found jobs the month I am writing: 3,907,000.

Number of vacancies still unfilled at the end of this month: 3,093,000.

Imagine we find ourselves in some U.S. city that we haven't been to, in ten years.

We had a friend there, and we wonder if he's still there; or has he moved, or maybe died. We decide to look him up in the phone book. We come up empty. No phone number for anyone by that name. We decide, therefore, that he doesn't live there anymore.

Well, we're wrong. He does still live there. It's just that, like 26.6 percent of all American homes, he's switched completely from a landline to a cell phone, and cell phones aren't listed in the local phone book.

So, what was our error? (*Hint: there are two errors here.*)

The first is, we chose the wrong method to try and find him.

The second, and more grievous error, is we falsely concluded that because we couldn't find him with our method, this meant that he didn't exist. Didn't exist *there*, at any rate. *Wrong!* It's stretching logic beyond the breaking point to think that "Can't find" = "doesn't exist." Think about the lifelong battle between ourselves and our car keys.

Okay, now fast-forward to a time when we're out of work. We are looking for a job. We turn to the Internet, and search all the job boards: Monster, CareerBuilder, LinkUp, Craigslist, Indeed, SimplyHired, and so forth. We can't find any work. What is it we all typically say at this point? Well, you know what we say: "There are no jobs out there. I've looked until I'm blue in the face." We've just made the same error, again, as we did with our friend and the phone book. We've assumed that "Can't find" = "doesn't exist." *Wrong!*

So, if you're out of work, survival job-hunting begins with a simple mantra. Write it out, stick it on your bathroom mirror, read it every morning while you're unemployed:

> Just because you can't find them doesn't mean they don't exist. You've got to change the way you're looking for them. Because there are *always* job vacancies out there.

Let's tackle right off the bat the most vexing question that then faces us regarding job-search: why do our elementary job-hunting skills work so well at finding those vacancies during good times, but come up empty during hard times such as we are presently in?

The answer to this begins with a profoundly overlooked fact. And that is, generally speaking, *employers and job-hunters search for each other in entirely different ways*. Actually, it's worse than that. Employers and job-hunters typically search for each other in almost *exactly opposite ways*. A chart of employers' preferences vs. job-hunters' preferences would come out looking something like the diagram on the next page.

Now comes the twist: during good times, when employers are having difficulty in filling a vacancy, *they will typically adapt to the job-hunter's preferences*, and search for employees in ways that job-hunters prefer: that is, they will post their vacancies on the Internet, and they will take the trouble to look at, and read, job-hunters' resumes. And we, the unemployed, are close to job-hunting heaven.

What we are not prepared for, is that during hard times, when employers are finding it much easier to fill a vacancy, as currently, *they will revert to their original preferences (in the diagram, choosing red #1, then #2, etc.)*. And when that happens, we can search the Internet or send out resumes until we're blue in the face, yet turn up nothing. Because during hard times employers mostly aren't using the job-hunters' favorite methods anymore, to broadcast their vacancies. Employers have gone

# Many If Not Most Employers Hunt for Job-Hunters in the Exact Opposite Way from How Most Job-Hunters Hunt for Them

**The Way a Typical Employer Prefers to Fill a Vacancy**

**1** **6**

From Within: Promotion of a full-time employee, or promotion of a present part-time employee, or hiring a former consultant for in-house or contract work, or hiring a former "temp" full-time. Employer's thoughts: *"I want to hire someone whose work I have already seen."* (A low-risk strategy for the employer.)

**Implication for Job-Hunters:** See if you can get hired at an organization you have chosen—as a temp, contract worker, or consultant—aiming at a full-time position only later (or not at all).

**2** **5**

Using Proof: Hiring an unknown job-hunter who brings proof of what he or she can do, with regards to the skills needed.

**Implication for Job-Hunters:** If you are a programmer, bring a program you have done—with its code; if you are a photographer, bring photos; if you are a counselor, bring a case study with you; etc.

**3** **4**

Using a Best Friend or Business Colleague: Hiring someone whose work a trusted friend of yours has seen (perhaps they worked for him or her).

**Implication for Job-Hunters:** Find someone who knows the person-who-has-the-power-to-hire at your target organization, who also knows your work and will introduce you two.

**4** **3**

Using an Agency They Trust: This may be a recruiter or search firm the employer has hired; or a private employment agency—both of which have checked you out, on behalf of the employer.

**5** **2**

Using an Ad They Have Placed (online or in newspapers, etc.).

**6** **1**

Using a Resume: Even if the resume was unsolicited (if the employer is desperate).

**The Way a Typical Job-Hunter Prefers to Fill a Vacancy**

back to their default position. And we, accustomed to job-hunting in good times, suddenly find that nothing is working.

Yet, it isn't for want of trying. We work like a dog, we send out resumes week after week, we search all the Internet job boards day after day, we turn to our Facebook, and LinkedIn, and Twitter pages for help, we network like crazy, we attend job-hunters' support groups week after week, but. . . . But, nothing happens. Everything that used to work, doesn't work anymore. For us, the unemployed, *that* is baffling, and if it goes on for many months, it is absolute hell. It is like turning the key in our faithful car, but for the first time in ten years, the motor won't start.

We conclude, of course, that there just aren't any jobs out there. Oh, but there are. As we saw at the beginning of this chapter. We just can no longer find them. So, what are we to do?

We have a remedy, fortunately. We can, in such times as these, start thinking like an employer, learn how employers prefer to look for employees, and figure out how to change our own job-hunting strategies so as to conform to *that*. In other words, *adapt to the employer's preferences*.

## VISITING THE FOREIGN COUNTRY CALLED "THE WORLD OF THE EMPLOYER"

This was an idea from the authors of a book called *No One Is Unemployable*.[1] They suggested that when you approach the world of business for the first time, you should think of it as like going to visit a foreign country; you know you're going to have to learn a whole new language, culture, and customs, there. Same with the job-market.

So, let's take a look at that world:

1. When it comes right down to it, there is no such thing as "employers." Employers are a rainbow, not just, say, blue. Not just any one color. They span a wide range of attitudes, wildly different ideas about how to hire, a wide range of ways to conduct hiring inter-

---

1. Debra Angel MacDougall and Elisabeth Harney Sanders-Park. The book was published by Worknet Training Services in 1997. A more current book of theirs is titled *The 6 Reasons You'll Get the Job: What Employers Look for—Whether They Know It or Not*, published in 2010 by Prentice Hall.

views, and as many different attitudes toward handicaps as you can possibly think of. Job-hunters' generalizations, like "Employers don't want someone with my background," are just not true. *Some* employers do want you. Your job is to find *them*.

2. There is a big difference between large employers (those with hundreds or thousands of employees) and small employers (alternately defined as those with 25 or fewer employees, those with 50 or fewer employees, or—the most common definition—those with 100 or fewer employees). The chief difference is that large employers are harder to reach, especially if the-person-who-has-the-power-to-hire-you (for the job you want) is in some deep inner chamber of that company, and the company's phone has a voice menu with eighteen layers.

3. There is a big difference between new companies or enterprises, and those that have been around for some time, as far as hiring is concerned. A study reported in *Time* magazine found that newer small companies (100 or fewer employees here) that were less than six years old created 4.7 million jobs in 2005, while older small firms created only 3.2 million jobs.[2] So when hiring is tight, you will want to concentrate on small firms, and newer small firms, at that.

4. Employers have the power in this whole hiring game; and this explains why parts of the whole job-hunting system in this country will drive you nuts. It wasn't built for you or me. It was built by and for *them*. And they live in a world different from yours and mine, in their head. (I said *foreign country*!) This results in the following six contrasts:

   a. You want the job-market to be *a hiring game*. But the employer regards it as *an elimination game*—until the very last phase. They're looking at that huge stack of resumes on their desk, with a view—first of all—to finding out who they can eliminate. Eventually they want to get it down to the "last person standing."

   b. You want the employer to be taking lots of initiative toward finding you, and when they are desperate they will. HR

---

2. "Briefing on the Economy," *Time*, April 11, 2011.

departments can spend hours and days combing the Internet looking for the right person. But generally speaking the employer prefers that it be you who takes the initiative, toward finding *them*.

c. In being considered for a job, you want your solid past performance—summarized on your written resume—to be all that gets weighed, but the employer weighs your whole behavior as they glimpse it from their first interaction with you, to the last. Employers operate intuitively on the principle of microcosm equals macrocosm. They believe that what you do in some small "universe" reveals how you will act in a larger "universe." Small "universes," in the hiring interview, are such things as: Are you late for the appointment? Do you let the interviewer talk half the time, or not? Do you treat everyone with respect and courtesy there, or not? Do you write a thank-you note after the interview—not only to them, but to the receptionist, secretary, and whoever else you interacted with, there—by name—or not? They watch you carefully in these particulars, during and after the interview, because they assume that each of these reveals, in microcosm, how you would act in a larger "universe," like: the job you are applying for! They scrutinize your past, as in your resume, for the same reason: *microcosm* (behavior in the past) *reveals macrocosm* (behavior in the future).

d. You want the employer to acknowledge receipt of your resume—particularly if you post it *right on their website*, but the employer generally feels too swamped with other things, to have time to do that, so only 45 percent do. A majority, 55 percent, do not. Don't take it personally.

e. You want to go into the interview with the employer curious to know more about *you*, but the employer is first of all curious about what you know about *them*. Employers don't like blind dates.

f. You want employers to save your job-hunt by increasing their hiring, and you want the government to give them incentives to do so. Unhappily, employers tend to wait to hire until they see an increased demand for their products or services. In the meantime, most do not much care for government incentives to hire, because they know such incentives always have a time limit, and once they expire, that employer will be on the hook to continue the subsidy out of their own pocket. What all this adds up to is that employers won't come to save you. The success of your job-hunt depends on you—with a little help from your friends. You must be in charge of it. You must plan it. You must direct it. You must know what works and what doesn't work. Your job-hunt is by its very nature a "self-directed search."

With this background concerning the differences between your world and the employers' world, we are ready to understand not only what are the five worst or five best ways for discovering those vacancies that are out there, but also *why* they are the worst or the best. (*Here comes a generalization.*) In general, it is risk that determines which job-hunting methods "employers" prefer. Most employers prize *low risk* in hiring—they prefer that they or someone they respect has actually seen the job-hunter perform, and can testify from their experience that this job-hunter would be a good hire. In-house promotion is their absolute preference. But referrals, particularly in-house referrals, are a gold standard. So is recommendation by some fellow employer or colleague whose opinions they trust.

Because of their fear of risk, employers tend to be much more focused on a job-hunter's experience than they are on his or her *potential*, or *skills*, or *knowledges*. They prefer to hire someone who has had past experience in this or related fields, rather than a career-changer who is new to the field and to the job. (*Good news: there are ways of getting around this, as we shall see later, in chapter 12.*) Of course there are sterling exceptions to what I have just said, but you have to hunt harder, to find them.

## JOB-HUNTING METHODS WERE NOT CREATED EQUAL

Now to our lists. But first a word about my methodology, such as it is. There is absolutely nothing scientific here. The statistics, the percentages, are guesses. My guesses.

That's because, on the one hand, we don't have much research comparing how well job-hunters' methods work. Researchers tend to study employers' behavior and preferences, but not job-hunters'.

On the other hand, if you are in this field for forty years, as I have been, and you keep your eyes open, you do run into a small study here, a small study there, that gives you a pretty good idea, over time, of what works, what doesn't, and to what degree. I watch for these all the time, but I don't keep records of what study, what year, who did it, and that kind of thing. Studies about job-hunters' behavior are notoriously "squishy," and not worth leaning too heavily on. So, I read this stuff, and then store just the basic statistics away in my head, so when it comes time to make guesses, I don't make them out of thin air. They are *educated* guesses, based on research and observation.

Now, when all is said and done, what difference do these odds make? Just this. There are 18 alternative ways of looking for work, as we have seen; but unfortunately, these alternatives were *not* all created equal. Some methods of hunting for jobs have a pretty good track record, and therefore will repay you for time spent pursuing them. But other methods have a pretty poor track record, and you can waste a lot of time, and energy, on them, with no results, if you're not careful. So, this is all about *conservation of energy. Your* energy. The lesson from all this is: don't waste your time or energy on the least effective job-hunting methods, unless you're one of these people who likes to bet against the odds, the bigger the better.

Here, then, are my educated guesses as to what percentage of job-hunters who use *each method* actually succeed thereby in finding a job.

You will notice that some of our country's favorite job-hunting strategies are on the list of *least effective*. I was as surprised as you.

## THE FIVE WORST WAYS TO LOOK FOR A JOB

### Only a 4 to 10% Success Rate

1. Looking for employers' job-postings on the Internet. Yeah, I know, you're somewhere between *surprised* and *shocked* at this finding. I was too. For now, we are talking about the Internet in just one of its capaci-

ties: as a place where job-hunters can find jobs, whether through posting their resume, or looking for employers' job postings, working through social media, websites, Twitter, or blogs. The question is, how helpful is *this* use of the Internet, and this use only?

The answer is: well, that depends.

You will hear stories of job-hunters who have successfully used the Internet to find a job. The stories are very impressive. Here are some examples.

A job-seeker, a systems administrator in Taos, New Mexico, who wanted to move to San Francisco posted his resume at 10 p.m. on a Monday night, on a San Francisco online bulletin board (*Craigslist.org*). By Wednesday morning he had over seventy responses from employers.

Again, a marketing professional developed her resume following guidance she found on the Internet, posted it to two advertised positions she found there, and within seventy-two hours of posting her electronic resume, both firms contacted her, and she is now working for one of them.

I get letters about this, too. "In May I was very unexpectedly laid off from a company I was with for five years. I did 100 percent of my job search and research via the Internet. I found all my leads online, sent all my resumes via e-mail, and had about a 25 percent response rate that actually led to a phone interview or a face-to-face interview. It was a software company that laid me off, and I am [now] going to work for a publishing company, a position I found online."

And: "Thanks to the Internet, I found what I believe to be the ideal job in [just] eight weeks—a great job with a great company and great opportunities. . . ."

So we see the Internet can do a marvelous job of making it possible for an employer and a job-hunter to get together, in a way that was rarely possible even fifteen years ago. Internet sites devoted to job-hunting— some experts say there are over 100,000 "job-boards" now—make it possible for job-hunter and employer to get together *faster* than ever before in history.

So, you'll want to try it. Of course, it doesn't always work. Aye, and there's the rub! It turns out, despite all the hype, that it actually doesn't work for a huge percentage of those who try it. Researchers have turned up the fact that out of every 100 job-hunters who use the Internet as their search method for finding jobs, 4 of them will get lucky and find a job thereby, while 96 job-hunters out of the 100 will not—if they use *only the Internet* to search for a job.

*Disclaimer: If you are seeking a technical or computer-related job, an IT job, or a job in engineering, finances, or healthcare, the success rate rises, to somewhere around 10 percent. But for the other 20,000 job-titles that are out there in the job-market, the success rate reportedly remains at about 4 percent.*

In better times, economically, it was common for job-hunters to believe that job-search on the Internet worked for most everybody, so when they found that it didn't work for them, they obsessed over the question: "What's wrong with *me*?" Result: lowered self-esteem, or even mammoth depression. Yuck!

In hard times, we expect that job-search on the Internet won't work well for just about everybody. Why? Because we think there just are no jobs out there. Okay, and why do we think that? The answer: Mythology.

> The common myth among job-hunters is that if an employer has a vacancy, they will post it on the Internet—on their own site, if nowhere else. *Not true.* Employers will only post their vacancies on the Internet, or anywhere else, if they are having trouble finding the kind of hire that they are looking for.

Otherwise, they fall back to their default position: filling it without advertising it. This creates what we might call an underground job-market, which historically has been called the "hidden job market." Because of this mythology, job-hunters think that if there are no postings, there are no jobs available. *Not true.* The vacancies have just gone underground.

## Only a 7% Success Rate

2. Posting or mailing out your resume to employers. This job-search method apparently has about a 7 percent success rate. That is, out of every 100 job-hunters who use only this search method, 7 will get lucky, and find a job thereby; 93 job-hunters out of 100 will not—if they use only resumes to search for those vacancies that are out there. This comes

as a shock to most job-hunters. Everyone and his brother tell us: a good resume will get you a job. It's virtually an article of faith among the unemployed. Why does everyone keep telling us this, if it's not true? Oh, why did everyone entrust their money to Bernie Madoff? Or why did so many people buy those incredibly risky financial instruments that led to the Recession? You tell me.

Resumes make you feel like they're out there, working for you. They make you feel as though you're really doing something about your job-hunt. But in fact they may be moribund or comatose. That is, they may not be getting read, at all, even when posted on an employer's own website. As for posting on general sites, well, they won't tell you their success rate, but back before this curtain of silence fell, Pete Weddle, an expert on recruiting, got some resume sites on the Internet to tell him how many employers actually looked at the resumes on their sites at that time. Sit down while I tell you the news from back then: A site that had 85,000 resumes posted, only 850 employers looked at any of those resumes in the previous three months before the survey. Another site with 59,283 resumes posted, only 1,366 employers looked at any, in the previous three months. Another site with 40,000 resumes, only 400 employers in three months. A site with 30,000 resumes, only 15 employers looked in, during the previous three months.

So, you post your resume on the Internet, confident that employers are reading them, when—in a depressing number of cases—nobody is. Some employers, in fact, hate resumes (I kid you not). So many lies, on so many resumes. Or at least exaggeration and distortion of job-hunters' actual experience and knowledge. As much as 82 percent of the time, according to some experts.

*(Anyway, the success rate is sad. And actually I'm being generous here with my reported percentage. One study suggested that outside the Internet only 1 out of 1,470 resumes actually resulted in a job. Another study said the figure was even worse: one job offer for every 1,700 resumes floating around out there. We do not know what the odds are if you post your resume on the Internet. We do know that once you post your resume on the Internet, it gets copied quickly by "spiders" from other sites, and you can never remove it completely from the Internet. There are reportedly at least 40,000,000 resumes floating around out there in the ether, like lost ships on the Sargasso*

Sea. No one's bothered to try to count how many of those 40,000,000 actually turned up a job for the job-hunter.)

## Only a 7% Success Rate

3. Answering ads in professional or trade journals, appropriate to your field. This search method, like the one above, apparently has about a 7 percent success rate. That is, out of every 100 job-hunters who use only this search method, 7 will get lucky and find a job thereby; 93 job-hunters out of 100 will not—if they use only this method to search for the vacancies that are out there.

## Only a 5 to 24% Success Rate

4. Answering local newspaper ads. This search method apparently has about a 5 to 24 percent success rate. That is, out of every 100 job-hunters who use only this search method, between 5 and 24 will get lucky and find a job thereby; 76 to 95 job-hunters out of 100 will not—if they use only this method to search for the vacancies that are out there.

*(The fluctuation between 5 percent and 24 percent is due to the level of salary that is being sought; the higher the salary being sought, the fewer job-hunters who are able to find a job using only this search method.)*

## Only a 5 to 28% Success Rate

5. Going to private employment agencies or search firms for help. This method apparently has about a 5 to 28 percent success rate—again depending on the level of salary that is being sought. Which is to say, out of every 100 job-hunters who use only this method, between 5 and 28 will get lucky and find a job thereby; 72 to 95 job-hunters out of 100 will not—if they use only this method to search for those vacancies that are out there.

*(The range is for the same reason as noted in #4. It is of interest that the success rate of this method apparently has risen slightly in recent years, in the case of women but not of men: before the recession, 27.8 percent of female job-hunters found a job within two months, by going to private employment agencies.)*

Other Job-Hunting Methods in the *Least Effective* Category: For the sake of completeness we should note that there are at least four other methods for trying to find jobs, that technically fall into this category of Worst Ways. Those four are:

Going to places where employers pick out workers, such as union halls. This apparently has about an 8 percent success rate. *(Only 11.9 percent of U.S. workers are union members,*[3] but it is claimed that those who do have access to a union hiring hall, have a 22 percent success rate. What is not stated, however, is how long it takes to get a job at the hall, and how short-lived such a job may be; in the trades it's often just a few days.)

Taking a civil service examination. This apparently has about a 12 percent success rate.

Asking a former teacher or professor for job-leads. This also has about a 12 percent success rate.

Going to the state or federal employment service office. This apparently has about a 14 percent success rate.

## THE FIVE BEST WAYS TO HUNT FOR A JOB

Okay, so much for the apparently least effective ways to hunt for the vacancies that are out there. But now, let's look at the other side of the coin. What are the job-hunting methods that have a better payoff, for the time and energy you invest in them?

Here are some educated guesses about the five best:

### 33% Success Rate

1. Asking for job-leads from: family members, friends, people in the community, staff at career centers—especially at your local community college or the high school or college where you graduated. You ask them one simple question: do you know of any job vacancies at the place where you work—or elsewhere? This search method apparently has about a 33 percent success rate. That is, out of every 100 people who use this search method, 33 will get lucky, and find a job thereby; 67 job-hunters will not—if they use only this method to search for those vacancies that are out there.

---

3. http://tinyurl.com/27c4z5

Whoa! This is one of the five best ways to look for a job? Well, yes; it's all relative. But to put things in perspective, do note that this method's success rate is almost five times higher than the success rate for resumes. *In other words, by asking for job-leads from your family and friends, you have an almost five times better chance of finding a job, than if you had just sent out your resume.*

## 47% Success Rate

2. Knocking on the door of any employer, factory, or office that interests you, whether they are known to have a vacancy or not. This search method apparently has anywhere up to a 47 percent success rate. That is, out of every 100 people who use only this search method, 47 will get lucky, and find a job thereby; 53 job-hunters out of 100 will not—if they use only this one method to search for work. But again, for perspective, note that *by going face-to-face* you have an almost seven times better chance of finding a job, than if you had just sent out your resume.

## 65% Success Rate

3. By yourself, using the index to your phone book's Yellow Pages to identify subjects or fields of interest to you in the town or city where you want to work, and then calling up or visiting the employers listed in that field, to ask if they are hiring for the type of position you can do, and do well. This method apparently has about a 65 percent success rate. That is, out of every 100 job-hunters or career-changers who use only this search method, 65 will get lucky and find a job thereby; 35 job-hunters out of 100 will not—if they use only this one method to search for them. For perspective, however, note that by doing *targeted phone calls by yourself,* you have a nine times better chance of finding a job, than if you had just sent out your resume.

## 70% Success Rate

4. In a group with other job-hunters, a kind of "job-club" or "job support group," using the phone book's Yellow Pages to identify subjects or fields of interest to you in the town or city where you are, and then calling up or visiting the employers listed in that field, to ask if they are hiring for the type of position you can do, and do well. This method is the same as the previous method, except here you work in a

group and you choose a partner to work with in identifying job-leads. Moreover, you share with the rest of the group what kind of job you are looking for. This method apparently has at best a 70 percent success rate. That is, out of every 100 job-hunters or career-changers who use only this search method, 70 will get lucky and find a job thereby; 30 job-hunters out of 100 will not—if they use only this one method to search for them. For perspective, however, note that by doing *targeted phone calls with a group to support you*, you have an almost ten times better chance of finding a job, than if you had just sent out your resume. Why does this method work better than doing it alone? Well, let's say you're in a job-club that has 48 other members. Once you tell them what you're looking for, you get an extra 48 pairs of eyes looking on your behalf, and an extra 48 pairs of ears listening on your behalf—all the time that they are out there looking for job-leads themselves.

*Note: the success rate for this approach has declined precipitously.* Nathan Azrin invented this method back in 1973. It had an 84 to 92 percent success rate; but there are virtually no "job-clubs" today that follow his model, and there's the problem.

Azrin's job-club was all about action, calling for the job-club to meet every single weekday, all day, doing phoning with partners in the morning, and going out and calling upon employers every afternoon.[4] Most groups that call themselves "job-clubs" today are only shadows of the Azrin model, and may more accurately be described as "job support groups." They tend to meet once weekly at best, for just two or three hours at a time, and devote their meetings to inspiration, pep talks, and exchanging job-leads; but the actual job-hunt occurs outside the group meeting. As a result, the success rate is as low as 10 percent.

Job support groups do have one sterling virtue, however, and that is, they provide community to the otherwise lonely job-hunter. This is very, very valuable. No one should have to job-hunt by themselves.

---

4. His detailed manual describing exactly how to do this has been out of print for years; but the desperate (and well-off) can find it for about $100 at alibris.com. It's called *The Job Club Counselor's Manual: A Behavioral Approach to Vocational Counseling*. Nathan Azrin is the author.

5. Doing an Inventory of Yourself. This doesn't sound like a job-hunting method, but it is. It was invented by the late Bernard Haldane, polished by the late John Crystal, and organized by Daniel Porot. It involves doing extensive homework on *yourself* before you go out there pounding the pavement. This method has an apparent 86 percent success rate, the highest by far of any job-hunting method. You know by now that this means out of every 100 job-hunters or career-changers who use this method, 86 will get lucky and find a job thereby; 14 job-hunters out of 100 will not—if they use only this method to search for vacancies. Such an effectiveness rate is astronomically higher than virtually every other job-hunting method there is. For example, doing homework on yourself works twelve times better than resumes, when you're looking for work. This means, that by doing the hard thinking this method requires, you have a 1,200 percent better chance of finding a job than if you just send out resumes!

This method revolves around three simple words: you do an inventory of your answers to What, Where, and How.

1. WHAT. This has to do with your skills, specifically your *transferable* skills. You need to inventory and identify what skills you have *that you most enjoy using.* I didn't say: *that you are best at,* or that are the most marketable. No, these are the ones you *enjoy* using the most. They are called your transferable skills, because they are transferable to any field/career that you choose, regardless of where you first picked them up. These are usually verbs—*the gerund form of verbs, actually*—like: analyzing, organizing, researching, communicating, etc.

2. WHERE. This has to do with job environments. Think of yourself as a flower. You know that a flower that blooms in the desert will not do well at 10,000 feet up—and vice versa. Every flower has an environment where it does best. In that sense, you are like a flower. You need to decide where you would most enjoy using your skills, because that is where you will do your most effective work. Experts call these your "fields of fascination," or just "fields." These are

usually nouns, like technology, finance, the arts, chemistry, automobiles, criminal justice, nursing, hospitality, etc.

3. HOW. You need to decide how to get where you want to go. This has to do with finding out the names of the jobs you would be most interested in, **and** the names of organizations (in your preferred geographical area) that have such jobs to offer, and the names of the people or person there who actually has the power to hire you. And, how you can best approach that person to show them how your skills can help them with their goals or challenges. How, if you were hired there, you would not be part of the problem, but part of the solution.

Why does this self-inventory work so well *as a job-hunting method?* Well, there are three reasons that I have observed, over the years:

a. If you do this self-inventory, you can then more accurately define to yourself just exactly what you're looking for, beneath the shifting shape of job-titles. In a brutal economy, job-titles like "accountant" just aren't detailed enough. New thinking is called for: as we saw earlier, you are not "an accountant" or "a construction worker" or whatever. *You are a person, who* . . . You are a person who has these skills and these experiences. You are a person who can describe yourself in alternative ways.

b. If you do this self-inventory, you can then more accurately describe to your family, friends, and networks just exactly what you're looking for, in detail. Not just *"Uh, I'm out of work; let me know if you hear of anything,"* but exactly what kind of "thing," and in what work setting.

c. Lastly, when you are facing, let us say, nineteen other competitors for a job you want—who superficially look equal to you in skills and experience—if you did this self-inventory, then you can accurately describe to employers exactly what is unique about you, and what you bring to the table that the others don't. These will usually turn out to involve adjectives or adverbs, what we normally call *traits.*

*There is one problem with this method, which we should note: It involves work.* "Thinking" kind of work. Most job-hunters therefore avoid it. Takes too much time. Demands too much thinking. It certainly is not for the lazy, nor for those looking for the easy way out of their unemployment situation. (Reality check, however: it actually can be done in a full weekend, or on six successive Monday nights, or whatever.)

## SOME GENTLE CAVEATS

Well, there's your list. The best and the worst. Now you know which methods are most effective—on two counts: that conserve your energy, and that are most likely to produce results in your job search. But keep in mind, when all is said and done:

1. *Job-hunting is an activity that repeats itself over and over again, in most people's lives.* Lucky you, if that is not the case; but the odds are overwhelming that it will be. According to experts, the average worker, under thirty-five years of age, will go job-hunting every one to three years. And the average worker over thirty-five will go job-hunting every five to eight years! And, in this process, so the experts say, we will each of us probably change *careers* three to five times, or more, over our lifetime.

2. *Job-hunting is not a science; it is an art.* Some job-hunters know instinctively how to do it; in some cases, they were born knowing how to do it. Others sometimes have a harder time with it, but fortunately for us in the U.S. and elsewhere in the world, there is help, coaching, counseling, and advice—online and off.

3. *Job-hunting is always mysterious.* Sometimes *mind-bogglingly mysterious.* You may *never* understand why things sometimes do work, and sometimes do not.

4. *There is no always wrong way to hunt for a job or to change careers.* Anything *may* work under certain circumstances, or at certain times, or with certain employers. There are only *degrees of likelihood* of certain job-hunting techniques working or not working. But it is crucial to know that likelihood, as we have just seen.

5. *There is no always right way to hunt for a job or to change careers.* Anything *may* fail to work under certain circumstances, or at cer-

tain times, or with certain employers. There are only *degrees of likelihood* of certain job-hunting techniques working or not working. But it is crucial to know that likelihood, as we just saw.

6. *Job-hunting always depends on some amount of luck.* Luck, pure luck. Having advanced job-hunting skills doesn't mean absolutely, positively, you will always be able to find a job. It does mean that you can get good at reducing the amount that depends on luck, to as small a proportion as possible.

## CONCLUSION

Job-hunting skills are defined as *advanced* when they take seriously the world of the employer, and try to enter into the mind of the employer. And understand *why* they do what they do.

As shown in the diagram at the beginning of this chapter, employers came to their preferences out of hard experience, measured by their desire, same as you, to conserve their energy. Their basic concern was and is, "How many applications will I have to run through, before finding someone to hire?" (The number of interviews they need to do to find a hire, once they've sifted through the applications, stays constant, around 5.4.) Okay, so with that background, this is their experience:[5]

If employers post their vacancy on a job-board such as CareerBuilder .com or Monster.com, they have to look through 219 applications from job-hunters who respond, before they find someone to hire.

If employers consider applications from job-hunters who come through social media sites, such as LinkedIn or Facebook, they have to look through 116 applications, before they find someone to hire.

If employers post their vacancy on their own website, they have to look through 33 applications from job-hunters who respond, before they find someone to hire.

If the job-hunter takes the initiative to find a very specific job, rather than waiting to find a vacancy, and does this, say, by typing the name of that job into a search engine, then sending resumes to companies they turn up that way whether or not they are known to have a vacancy,

---

5. From an analysis, released in April 2011, by Jobs2web, Inc., of 1,300,000 job applications and 26,000 hires in 2010.

employers only have to look through 32 applications, before they find someone to hire.

And if the job-hunter takes even more initiative, chooses a company where they'd like to work, and gets a referral (i.e., gets some employee within that company to recommend them), employers have to look through only 10 such applications, before they find someone to hire.

Now you understand.

## Discussion

*Job-hunter: Since the information in this chapter is so crucial for our survival in today's world, why do you think this stuff isn't taught in high schools and colleges?*

Career-counselor: Well, it certainly should be! The reasons why it's not, make up a very long list. You can choose between: because the teachers don't know these facts, because the teachers haven't had to job-hunt recently themselves, because they think the function of a school is to teach ideas, not practical manuals like how to fix a car, or how to run their job-hunt successfully, or how to find an appropriate friend or (eventually) a mate, and so on.

*Job-hunter: I think inertia enters in, too. "This is the way we've always done it, and we don't see any reason to change."*

Career-counselor: Yes, and don't forget budgets. Education is the victim of a lot of belt-tightening these days, and of course the first staff to be let go are the ones who are experts on how to relate education to the world of work. That's often regarded as "nice but not necessary" information.

*Job-hunter: What's the remedy for this missing part of our education?*

Career-counselor: Learn it on your own; and then go teach at least one other person.

*He or she who gets hired is not necessarily the one who can do that job best; but, the one who knows the most about how to get hired.*

RICHARD LATHROP

in his classic *Who's Hiring Who?*

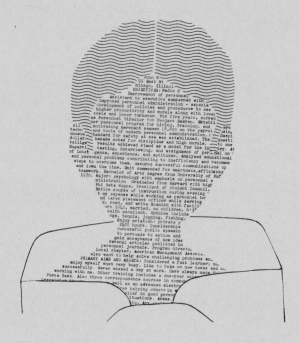

# Chapter 6. Do I Really Need a Resume?

In "the old days" before the Internet became popular with job-hunters, the only way an employer could learn much about you was from a piece of paper that you yourself wrote—with maybe a little help from your friends—called your resume, or C.V., which is an academic term meaning "curriculum vitae." On that paper was a summary of where you had been and all you had done. From that piece of paper, the employer was supposed to guess what kind of person you are and what kind of employee you'd be.

The good thing about all this, from your point of view, was that you had control over what went on that piece of paper; you could omit anything that was embarrassing, or anything from your past that you have long since regretted. Short of their hiring a private detective, or talking to your previous employers, employers couldn't find out much else. You had absolute control over how much they could know about you. That was nice. But now those days are gone forever.

## IN THIS TWENTY-FIRST CENTURY: GOOGLE IS YOUR NEW RESUME

There is a new resume in town, and it's called *Google*. All any employer has to do is type your name into a search engine like Google, and bamo! If you've been anywhere near the Internet (and 82 percent of us in the U.S. have)—if you've posted anything on Facebook, Twitter, MySpace, YouTube, or if you have your own website or webcasts or photo album or blog, or if you've been on anyone else's Facebook page, every aspect of you may be revealed. You no longer control how you come across to an employer. So naturally, a vast majority of employers now Google your name—*yes, Google has become both noun and verb*—before they'll consider hiring you.

So, if they do that with your name, what will they see? They'll see those impressive achievements you've done, where you far exceeded people's expectations—they're there. But, depending on your privacy settings, they may also see those playful photos you've allowed your friends to post on your Facebook page, or theirs, that make you look like an idiot. They're there, too. And the indiscreet comments you made when you were upset about this or that. And more. All these things, together, comprise your new resume, a richer body of data about you than your old classic resume ever aspired to be. And from this, now, prospective employers can better guess what kind of person you are and what kind of employee you'd be.

Or at least they think they can. Heaven help you if you Google yourself and recoil with horror at the distorted picture of you that emerges en toto. There's your new resume, using the word *resume* loosely. *Bye, bye, control.*

Is there anything you can do about this new Google resume of yours? Well, yes, actually there are four things you can do. They are: edit, fill in, expand, and add. Let's see what these mean.

Edit. First of all, think of how you would like to come across, when you are being considered for a job. Make a list of adjectives you'd like the employer to think of, when they consider hiring you. For example, how about: professional? experienced? inventive? hard-working? disciplined? honest? trustworthy? kind? What else? Make a list.

Then Google yourself and read over everything the search engine pulls up about you. Weigh what this or that suggests. Go over any pages you have put up on social sites like Facebook, MySpace, or YouTube, and remove anything you posted there, or allowed others to post, that contradicts the impression you would like to make, anything that might cause a would-be employer to think, "Uh, let's not call them in, after all." Look particularly for unflattering pictures or four-letter text.

If you don't know how to remove an item from a particular site, type or speak the following into a search engine like Google: "how to remove an item from my Facebook page" or whatever. I'd tell you right here how to do this, but the last time I looked, it took about nineteen steps to do a thorough "scrub" on Facebook, for example; and I'm sure those instructions will be outdated by the time you read this. You want *current* information; so look at the date on any items the search engine pops up. Pick the most recent, before looking at the suggested posts that are further back in time.

Do this "scrub" on any and every site that you know you're on. You should have no trouble finding detailed instructions for any site. The site itself may not tell you, but I guarantee you're hardly the first one with this need, so someone clever has already figured out how to do it, and posted the answer.

Now to the second thing you can do about your new Google resume:

Fill In. On any of these sites, but on the professional social network sites in particular (like LinkedIn or Plaxo), if they allow you to fill out a profile, fill it out completely. I mean *completely*; cross every t, and dot every i. Leave no part of the profile blank unless you have a very good reason. If you're on Twitter, fill out your bio completely there (69 percent of all users already have).

More importantly, *be sure* to keep each profile up-to-date. Really up-to-date. There is nothing that makes you look less professional than having an obviously outdated profile.

Last thought here: I mentioned LinkedIn; be sure to get on it, if you're not already. More than a 100 million other people have, and now it's become the first social media site to go public. It's the site of first resort when some employer is curious about you. It allows corporate and agency headhunters to avoid advertising an open position, but nonetheless to go "trolling" on LinkedIn for what employers call "passive job-seekers." *You ain't lookin' for them, but they're sure lookin' for you.* Of course, you have no control over whether they find you, except for being sure you have a completely filled-out profile. (They search by keywords.)

Now to the third thing you can do about your new Google resume:

Expand. Expand your presence on the Internet. How to do this? Several ways.

**Forums.** Professional sites like LinkedIn have forums, or groups, organized by subject matter. Other social networking sites, like Facebook, have pages devoted to particular subjects. Look through the directory of those groups or forums, choose one or two that are related to your industry or interests, and after signing up, speak up regularly *whenever you have something to say that will quietly demonstrate you are an expert in your chosen subject area.* Otherwise, keep quiet. Don't speak up about just anything. You want to be seen as a specialist—knowledgeable, and focused. You want to get noticed by employers when they're searching for expert talent *in your field or specialty.*

**Blogs.** Start a blog (short for "web log," as you probably know), if you don't already have one.[1] It doesn't matter what your expertise, if it's related to the job you are looking for, do a blog, and update it regularly. And if you don't know how to blog, there are helpful sites such as Blogger.com at http://tinyurl.com/294vgzr, which can give you detailed instructions.

If you already have a blog, but it roams all over the countryside in terms of subject matter, then start a new blog that is more narrowly preoccupied with your particular area of expertise. Post helpful articles there, focused on action steps not just thoughts. Let's say you are an expert plumber; you can post entries on your blog that deal with such problems as "how to fix a leaky toilet," etc. Generally speaking, employers are looking for blogs that deal with concrete action, rather than lofty philosophical thought. Unless, of course, they represent a think tank.

**Twitter.** Some experts claim that blogs are so *yesterday.* Communication is moving toward *brief,* and *briefer.* Texting has become wildly popular.[2] So has Twitter. Twitter allegedly has over 20 million users, though in truth 2.2 percent of Twitter users generate 60 percent of all those "tweets."[3] Twitter's advantage is that it has hashtags,[4] and Google is indexing all those tags and "tweets." Savvy employers know how to do Twitter searches on Google (or on Twitter itself, for that matter). All you have to figure out is what hashtags employers are likely to look for, when they want to find someone with your expertise and experience.

**Videos.** Presentation is not only getting briefer, but it is moving more and more toward the visual, these days. People like to *see* you, not just

---

1. As of February 16, 2011, there are 156 million blogs in the U.S.
2. Over 150 billion text messages are sent per month, in the U.S. And that was back in 2009.
3. http://tinyurl.com/4ywf2yf
4. http://tinyurl.com/2crj55

read you. You could guess that just from the enormous popularity of YouTube. As for shooting the videos, the Flip video camcorder used to be the most popular and inexpensive way to record yourself; but this year it was allowed to go belly-up. Sad! It was displaced, as you might guess, by smartphones, which usually can do video, and sometimes rather surprisingly good video.

As for where to post your video, once you have it, there is the obvious— YouTube—of course; for other possibilities see Friday Traffic Report's list at http://tinyurl.com/yjnokur.

Now to the fourth and final thing you can do about your new Google resume:

**Add.** The old classic resume still has its uses. It will take any employer or HR department some time to sift through all the stuff about you that may appear when they do a Google search. You would help them by summarizing and organizing the pertinent information about yourself. You do this by composing an old classic resume.

Here's an outline you may find useful for gathering that information about yourself:

## A STARTER KIT, FOR WRITING YOUR RESUME

*This is adapted, with the written permission of my friend Tom O'Neil, from an original document of his, which was and is copyright protected under the New Zealand Copyright Act (1994) © cv.co.nz 2001. You may contact Tom at www.cv.co.nz.*

A resume is about your past. Here is a framework for recalling that past.

If you cannot think of any achievements under the categories below, don't be concerned, as the Flower Exercise in chapter 13 will help you greatly.

For now, think of your working and personal experiences and skills that you believe you possess innately, or have learned. Which ones are you proud of? What things have you done in your life or work experience that no one else has done? Take some blank sheets of paper and fill in any answers that occur to you, please.

*It is important to be quantitative when you do this (e.g., mention dates, percents, dollars, brand names, etc.).*

### Volunteer, Community, and Unpaid Work

1. Have you completed any voluntary or unpaid work for any organization or company? (e.g., church, synagogue, mosque, school, community service, or special needs organization)

### Educational

2. Did you work while you were studying? If so, did you receive any promotions or achievements in that role?
3. Were you given any scholarships?
4. Were you involved in any committees, etc.?
5. Did you win any awards for study?
6. Did you have any high (e.g., A or A+) grades? If so, what were the subjects—and grades?

### Sales or Account Management

Have you ever been in sales? If so, what were some of your achievements? For example:

7. Have you ever consistently exceeded your set budget in that role? If so, by what percent or dollar value?
8. Have you exceeded your set budget in a particular month(s)/quarter(s) in a role? If so, by what percent or dollar value?
9. What level were you, compared to other sales professionals in your company? (e.g., *"Number three out of twenty on the sales team."*)
10. Have you ever increased market share for your company? If so, by what percent or dollar value?
11. Have you ever brought in any major clients to your company?
12. What major clients are/were you responsible for managing and selling to?
13. Did you ever manage to generate repeat business or increase current business? If so, by what percent or dollar value?

14. Have you won any internal or external sales awards?

15. Did you develop any new successful promotional or marketing ideas that increased sales?

## Administration, Customer Services, and Accounts

Have you ever been in customer service or helped run a business unit? If so:

16. Did you assist in reducing customer complaints, etc.?

17. Did you set up or improve any systems and/or processes?

18. Was there a quantifiable difference in the company or business unit when you first joined the business or project and when you completed the project or left the business?

19. Did you take any old administration or paperwork-based systems and convert them into an IT-based system?

## Responsibility

20. Have you ever been responsible for the purchase of any goods or services in some job? (e.g., air travel or PC acquisition)

21. Have you ever had any budget responsibility? If so, to what level? (e.g., *"Responsible for division budget of $200,000 per annum."*)

22. Have you ever been responsible for any staff oversight? If so, in what capacity and/or how many staff members were you responsible for?

23. Were you responsible for any official or unofficial training? If so, what type, for whom, and how many people have you trained? (e.g., *"Responsible for training twelve new staff in customer service as well as in using the in-house computer system."*)

24. Were you responsible for any official or unofficial coaching or mentoring of other staff?

## Events or Conference Planning or Logistical Management

25. Have you organized any events or conferences? If so, how large were they (both people attending and total budget if possible) and where and when was the event(s) held?

26. Have you been involved in any major relocation projects?

27. Have you had responsibility with regard to any major suppliers? If so, who?

### Computers, Internet

28. What systems, software, and hardware experience do you have? Desktop, notebook, mobile, smartphones? And how deep is your expertise with any of these?

29. What software have you utilized? Or what software have you developed? Apps? Systems software?

30. Have you developed any websites? If so, what were they, and did they positively affect any business you were doing? Are you on LinkedIn, Plaxo, Twitter, Facebook, YouTube, etc., and if so how deep an expertise do you have with any of these sites?

31. Were you involved in any special projects that were outside of your job description?

### Mechanical

32. Other than computers, have you had experience on any kinds of machines or equipment? Please list them together with the number of years.

33. If you ever worked on transportation devices, what was the airplane, farm equipment, truck, car, machine, or bike brands that you serviced, maintained, or repaired?

### Building, Construction, Electrical, and Plumbing

34. If you ever worked in those fields, were there any major projects you have worked on? How much did the project(s) cost? (e.g., *"Reception refurbishment—ABC Bank [Auckland Central Head Office] $1.2m."*)

### General

35. How long have you spent within any industry? (e.g., *"Twelve years' experience within the fashion industry."*)

36. Were you promoted in any of your roles? If so, in what years and to which roles?

37. Was extra authority awarded to you after a period of time within a role? (e.g., *"Commenced as receptionist; then, after three months, awarded by being given further clerical responsibilities including data entry and accounts payable."*) It is not necessary that these responsibilities awarded to you should have changed your job title and/or salary.

38. Have you been asked to take part in, or lead, any trainee management courses or management development programs?

39. Were you asked to get involved in any special projects outside your job description? Or, did you ever volunteer for such? What was the result?

## Positive Feedback

40. Have you ever received any written or verbal client, customer, or managerial commendations or letters of praise?

41. Can you think of any occasions where you gave excellent customer service? If so, how did you know the customer was satisfied? (Also: What was the outcome? How did it benefit the company?)

42. Did you receive any awards within your company or industry? (e.g., *"Acknowledged for support or service of clients or staff, etc."*)

## Memberships

43. Have you been a representative on any committees (e.g., health and safety committee)? Any special responsibilities there?

44. Do you belong or have you belonged to any professional clubs such as Toastmasters, Lions, or Rotary?

## Published or Presented Work

45. Have you had any articles, papers, or features published in any magazines, journals, or books? If so, what publications and when? Have you written any books?

46. Have you presented any topics at any conferences or completed any public speaking? If so, what subjects have you talked about and how large was the audience? List in detail.

**Looking Ahead**

- What value do you think you would add to a potential employer's business? How would you be "a resource" or even "a resource-broker" for them, rather than just "a job beggar"? What kind of problems are you good at solving?
- How do you think you would stand out compared to other applicants who have about the same qualifications as you have?


That should give you a good start. Modify the list any way you want to—add items and questions to it, change the wording, whatever.

If you need additional guidance, search Google for the topic "how to write a resume" or "tips on writing a resume" or "keywords on an electronic resume" or "examples of resumes." This will not only turn up free resources and advice on the Internet and for-fee resources, such as professional resume writers, but also the names of books, if you want to get very thorough. You should look particularly for resume books by Yana Parker and Susan Whitcomb.

As for what is the proper form for a resume, there are no rules. The only question is: is there a particular place or kind of place where you'd like to work, and if so, will the person there who has the power to hire you for the kind of job you want, be persuaded to invite you in? If the answer is, Yes, then it matters not what form your resume took.

To illustrate my point, I used to have a hobby of collecting "winning" resumes—that is, resumes that had actually gotten someone an interview and, ultimately, a job. Being playful by nature, I would show these without comment, to employer friends of mine, over lunch. Many of them didn't like these winning resumes at all. "That resume will never get anyone a job," they would say. Then I would reply, "Sorry, you're wrong. It already has. I think what you mean is that it wouldn't get them a job *with you*."

The resume reproduced on the following page is a good example of what I mean; it's dated, but it's still my favorite:

E.-J. DYER          Street, City, Zip          Telephone No.

I SPEAK
THE LANGUAGE
OF
MEN
MACHINERY
AND
MANAGEMENT
. . .

OBJECTIVE:        Sales of Heavy Equipment

QUALIFICATIONS    * Knowledge of heavy equipment, its use and maintenance.
                  * Ability to communicate with management and with men in the field.
                  * Ability to favorably introduce change in the form of new equipment
                    or new ideas . . . the ability to sell.

EXPERIENCE        * Maintained, shipped, budgeted and set allocation priorities for 85 pieces
                    of heavy equipment as head of a 500-man organization (1975–1977).
Men and
Machinery         * Constructed twelve field operation support complexes, employing a
                    100-man crew and 19 pieces of heavy equipment (1965–1967).
                  * Jack-hammer operator, heavy construction (summers 1956–1957–1958).

Management        * Planned, negotiated and executed large-scale equipment purchases on
                    a nation-to-nation level (1972–1974).

Sales             * Achieved field customer acceptance of two major new computer-
                    based systems:
                    —Equipment inventory control and repair parts expedite system (1968–1971)
                    —Decision makers' training system (1977–1979)
                  * Proven leader . . . repeatedly elected or appointed to senior posts.

EDUCATION         * B.A. Benedictine College, 1959 (Class President; Yearbook Editor;
                    "Who's Who in American Colleges")
                  * Naval War College, 1975 (Class President; Graduated "With Highest
                    Distinction").
                  * University of Maryland, 1973–1974 (Chinese Language).
                  * Middle Level Management Training Course, 1967–1968
                    (Class Standing: 1 of 97).

PERSONAL          * Family: Sharon and our sons Jim (11), Andy (8) and Matt (5) desire to
                    locate in a Mountain State by 1982, however, in the interim will consider
                    a position elsewhere in or outside the United States . . . Health: Excellent . . .
                    Birthdate: December 9, 1937 . . . Completing Military Service with the rank
                    of Lieutenant Colonel, U.S. Marine Corps.

SUMMARY           A seeker of challenge . . . experienced, proven and confident of
                  closing the sales for profit.

Jim Dyer, who had been in the U.S. Marines for twenty years, wanted a job as a salesman for heavy construction and mining equipment, thousands of miles from where he was then living. He devised the resume you see, and had just fifteen copies made. He mailed them out, he said, "to a grand total of seven before I got the job in the place I wanted!"

Like the employer who hired him, I loved this resume. Yet some of the employers I showed it to (*over lunch, as I said*) criticized it for using a picture or for being too long, or for being too short, etc. In other words, had Jim sent that resume to *them*, they wouldn't have invited him in for an interview.

Some employers will like your resume, some won't. Trouble is, you don't know which employer likes *what*. That's why many job-hunters, if they use resumes, pray as they mail their resume: *Please, dear God, let them be employers who like resumes in general, and may the form of my resume appeal to those employers I care about, in particular.*

Whatever form you decide on, write it and then post it *everywhere* online: on the omnibus job boards, famous job boards, community bulletin boards, and niche sites. For lists of such sites, go to Quintessential Careers' website at http://tinyurl.com/3nnqhse.

There are resume distribution services that can do this blanket posting for you, if you wish, often without a fee (see www.forward yourresume.com for evaluations of such services).

Post your resume, above all, on the actual website of companies that interest you, if they have a site, and if their site permits that. (You *have* already chosen companies or organizations that interest you, I hope—whether or not they have any known vacancies.)

If you post your resume on the sites of particular employers, large or small, don't count on any acknowledgment or reply. Just post the thing, cross your fingers, and pray it has come to the right place at the right time.

This strategy—planting your resume on the Internet midst all the other stuff that an employer will find if they Google you—will work better with small companies than with large, and with *new* small companies, especially.

But remember this: once your resume is posted on the Internet, there is really no way for you to ever take it down. Even if the site you initially post it on *promises* timely removal, you have no control over digital "spiders" that may come in stealthily, and copy it, often multiple times. One way or another, your resume may hang out there in cyberspace for the next one hundred years. So, make sure you're pleased with it, before posting. And I mean *very* pleased!

Incidentally, if you're blanketing the Internet with your resume, be cautious about including any stuff on the resume that would help someone locate you, particularly if you're a female. No, I'm not being sexist. It's just that there are some sick people out there. Sick in the head, that is. So, I'd leave out my address and home phone number if I were you. You can give that information to any employer who actually contacts you for an interview. But only then. For now, just give them *some way* to get in touch with you. Just your e-mail address is probably best.

## TARGETING PARTICULAR EMPLOYERS

If you are planning on approaching particular employers, and not just posting your resume on job sites, then keep in mind that a resume is best not sent solely by e-mail these days. That route has been overused, and abused; in fact, many employers, leery of viruses, will not even open e-mail attachments (such as your resume). Of course, you can always get around that by copying and pasting your resume into the body of the e-mail. But then it will be unformatted, and neither it nor you will come across the way you want to. So send it by e-mail if you must, but always send a nicer version of it by the postal service, or UPS, or FedEx, etc.

If you're going to mail a resume to a particular employer pay attention to the paper you write or print it on. Picture this scenario: an employer is going through a whole stack of resumes, and on average he or she is giving each resume about eight seconds of their time (true: we checked!). Then that resume goes either into a pile we might call "Forgeddit," or a pile we might call "Bears further investigation." And what is that employer's first contact with your resume? It's through the fingers. A resume on paper first presents itself to the employer's sense of touch, before it presents itself to their eyes. By the message from their fingers they are either prejudiced in your favor before they even start reading, or prejudiced against you. Before their eyes read even one line. Usually they are not even aware of this.

So, you want the paper to feel good. That usually means using paper weighing at least 28 pounds (a paper's weight is on every package). And you want it to "read good"—so be sure it's nicely laid out or formatted, as they say, using a decent-size font, size 12 or even 14 (makes it faster to read), etc.

As for boiling down your resume so that it isn't too long, what advice can I give you? Well, you ought to have some intention for that resume. I said previously that your intention *might be* just to collect and organize all pertinent information about yourself in one place, in contrast to your so-called Google resume, where the information about you may be scattered all over the lot.

But if you're targeting particular employers, individually, then your resume can have only one intention and purpose: to get yourself invited in, for an interview. Nothing more.

This truth, however, is not widely understood. Most job-hunters (and even a few resume writers) assume a resume's purpose is to "sell you," or secure you a job. No, no, no. Its *only* purpose is to get you an interview. Believe me!

Selling is what you do after you're in the interview room. It's *your* task, when you're face to face, not that piece of paper's.

So, forget about selling yourself, for the moment; just read over *every single sentence* in your resume and evaluate it by this one standard: "Will this item help get me invited in? Or will this item seem too puzzling, or off-putting, or a red flag?" If you doubt a particular sentence will help you get invited in for an interview, then omit that sentence.

If there is something you feel you will ultimately need to explain, or expand upon, save that explanation for the interview, also.

Your resume is, above all, no place for "true confessions." (*"I kind of botched up, at the end, in that job; that's why they let me go, as I'm sure they'll tell you when you check my references."*) First of all, don't give references until the end of the interview. And save true confessions also for the interview, near the end of the interview at that, and only if you're confident at that point that they really want you. Ditto for discussing any nonobvious handicap you may have. Discuss what you can do—that you can perform the tasks required—not what you can't do. Unless and until they have said they really want you.

## DEPENDING ON RESUMES MAY BE INJURIOUS TO YOUR HEALTH

There are three dangers that arise from resumes. The dangers arise not from using them, but from *depending*, absolutely depending, on them to get you an invite to an interview:

1. Resumes may create depression in you, and vastly lower your self-esteem. This is the greatest danger, by far, of depending on resumes. Why depression? Well, if it were just a matter of trying a job-hunting method that didn't work very well, that might be okay. You pick yourself up, and go on, still keeping a good self-esteem. But in fact, the danger of resumes is that *if* you believe in them, and they don't work for you, you start to think something is really, really wrong with *you*. And if some of your friends tell you their resume actually got them a job (not true: it actually got them an interview), you may feel lower than a snake's belly. Many job-hunters never snap out of the depression and feelings of worthlessness that follow. *"Ten thousand people in my town found a job using a resume, and I'm the only one who didn't!"* Or some fantasy like that. Every resume should carry a warning label, addressed not to *them* but to you: "Depending on this may be hazardous to your mental health."

2. Resumes make you feel like they're out there, working for you. They make you feel as though you're really doing something about your job-hunt. But in fact they may be moribund or comatose. That is, they may not be getting read, at all, even when posted on an employer's own website, as we saw in the previous chapter. Some employers, in fact, hate resumes (I kid you not; they're tired of sifting through all those exaggerations, all those unsubstantiated claims, all those outright lies—in anywhere between 30 and 80 percent of the resumes they receive). Other employers love resumes, but not for the reasons you think. They love them because they offer an easy way to cut down the time employers have to spend on job-hunters. Remember, for the employer, hiring is essentially an elimination game: in a large organization, they're looking for a reason—any reason—to cut their stack of resumes down to manageable size. As mentioned, it only takes a skilled

human resource person about eight seconds to scan a resume (thirty seconds, if they're really dawdling), so getting rid of fifty job-hunters—I mean getting rid of fifty *resumes*—takes only half an hour or less. Whereas, interviewing those fifty job-hunters in person would have taken a minimum of twenty-five hours. Great time savings—for them!

3. Resumes may cause you to give up your job-hunt prematurely. Resumes can be a useful part of anybody's job-hunt, but they should never be your entire plan. You can send out tons of resumes, or post them on every resume site on the Internet, and not get a single nibble. Bummer! As we saw in chapter 1, you need alternatives. You need resumes *and*. . . . A resume is one way to get yourself invited in for an interview, but there are other ways, even preferred ways. Know what they are. For example: getting introduced there, by a mutual acquaintance or friend (a contact of yours, a business contact, a personal contact or friend, a family contact, or anyone you've ever met and know well enough to have their name and address or phone number).

## ALTERNATIVES TO A CLASSIC RESUME

Many experts suggest that instead of sending a resume, you send just a "cover letter," summarizing all that a longer resume might have covered. If you don't know what a cover letter is, or how to write it, the Internet can rescue you handily. Just type "cover letters" into your favorite search engine. You'll be surprised at how many tips, examples, etc., you find. Look particularly for Susan Ireland's Cover Letter Guide at http://susanireland.com/letter/how-to. It's free. Incidentally, recent surveys have revealed that many employers prefer a cover letter to a resume.

Another alternative to a classic resume is a Job or Career Portfolio. A portfolio may be electronic (posted on the Internet) or on paper/ a notebook/in a large display case (as with artists), demonstrating your accomplishments, experience, training, commendations or awards, from the past. Artists have a portfolio, with samples of their work. You probably knew that. But portfolios are equally apt in other fields.

Instead of "portfolio" we might just call them "Evidence of What I Can Do and Have Done," or "Proof of Performance." For guidance on how to prepare a job-portfolio, and what to include, type "job portfolios" into Google; you'll get a wealth of tips and information. I particularly recommend Martin Kimeldorf's site, http://amby.com/kimeldorf/portfolio.

## CONCLUSION

Okay, let's go over it, one more time: do you really need a resume?

Well, no you don't, and yes you do.

You already have a resume if you've been posting any stuff on the Internet. That resume is called Google.

You've got to clean up *that* resume, edit, fill in, expand, and add to it.

But that, alone, is not enough. You need to supplement what's already there, by organizing the most pertinent information about you—whether it's on the Internet or not—by writing the old kind of resume.

You can and should post it everywhere on the Internet, but if you decide to send it to particular employers, then you need to edit it before sending it to those employers. The principle by which you judge every sentence in it is, *will it get me invited in for an interview?*

These ancient truths reign, over all:

**The primary purpose of a resume is to get yourself invited in for an interview** (*with a prospective employer, of course*).

**The primary purpose of that interview is to get yourself invited back for a second interview.**

If you keep these two simple truths always in front of you, as you go about your job-hunt or career-change, you will be ahead of 97 percent of all other job-hunters or career-changers.

Wild Life, by John Kovalic, © 1989 Shetland Productions. Reprinted with Permission.

*What is success?*
*To laugh often and much;*
*To win the respect of intelligent people*
*and the affection of children;*
*To earn the appreciation of honest critics*
*and endure the betrayal of false friends;*
*To appreciate beauty;*
*To find the best in others;*
*To leave the world a bit better, whether by*
*a healthy child, a garden*
*patch or a redeemed social condition;*
*To know even one life has breathed*
*easier because you have lived;*
*This is to have succeeded.*

BESSIE ANDERSON STANLEY, 1904
TRADITIONALLY ATTRIBUTED TO
RALPH WALDO EMERSON (1803–1882)

# Chapter 7. Networking in This Age of Social Media

If someone out of work knows only three words about their impending job-hunt, I'm willing to bet those three words will be: *resumes, interviews,* and *networking.*

If there's one really overworked word in the whole of job-hunting, it's that last one: *networking.* It's used by more job-hunters, and with the least understanding of what it really is for, than any other word that I can think of, in job searching.

Job-hunters will go blindly to group meetings—job support groups, business presentations, college reunions, even beer parties or cocktail parties—and when you ask them what they're doing, they will say, "I'm networking. Isn't that what I'm supposed to be doing?"

Job-hunters will collect people's business cards day after day, week after week, convinced that this will pay off down the line. They approach networking as something almost magical, based on the flimsy belief: *"He or she who ends up with the most business cards, will be most successful in their job-hunt."*

Job-hunters will "friend" reflexively on Facebook and "link" with everyone they can think of on LinkedIn, trying to collect as many names as possible.

And if you ask them *why* they are doing this, they will reply that they've been told that that is what they are supposed to do, when they're looking for work: *networking.*

# THE VIRTUES OF NETWORKING

I certainly understand where this preoccupation with *networking* came from. I have made it a hobby for years to ask people I encounter in my daily life, "How did you get your job here?" Waiters and waitresses, retail store clerks, supermarket check-out people, computer store sales-people—you name it.

And nine times out of ten, they will say that some *person*—friend, family member, school chum, doctor, some friend on Facebook, some link on LinkedIn, some total stranger they accidentally met—got them that job. Either that person worked there, too, or used to work there, or knew somebody who worked there.

So, it all comes down to this: when you set out job-hunting, there is a gap between you and a job. That gap may be filled by anything: a job posting on the Internet, your resume, you name it.

Most often, however, it is filled by a person. Yes, into that gap comes a person. A person who is a kind of bridge. A bridge between you and an employer you're interested in. They know *you*; they know *them*. They thus bridge the gap between you and them. Your chances of getting a job there, increase. Thanks to this "bridge-person." That is how most jobs get filled.

> *Knowing this when you first begin your job-hunt, you will of course give priority to searching for such "bridge-persons," even before you know what you are going to need them for. That search is called networking. It is the collection of names now, for the purpose of picking out from among them the "bridge-persons" you discover you will need, later. (Incidentally, before social media became popular these people were called "your contacts." Now they are more popularly called "your links" or "friends." I prefer to call them, as is obvious, your "bridge-people.")*

# THE DEFECTS OF NETWORKING

A "bridge-person" is always very specific to a particular job, person, or organization. No one is a "bridge" to everyone. They've got to know you. They've got to know this other specific person. You'll probably need a different "bridge" to each employer that interests you. So, unless or until you've done the necessary homework so you can define *who*, networking is little better than just blind luck.

The plea that job-hunters traditionally use early on, with their network—when they haven't yet figured out where they're trying to go next with their lives—is to say to their network, "I'm out of work. If you hear of *anything*, please let me know."

It's hard to know who would be a useful bridge-person between *you* and *anything*. You need to be more specific.

Otherwise, searching for a bridge to *anything* ends up being a bridge to nowhere. Your carefully collected stack of business cards is left just blowin' in the wind.

Many job-hunters don't care for networking, because it feels like they're just *using people*. This is a common feeling among ethical people. That kind of sesnsitivity is of course to be saluted and celebrated, in a world that all too often revolves around *me*.

But let's step back a little, and think about human relationships. For, *networking* is just one activity between humans, isn't it? Let's think, for a moment, about all human relationships. The first thing that strikes us is that we are born for *community*. Fish swim in water, humans swim in a social context. From our birth, we are part of a community. By definition, a community is a bunch of people who have something in common. That may be: a common blood bond, a common geography, common interests, common problems, common identity, common goals, and so on. Bound together by what we have in common, we then interact with each other, complement each other, supplement each other.

When we encounter problems, we may be able to solve them by ourselves: *just me, myself, and I*. But sometimes, problems can only be solved when two or more people work together on that problem. We may each have one piece of the solution in our hands, but only one piece.

So, we need each other. And as we grow older and mature, we learn that there are two sides to every relationship: not just *take*, but also *give*. Not just *give*, but also *take*. Here are some examples:

| Your Relationship | What You Give to Them | What They Give to You |
|---|---|---|
| To Your Mother and Father | Devotion, love, time, thanks, and (in their old age) care | Love, nurture, upbringing, teaching, support when you are out of work |
| To Your Brothers & Sisters | Time, listening, loyalty | Staying in touch, play, joy |
| To Your Teachers or Professors | Curiosity, willingness to learn, your opinions, attention | Their experience, training, knowledge, resources, perspective |
| To Your Partner or Mate | Love, time, priority, faithfulness, support, equality, openness to their insights, children (it may be) | Love, time, priority, faithfulness, support, equality, openness to their insights, children (it may be) |
| To Your Children | Love, nurture, upbringing, teaching, support when they are out of work | Love, celebration, thanks, shared lives, and (in your old age) care |
| To Your Close Friends | Your time, laughter, wisdom, playfulness, your car keys (when out drinking together) | Their time, their wisdom, ideas, companionship, affection |
| To Your Co-workers | Help with their difficulties at work, tasks too big for them | If they're there when you first arrive, teaching you the ropes |
| To Your Boss | Your time, your talents, your skills, and experience, plus dependability | Money (certainly), appreciation for what you've done there (sometimes) |
| To Your Acquaintances | Encouragement, appreciation | Ideas, support, their experience and learnings |
| To Your Network | What you've learned from your Informational Interviewing within their industry | Information, and (in some cases) a bridge between you and an organization you are trying to get into |

I can illustrate the final entry on this chart—your relationship to your network—very simply. When we are out of work, we begin collecting names for two purposes down the road: information, and introduction.

I've been talking as though the *introduction* side of networking—finding "bridge-people" who bridge the gap between you and a job—is the only purpose of networking. But clearly it isn't. There is also the *information-gathering* side of networking, preceding the need for any introductions. Its $64,000 question is: *is this a place where I could put my talents, gifts, skills and experience to their best and most effective use?*

A job-hunter named Bill N. had worked for a number of years in retail; now he was debating moving over to the oil industry. That meant, he had to first learn a lot, because he knew virtually nothing about the oil industry. So, he went from person to person who worked at companies in that industry, just seeking information about the industry. But the more of these "informational interviews" he conducted, the more he knew. In fact, coming down the home stretch—still interviewing people at companies in that industry—he found he now knew more than they usually did, about their competitors. He was therefore able to give them an overview that they had never had the time to go gather, themselves.

In other words, he was no longer just gathering information, he was also dispensing it. His networking was no longer just *take*; it was also *give*. He no longer felt that networking was just *using people*. It had become a two-way street.

So when you are out of work, and you begin networking, all you need is the firm resolve that you *will* find ways to *give* as well as *take* from the people you approach, and you too need no longer feel that networking is just *using* people.

## NETWORKING IN THESE DAYS OF SOCIAL MEDIA

Networking has greatly changed from what it was, oh, even ten years ago. I said earlier that fish swim in water, humans swim in a social context. With the advent of social media on the Web, we are no longer just swimming in a pool; we have moved to an ocean.

Thanks to social media sites like *Facebook, Twitter, LinkedIn, Yelp, YouTube, TripAdvisor, Wikipedia, MakeProjects, GroupMe,* and similar—communities gather,[1] share information, make recommendations, aid decision-making, foster cooperation and invention, plus new ways to work,[2] and new ways to get in touch with each other—it is an ocean indeed.

---

1. Many of the social media sites create groups you can join. As a consequence, 82 percent of social network users and 85 percent of Twitter users participate in groups, according to the Pew Internet and American Life Project's 2011 survey.
2. Social media is beginning to change the way work is done. See www.menloinnovations .com where all work—all work—is done in pairs.

> *Information and Introduction. It's so much easier now to do net-working as information-gathering, or networking as a search for "bridge-people," than was ever possible before. It used to be an agonizing desperate search for the right people. Now, for anybody with even a modest acquaintance with social media, that search is one hundred times easier. Faster. More accurate. And, less time-consuming.*

Here are a few background thoughts about social media:

1. Mastery of social media is becoming important to employers, with the result that there are actually job-titles for people with this expertise: *online community manager, social media analyst, chief social media officer,* and even *chief listening officer* (responsible for seeing the company actually listens, and responds, to what's being said out there—something that Toyota, for example, failed to do, according to a recent study[3]).

2. There are tools for creating social networks where none existed before, particularly within your own company, like https://yammer.com.

3. Each social media site has a different scope, a different emphasis, and a different audience. Look for the things that matter to you. Choose a site appropriately. If you have a particular issue, and you just don't know how to find the appropriate social site, do a search on Google. For example, if ex-military who are hunting for help in getting back into civilian life, Google "ex-military job-hunting" they will turn up a number of sites to help them with that job-hunt, such as: www.jobswap.com, www.dol.gov/vets, LinkedIn.com (hashtag[4] #US Army), www.hireds.com, http://fedshirevets.gov, and www.woundedwarriorproject.org.

4. You can stay up-to-date on social media developments, by sub-scribing to the free daily e-mail called *Smartbrief on Social Media.* Sign up at www.smartbrief.com/socialmedia.

---

3. A study reported in the May 23, 2011, issue of the *New York Times.*
4. If you don't know what this is, see http://en.wikipedia.org/wiki/Hashtag#Hashtags.

5. For an extensive list of current social networking websites go to http://tinyurl.com/k2jhx. You can click on the little icon immediately beneath "Global Alexa Page Ranking" and get them listed in their order of popularity (from "Most Popular" down to "Least Popular").

Now let's look at some of the most popular social media sites, and see how they might be helpful with your *networking*:

## LinkedIn

Website url: www.linkedin.com

Background: Business-oriented networking website. 100+ million users worldwide, with more than 44 million of them in the U.S.

General Description: 70 to 90 percent of employers, depending on which survey you look at, use LinkedIn for trolling in general, or researching a job-hunter in particular.

Usefulness to Job-Hunters:

1. LinkedIn allows you to post a mini-version of your resume, which they call your Profile. (*Be sure it is as complete as you can possibly make it! LinkedIn says you are 40 times more likely to be approached if your profile is complete, than if it is not.*)

2. LinkedIn allows you to have recommendations from any of your links. So, don't just sit there; encourage those who know you well to post a recommendation of you or your work: 85 percent of employers say a positive online reputation influences their hiring decisions.

3. LinkedIn enables you to click on "Companies," and then elect to "follow" particular companies that interest you.

4. LinkedIn has "Jobs" at the top of its homepage. Click on it, and see what openings LinkedIn knows about, currently.

5. LinkedIn lets you search for particular job vacancies, using the Advanced Search Option, by keyword, location—country, postal code, miles from a location—experience level, industry, company, job-title, job function, and date posted.

6. LinkedIn allows you to search for people in particular business fields where you are, regardless of whether you know them or not.

7. LinkedIn tells you who might be "bridge-people" (they call them "inside connections" here) for particular companies. How? *JobInsider*, which is part of the Browser Toolbar for Firefox, or Internet Explorer. If you have access to either of these Web browsers, click on "Tools" at the bottom of any LinkedIn page, and choose *JobInsider*. Then when you are browsing *Monster, CareerBuilder, HotJobs, Craigslist, Dice, Vault, and the like*, if you click on a particular company's ad, it will identify people you are linked to, who work at that company, or people in your groups, whom you can ask to be introduced to. This is explained in a video at http://tinyurl.com/3kt5mv8.

8. While LinkedIn is free, they have a Premium membership (of course), where—for either $30 or $50 a month (choose one)—you get extra attention and privileges.

9. For more detailed ideas on LinkedIn and job search, the best article IMHO is by Guy Kawasaki, which you can find at http://tinyurl.com/3thvknr. He has a related blog for small businesses on LinkedIn, at http://tinyurl.com/yevgehz.

## LinkUp

Website url: http://linkup.com

Background: This is a job-search engine, *not to be confused with LinkedIn.*

General Description: This site pulls job openings only from employers' websites (21,000 at current count).

Usefulness to Job-Hunters: If you live in areas covered by LinkUp, you may find a job opening here.

## Facebook

Website url: www.facebook.com

Background: Hugely popular; 600 million users worldwide.

General Description: The world's largest social media site (but you probably already knew that).

Usefulness to Job-Hunters:

1. Facebook lets you sign up on pages devoted to Job-hunting and Careers. For example, www.facebook.com/jobhunting.

2. Facebook has an app that enables you to hunt for people who work at a particular company or organization, or who share a particular interest of yours: www.facebook.com/profile-search.

3. Facebook has an app that enables you to see where your friends work, and helps you build a professional network, plus discover job openings: http://apps.facebook.com/careeramp.

4. Facebook has an app that enables you to do networking, find friends of friends, and search millions of job listings: http://branchout.com.

## Twitter

Website url: http://twitter.com

Background: A social networking and micro-blogging site; 8 percent of Internet users are on Twitter.

General Description: Allows you to send micro-messages using 140 characters or fewer.

Usefulness to Job-Hunters:

1. Twitter will take a background. When you are out of work, you can convey your status in that background (tastefully, professionally). For a tutorial on how to do this, go to http://tinyurl.com/5obsoue.

2. Twitter will take a bio. Mention what you're looking for, there. You have 160 characters, so practice the art of succinctness. Put a link to an online resume in your bio.

3. Twitter will take an avatar. Make it professional looking.

4. Twitter has a "follow" option. Follow anyone who is helpful to your job-hunt. If you don't have a clue, follow Susan Joyce of job-hunt.org, Internet expert Joel Cheesman of

http://cheesman.typepad.com, and/or Guy Kawasaki (you can follow his top ten per day from @guykawasaki10).

5. Tweet about your job search. Be *sure* you know you've done your homework first, and can state *exactly* what kind of work you're looking for.

6. Put a link in some of your tweets to your website, if you have one. *If you don't have one, and you are an expert in some area of knowledge or performance, start your own website. See* http://bravenet.com *for free help, or* www.bluehost.com *for inexpensive hosting ($6 a month).* Establish yourself as an expert in your field on Twitter.

7. Sign up at www.twitjobsearch.com to locate various job-opportunities around the world. Choose what they call "channels" and then receive instant notification of jobs thereafter. Also sign up at http://tweetmyjobs.com.

## Texting

Website url: None. You choose a phone number on your contacts list, and then select "Send text."

Background: Wildly popular.

General Description: Text messaging between mobile phone users. Allows you to send brief text messages (160 English characters or less) using the Short Message Service (SMS) or more ambitious messages containing image, video, and sound content (known as MMS messages).

Usefulness to Job-Hunters: Infinite number of occasions where you need instant help, texting is very useful. For example, you're on your way to an interview and you suddenly think of a question you might be asked, that you don't know how to answer. You can text a more experienced friend and get the answer before you even arrive at the door of the interview. Moreover, it's helpful to have that answer spelled out on your mobile screen, as you go up in the elevator (tall building??) so you can practice.

## Yelp

Website url: https://yelp.com *(https as opposed to http in any site's url, means their information is heavily encrypted [128 bit], which is considered unhackable).*

Background: Has more than 40 million unique visitors per month.

General Description: Community reviews of various businesses.

Usefulness to Job-Hunters: If there is a particular business or organization you are interested in, you may find feedback about it, here.


## Stack Exchange

Website url: http://stackexchange.com

Background: A network of 51 question and answer sites, with a community contributing, answering, evaluating, and voting; same genre as Quora, Aardvark, Answers.com, etc.

General Description: Useful for finding fast answers to puzzling questions.

Usefulness to Job-Hunters: When you're trying to find something, someone, some business, this is a good place to go to, and see if they know the answer, without your having to do detailed research *forever.* Great time-saver.


## Skype

Website url: www.skype.com

Background: Over 665 million registered users, bought by eBay in 2005, Microsoft in 2011.

General Description: Telephone calls over the Internet, utilizing both voice and video; free if the hookup is between registered users.

Usefulness to Job-Hunters: You can use video interviewing for informational interviewing with members of your network who live far away. More important, if an employer lives in another country of interest to you, and you or they want to do an interview, this is an inexpensive way to do it. If an employer can only talk to you over the phone, this at least adds video to your phone call, if the employer is also a Skype user. You can find interview tips on the web at sites such as Alison Doyle's http://tinyurl.com/nmbt5r.

## YouTube

Website url: www.youtube.com

Background: Wildly popular; 375 million unique visitors offered 75 billion video streams in 2011.

General Description: You can find a video on almost any subject, or post a video of your own, thus saving you from using up bandwidth on your own website (if you have one).

Usefulness to Job-Hunters: You can post a video resume, you can demonstrate your skills in a demonstration video you shoot, and post, etc. You can create your own channel through a widget (www.widgetbox.com/widgets). Widgets can be embedded on all your other sites, as well. You might even find some videos devoted to job-hunting techniques, such as: http://tinyurl.com/4ynl42n. (smile)

## Blogs

Website url: if it's your blog, you know the url. If you're looking for someone else's, do a search through Google, or Technorati (below).

Background: 133 million blogs, averaging 900,000 posts a day according to Technorati (http://technorati.com)—the central headquarters for all things blog.

General Description: At their best, blogs offer an expert's advice and wisdom.

Usefulness to Job-Hunters: If you can find a blog on your particular field or industry, you may discover openings through that blog. Also consider starting your own blog related to the field in which you are you looking for work, where—if you keep your blog focused—you can develop a reputation as an expert in your specialty, thus attracting the attention of prospective employers—maybe. *(Possible but not likely; still, you never know. It's worth trying!)* Remember, the Web is the modern way to attract attention to yourself. A blog, carefully managed, can ideally serve that purpose. Of course, you are only one out of 133 million blogs, so don't put all your eggs in this basket.

## Online Universities

Website url: www.phoenix.edu; www.kaplan.edu; www.capella.edu

Background: According to Global Language Monitor's July 2010 ranking, the three top online universities are the University of Phoenix, Kaplan University, and Capella University.

General Description: Offers both courses and degree programs, either by yourself or interacting with an instructor or other students online.

Usefulness to Job-Hunters: You can go to school online, get trained in new skills, etc., while still pursuing your job-hunt. For example, you can get trained in such skills as using a computer or particular software programs, accounting, marketing, business plans, etc. You can even get a college degree while job-hunting.

## THE FUTURE IS COMING AT US, FAST

These are some of the principal sites that job-hunters are turning to, today. But what of tomorrow? Tomorrow is populated with clouds, and apps, and QR tags, and new technologies, as yet undreamed. And one thing you can be sure of: with so many people out of work—not only here, but around the world—some bright souls are going to figure out how to make these serve job-hunters and career-changers, whatever else they may do. Maybe one of those bright souls will even turn out to be You.

# DANGERS OF LIVING IN A
# SOCIAL MEDIA WORLD

Social media sites are wonderful. And useful. Amazingly so. But entering social networks is like setting out to explore a mysterious forest. There is much there that is awe-inspiring, and beautiful to behold; you will be so glad you set out on this journey.

But also, there are dangers lurking in that forest: wild beasts, often ravenous ones.

The first beast is called *Identity Theft*. You must take care not to give your Social Security number or credit card information to any site whose url does not begin with *https*. That is is important. Just *http* won't do. You want a secure site, one whose url begins with https, which means it's encrypted (128 bit) and virtually unhackable. But be warned: this beast usually tries to lure you into its lair by offering to give you something for practically nothing, or to claim to straighten out something that is wrong with your bank account, or credit card, or financial records. Don't give them the information they ask for. If you think something might genuinely be wrong, disconnect from the site giving you that warning, and once you're free of them, go dial the Internet address of the bank, or whatever, using a lookup through Google. Never use the site *the beast* suggests.

The second wild beast waiting for you in the social media forest is called *Fraud*. This beast takes the initiative in approaching you, and basically offers you money you know you're not entitled to, or asks you to deposit money for them (their check is always bogus) and give them back a portion of it (before their check bounces!). In the U.S. the FBI maintains a helpful list of fraudulent schemes, and what you can do to avoid being suckered (www.fbi.gov/scams-safety/fraud).

The third beast is called *Unwarranted Charges on Your Bill*. You get a notice to call them back about *anything*—an "undeliverable package," or whatever. When you call that phone number (area codes 284, 473, 649, 664, 784, 809, or 876) you are calling the Caribbean, and the charges will probably run you $50 or more on your next phone bill. And if you sign up for some service or subscription online, always study your credit card bill monthly, to see if they are continuing to charge you multiple times, when you thought it would only be once.

The fourth beast is called *False Reviews.* You will have to be on your guard against this one if you have your own business and/or your own website. Competitors may (can) pay someone to post rave reviews on their site (but not yours) or negative reviews on your site. Where do they go shopping for such helpful(!) people? Oh, from among their loyal friends, or by going to such otherwise innocent sites as fiverr (http:// fiverr.com) and hiring someone to do it for them.

The fifth beast is called *Rumors.* You know, such things as "Steve Jobs is giving away trial iPads for $15"—that sort of thing. Go to www .snopes.com to find out what's true, and what isn't.

The sixth and final beast is *The Social Media Site That Will Not Die.* You go social, you try it out for a while, you want to terminate your account there, but you just can't. You try everything, but nothing works. What now? Well, fortunately, there is a site designed to help you precisely with that problem. It's called http://suicidemachine.org. Its sole mission is to help you get off social media sites you no longer want to be on; it works, too! (A similar site, Seppukoo, died in February of 2011. R.I.P.)

## GETTING OFF THE INTERNET AND OUT INTO THE WORLD

Networking's aim is to locate actual people. And after you have done your homework on yourself (chapter 13), and know what information you need, or what company you want an introduction to, you're going to have to get out there and actually meet some of those people. Appointments, made beforehand, are virtually mandatory. Everyone in today's world has their own life, their own plans, and you (usually) don't want to just drop in unannounced. Yet, this is where many of us freeze.

First of all, we don't know how to approach these people face-to-face. I think I can help you there. If it's information you're seeking, you send them an introductory note, letting them know how you're connected to them and asking them whether they'd be willing to meet up with you for an eighteen-minute informational interview. That note, sent by e-mail preferably, can run something like this:

"I'm in need of more information about *xxx,* than I've been able to find out so far. I'm told you could be really helpful to me. I'm wondering if you could spare eighteen minutes of your time this week or next, for me to come over and ask you these questions I have about *xxx*. I'm not looking for a job at the moment, I'm just trying to find information, at the present. Could I make a brief appointment with you? I'm very good about observing time limits. I only need eighteen minutes, but I'd like it to be in person rather than just over the phone or through e-mails. Thanks very much for your courtesy."

Make *sure* it's really information you want, and don't *under any circumstances* think this is just some clever way to get in and then ask for a job. You will spoil it for everyone who comes after you, if you turn out just to be a trickster.

If, on the other hand, it's not information you need, but you're at the point where you've found a company or vacancy that interests you, and now what you want is an introduction, your note might be more along these lines:

"You and I [*here you mention what you two have in common—same college, same town or city you grew up in, same interest, same love of movies or whatever, etc.*]. And I'm told you know the people over at [*here you mention the name of the organization or company*]. Do you think we could meet for coffee or something, as I have a few matters I need your advice on. I'll stick strictly to our time limit. I only need twenty minutes. Thanks for your courtesy, if you can do this for me; I really appreciate it."

If they respond, "Sure," then prepare your questions carefully before going over there, write them out—to avoid nervous amnesia—dress well, get there early, appear on their doorstep only at the appointed time (or two minutes before), and relax.

Now, what's going to torpedo you? What handicap lies in wait? Oh, any number of things, but I think "shyness" heads the top of the list. Call it anything else if you will—fear, anxiety, nervousness, sweating— but "shyness" is the historic word for it. We who are absolute experts in using and manipulating Facebook, LinkedIn, and the other social media, turn into jellyfish when it comes to actually going face-to-face with our network, or with an employer.

Yup, a lot of us who are shy would never think to use that word to describe ourselves. But actually, an incredible number of us are or have been shy at some point in our lives. Surveys have found as many as 75 percent of us have been painfully shy at some point in our lives. (*This always comes as a great surprise to my European friends, because they picture*

*Americans as assertive, aggressive, and similar words. Ah, some of us are, I guess. But that's not who most of us are, especially when we're out of work.)*

So, what to do?

---

## SHYNESS VS. ENTHUSIASM

Throughout the job-hunt and career-change, the key to "Informational Interviewing" is not found in memorizing a dozen questions about what you're supposed to say.

No, the key is just this one thing: now and always, make *sure* you are talking about something you feel *passionate about.*

**Enthusiasm** is the key—to *enjoying* "interviewing," and conducting *effective* interviews, at any level. What this exercise teaches us is that shyness always loses its power and its painful self-consciousness—*if* and *when* you are talking about something *you love.*

For example, if you love gardens you will forget all about your shyness when you're talking to someone else about gardens and flowers. *"You ever been to Butchart Gardens?"*

If you love movies, you'll forget all about your shyness when you're talking to someone else about movies. *"I just hated that scene where they . . ."*

If you love computers, then you will forget all about your shyness when you're talking to someone else about computers. *"Do you work on a Mac or a PC?"*

That's why it is important that it be your enthusiasms that you are exploring and pursuing in these conversations with others.

---

The late John Crystal often had to counsel the shy. They were often *frightened* at the whole idea of going to talk to people for information, never mind for hiring. So John developed a system to help the shy. He suggested that before you even begin doing any Informational Interviewing, you first go out and talk to people about *anything* just to get good at *talking to people.* Thousands of job-hunters and career-changers have followed his advice, over the past thirty years, and found it really helps. Indeed, people who have followed John's advice in this regard have had a success rate of 86 percent in finding a job—and not just any job, but *the* job or new career that they were looking for.

Daniel Porot, Europe's premiere job-hunting expert, has taken John's system, and brought some organization to it. He observed that John was really recommending three types of interviews: this interview we are talking about, just for practice. Then Informational Interviewing. And finally, of course, the hiring-interview. Daniel decided to call these three the *"The PIE Method,"* which has now helped thousands of job-hunters and career-changers in both the U.S. and Europe.[5]

Why is it called *"PIE"*?

**P** is for the *warm-up* phase. John Crystal named this warm-up "The Practice Field Survey."[6] Daniel Porot calls it **P** for *pleasure.*

**I** is for "Informational Interviewing."

**E** is for the employment interview with the-person-who-has-the-power-to-hire-you.

How do you use this **P** for *practice* to get comfortable about going out and talking to people *one-on-one?*

This is achieved by choosing a topic—*any* topic, however silly or trivial—that is a pleasure for you to talk about with your friends, or family. To avoid anxiety, it should not be connected to any present or future careers that you are considering. Rather, the kinds of topics that work best, for this exercise, are:

- **a hobby** you *love,* such as skiing, bridge playing, exercise, computers, etc.
- **any leisure-time enthusiasm** of yours, such as a movie you just saw, that you liked a lot
- **a long-time curiosity**, such as how do they predict the weather, or what policemen do
- **an aspect of the town or city you live in**, such as a new shopping mall that just opened

---

5. Daniel has summarized his system in a book published here in the U.S. in 1996: it is called *The PIE Method for Career Success: A Unique Way to Find Your Ideal Job,* published by JIST Works, Inc. It is a fantastic book, and I give it my highest recommendation. Daniel has a wonderful website of "career games," at www.careergames.com.
6. If you want further instructions about this whole process, I refer you to "The Practice Field Survey," pp. 187–196, in *Where Do I Go from Here with My Life?* by John Crystal and friend, published by Ten Speed Press.

- **an issue** you feel strongly about, such as the homeless, AIDS sufferers, ecology, peace, health, etc.

There is only one condition about choosing a topic: it should be something you *love* to talk about with other people; a subject you know nothing about, but you feel a great deal of enthusiasm for, is far preferable to something you know an awful lot about, but it puts you to sleep.

Having identified your enthusiasm, you then need to go talk to someone who is as enthusiastic about this thing, as you are. *For best results with your later job-hunt, this should be someone you don't already know.* Use the Yellow Pages, ask around among your friends and family, *who do you know that* loves *to talk about this?* It's relatively easy to find the kind of person you're looking for.

You love to talk about skiing? *Try a ski-clothes store, or a skiing instructor.* You love to talk about writing? *Try a professor on a nearby college campus, who teaches English.* You love to talk about physical exercise? *Try a trainer, or someone who teaches physical therapy.*

Once you've identified someone you think shares your enthusiasm, you then go talk with them. When you are face-to-face with your *fellow enthusiast*, the first thing you must do is relieve their understandable anxiety. *Everyone* has had someone visit them who has stayed too long, who has worn out their welcome. If your *fellow enthusiast* is worried about you staying too long, they'll be so preoccupied with this that they won't hear a word you are saying.

So, when you first meet them, ask for *ten minutes of their time, only.* Period. Stop. Exclamation point. And watch your wristwatch *like a hawk,* to be sure you stay no longer. *Never* stay longer, unless they *beg* you to. And I mean, *beg, beg, beg.*[7]

Once they've agreed to give you ten minutes, you tell them why you're there—that you're trying to get comfortable about talking with people, for information—and you understand that you two share a mutual interest, which is . . .

*continued on page 112*

---

7. A polite, "Oh, do you have to go?" should be understood for what it is: politeness. Your response should be, "Yes, I promised to only take ten minutes of your time, and I want to keep to my word." This will almost always leave a *very* favorable impression behind you.

| Initial: | Pleasure<br>**P** | Information<br>**I** | Employment<br>**E** |
|---|---|---|---|
| Kind of Interview | Practice Field Survey | Informational Interviewing or Research | Employment Interview or Hiring Interview |
| Purpose | To Get Used to Talking with People to Enjoy It; to "Penetrate Networks" | To Find Out If You'd Like a Job, Before You Go Trying to Get It | To Get Hired for the Work You Have Decided You Would Most Like to Do |
| How You Go to the Interview | You Can Take Somebody with You | By Yourself or You Can Take Somebody with You | By Yourself |
| Who You Talk To | Anyone Who Shares Your Enthusiasm About a (for You) Non-Job-Related Subject | A Worker Who Is Doing the Actual Work You Are Thinking About Doing | An Employer Who Has the Power to Hire You for the Job You Have Decided You Most Would Like to Do |
| How Long a Time You Ask For | 10 Minutes (and DON'T run over— asking to see them at 11:50 a.m. may help keep you honest, since most employers have lunch appointments at noon) | Ditto | Ditto (or 22 minutes; but notice the time, and keep your word) |
| What You Ask Them | Any Curiosity You Have about Your Shared Interest or Enthusiasm | Any Questions You Have about This Job or This Kind of Work | You Tell Them What It Is You Like * about Their Organization and What Kind of Work You Are Looking For |

| | **Pleasure** | **Information** | **Employment** |
|---|---|---|---|
| **Initial:** | **P** | **I** | **E** |
| What You Ask Them (continued) | If Nothing Occurs to You, Ask: **1.** How did you start, with this hobby, interest, etc.? **2.** What excites or interests you the most about it? **3.** What do you find is the thing you like least about it? **4.** Who else do you know who shares this interest, hobby, or enthusiasm, or could tell me more about my curiousity? **a.** Can I go and see them? **b.** May I mention that it was you who suggested I see them? **c.** May I say that you recommended them? Get their name and address. | If Nothing Occurs to You, Ask: **1.** How did you get interested in this work and how did you get hired? **2.** What excites or interests you the most about it? **3.** What do you find is the thing you like the least about it? **4.** What kinds of challenges or problems do you have to deal with in this job? **5.** What skills do you need in order to meet those challenges or problems? **6.** Who else do you know of who does this kind of work, or similar work but with this difference_____? Get their name and address. | You tell them the kinds of challenges you like to deal with. What skills you have to deal with those challenges. What experience you have had in dealing with those challenges in the past. |
| **Afterward:** That Same Night | SEND A THANK-YOU NOTE. | SEND A THANK-YOU NOTE. | SEND A THANK-YOU NOTE. |

Then what? Well, a topic may have its own unique set of questions. For example, I love movies, so if I met someone who shared this interest, my first question would be, "What movies have you seen lately?" And so on. If it's a topic you love, and often talk about, you'll *know* what kinds of questions you begin with. But, if no such questions come to mind, no matter how hard you try, the following ones have proved to be good conversation starters for thousands of job-hunters and career-changers before you, no matter what their topic or interest.

So, look these over, memorize them (*or copy them on a little card that fits in the palm of your hand*), and give them a try:

## Questions Shy People Can Practice With

*Addressed to the person you're doing the Practice Interviewing with:*

- How did you get involved with/become interested in this? ("*This*" is the hobby, curiosity, aspect, issue, or enthusiasm, that you are so interested in.)
- What do you like the most about it?
- What do you like the least about it?
- Who else would you suggest I go talk to who shares this interest?
- Can I use your name?
- May I tell them it was you who recommended that I talk with them?
- *Then, choosing one person from the list of several names they may have given you, you say,* "Well, I think I will begin by going to talk to this person. Would you be willing to call ahead for me, so they will know who I am, when I go over there?"

Incidentally, during *this* Practice Interviewing, it's perfectly okay for you to take someone with you—preferably someone who is more outgoing than you feel you are. And on the first few interviews, let them take the lead in the conversation, while you watch to see how they do it.

Once it is *your turn* to conduct the interview, it will by that time usually be easy for you to figure out what to talk about.

Alone or with someone, keep at this Practice Interviewing until you feel very much at ease in talking with people and asking them questions about things you are curious about.

In all of this, *fun* is the key. If you're having fun, you're doing it right. If you're not having fun, you need to keep at it, until you are. It may take seeing four people. It may take ten. Or twenty. You'll know.

## CONCLUSION

In this post-recessionary world, networking is an essential job-finding survival skill. If you want to survive in this new world, you must master it. Fortunately, with the social media world in which we now swim, as a culture, this is much easier than it ever used to be. So many useful, helpful Internet sites. But they all depend, for their effectiveness, on your having done your homework . . . on yourself. Upon completing a self-inventory so that you know just exactly what you are looking for. Chapter 13 waits for you, ahead, to help you do just that.

And now, on to Interviewing.

# THE TEN GREATEST MISTAKES
## MADE IN JOB INTERVIEWS

*Whereby Your Chances of Finding a Job Are Greatly Decreased*

I. Going after large organizations only (such as the Fortune 500).

II. Hunting all by yourself for places to visit.

III. Doing no homework on an organization before going there.

IV. Allowing the Human Resources department to interview you (their primary function is to look for reasons to screen you OUT).

V. Setting no time limit when you first begin the interview, and then overstaying your welcome.

VI. Letting your resume be the only agenda discussed during the job-interview.

VII. Talking primarily about yourself throughout the interview, and what benefit the job will be for you.

VIII. Failing to give examples of the skills you claim you have.

IX. Basically approaching the employer as if you were a job beggar, hoping they will offer you any kind of a job, however humble.

X. Not sending a thank-you note right after the interview.

# Chapter 8. Sixteen Tips About Interviewing

There are three types of interviews, as we saw in the previous chapter:

*Interviews for fun or practice, done with people who are passionate about the same thing you are;*

*Interviews for information, done with information specialists, experts in the industry that interests you, or employees holding down the same job as you are exploring; and*

*Interviews for hire, done with employers in general, and the person who has the power to hire you for the job you want, in particular.*

This chapter is about this third kind of interview, the one for hire. Here are sixteen tips about that kind of interview:

## TIP #1

**An interview** resembles dating, more than it does buying a used car (*you*). An interview is analogous to two people trying to decide if they want "to go steady."

**An interview** is not to be thought of as marketing yourself: i.e., selling yourself to a half-interested employer. Rather, an interview is part of your research, i.e., the *data-collecting process* that you have been engaged in, or should have been engaged in, during your whole job-hunt. While you are sitting there, with the employer, the question you are trying to find an answer to is: "*Do I want to work here, or not?*" You use the interview to find out. Only when you have concluded Yes, do you then turn your energy toward *selling* yourself.

An interview is not to be thought of as a test. It's a *data-collecting process* for the employer, too. They are trying to decide if you fit. They are using the interview to find out *"Do I want him or her to work here? Do they have skills, knowledge, or experience that I really need? Do they have an attitude toward work, that I am looking for? And, how will they* fit in *with my other employees?"*

## TIP #2

**An interview** should be prepared for, *before* you ever go in, by taking these three steps:

1. Research the organization or company, before going in. Go to their website if they have one, and read everything there that is "About Us." If your town has a public library, ask your local librarian for help in finding any news clippings or other information about the place. And, finally, ask all your friends if they know anyone who ever worked there, or works there still, so you can take them to lunch or tea or Starbucks and find out any *inside* stories. All organizations love to be loved. If you've gone to the trouble of finding out as much about them as you can, they will be flattered and impressed, believe me—because most job-hunters never go to this amount of trouble. Most just walk in the door, knowing nothing about the organization. I knew a man who ran a large organization in Virginia; he said to me, *"I'm so tired of people coming in here, saying, Uh, what do you do here? that the next person who comes in here and has done some prior research on us, I'm going to offer a job."* He called me a week later to say, *"I kept my word."*

2. When it is you who is taking the initiative in setting up the interview, specify the time you are asking of them—unless they ask you to stay longer. Experts recommend you only ask for twenty minutes, and observe this commitment *religiously.* Watch your watch or timepiece like a hawk! Stay aware of the time, and don't stay one minute longer than the twenty minutes, unless the employer *begs* you to—and I mean, *begs.* Always prepare to end it at the time you specified, with, *"I said I would only take twenty*

*minutes of your time, and I like to honor my agreements."* This will always make a big impression on an employer!

3. As you go to the interview, keep in mind that if this is the person-who-actually-has-the-power-to-hire-you, then they are just as anxious as you are. Why? Because, the hiring-interview is not a very reliable way to choose an employee. In a survey conducted some years back, among a dozen top United Kingdom employers,[1] it was discovered that the chances of an employer finding a good employee through the hiring-interview was only 3 percent better than if they had picked a name out of a hat. In a further ironic finding, it was discovered that if the interview was conducted by someone who would be working directly with the candidate, the success rate dropped to 2 percent below that of picking a name out of a hat. And if the interview was conducted by a so-called human resources expert, the success rate dropped to 10 percent below that of picking a name out of a hat.

No, I don't know how they came up with these figures, and maybe they are flat wrong, but I don't think so. They are totally consistent with what I have learned about the world of hiring during the past forty years. I have watched so-called experts make *wretchedly* bad choices about hiring *in their own office*, and when they would morosely confess this to me some months later, over lunch, I would playfully tease them with, "If *you* don't even know how to hire well for your own office, how do you keep a straight face when you're called in as a hiring consultant by another organization?" And they would ruefully reply, "We *act as though* it were a science." Well, let me tell you, dear reader, hiring is *not* a science. It is a very, very hazy art, done ineptly by most of its employer-practitioners, in spite of their own past experience, their very best intentions, and their carloads of good will.

## TIP #3

What this adds up to, is that the hiring-interview is not what it seems to be. It seems to be one individual (*you*) sitting there, scared to death,

---

1. Reported in the *Financial Times Career Guide* 1989 for the United Kingdom

while the other individual (*the employer*) is sitting there, blasé and confident. But what it really is, is two individuals (*you* and *the employer*) sitting there supremely anxious. It's just that employers have learned to *hide* their fears better than you have, because they've had more practice. But this employer is, after all, a human being just like you. In most cases, they were *not* hired to do *this*. It got thrown in with all their other duties. And they dread making the wrong decision.

The employer's fears include *any* or *all* of the following:

A. That you won't be able to do the job: that you lack the necessary skills or experience, and the hiring-interview won't uncover this.

B. That if hired, you won't put in a full working day, more often than not.

C. That if hired, you'll take frequent sick days, on one pretext or another.

D. That if hired, you'll only stay around for a few weeks or at most a few months, until you find a better job that you can go get.

E. That it will take you too long to master the job, and thus it will be too long before you're profitable to that organization.

F. That you won't get along with the other workers there, or that you will develop a personality conflict with the boss.

G. That you will only do the minimum that you can get away with, rather than the maximum that the boss is hoping for. Since every boss these days is trying to keep their workforce smaller than it was before the Recession, they are hoping for the maximum productivity from each new hire.

H. That you will always have to be told what to do next, rather than displaying initiative—that you will always be in a responding mode, rather than an initiating mode (and mood).

I. That you will have a disastrous character flaw not evident in the interview, and turn out to be either dishonest, or irresponsible, a spreader of dissension at work, lazy, an embezzler, a gossip, a sexual harasser, a drunk, a drug-user or substance abuser, a liar, incompetent, or—in a word—*an employer's worst nightmare.*

J. (*If this is a large organization, and your would-be boss is not the top person*) that you will bring discredit upon them, and upon their department/section/ division, etc., for ever hiring you in the first place—making them lose face, possibly also costing them a raise or a promotion from the boss upstairs.

K. That you will cost a lot of money, if they make a mistake by hiring you. Currently, in the U.S. the cost to an employer of a bad hire can far exceed $50,000, including relocation costs, lost pay for the period for work not done or aborted, and severance pay, if *they* are the ones who decide to let you go. (*Put "cost of a bad hire" into a search engine like Google and you will see figures ranging from fifteen times the hire's monthly salary to five times the hire's annual salary.*)

No wonder the employer interviewing you is as anxious as you are. In your heart, be as compassionate toward them, as you hope they will be toward you. Forget the title—"employer" or "employee"—both of you are just *persons*.

## TIP #4

During the interview, determine to observe "the 50-50 Rule." Studies have revealed that, in general, the people who get hired are those who mix speaking and listening fifty-fifty in the interview. That is, half the time they let the employer do the talking, half the time in the interview they do the talking. People who didn't follow that mix, were the ones who didn't get hired, according to the study.[2] My hunch as to the *reason* why this is so, is that if you talk too much about yourself, you come across as one who would ignore the needs of the organization; if you talk too little, you come across as trying to hide something about your background.

## TIP #5

In answering the employer's questions, observe "the twenty-second to two-minute rule." Studies[3] have revealed that when it is your turn to speak or answer a question, you should plan not to speak any longer than

---

2. This one was done by a researcher at Massachusetts Institute of Technology, whose name has been lost in the mists of time.
3. This one was conducted by my friend and colleague, Donal Porot, of Geneva, Swtizerland.

two minutes at a time, if you want to make the best impression. In fact, a good answer to an employer's question sometimes only takes twenty seconds to give. (But not less than that, else you will be assumed to be "a grunter," without any communication skills.)

## TIP #6

Determine to be seen as a part of the solution, not as a part of the problem. Every organization has two main preoccupations for its day-by-day work: the problems—they generally prefer "challenges"—they are facing, and what solutions to those challenges their employees and management are coming up with. Therefore, the main thing the employer is trying to figure out during the hiring-interview with you, is: will you be part of the solution there, or just another part of the *problem*.

In trying to answer this concern, you should figure out prior to the interview how a *bad* employee would "screw up," in the position you are asking for—such things as *come in late, take too much time off, follow his or her own agenda instead of the employer's, etc.* Then plan to emphasize to the employer during the interview how much you are the very opposite: your sole goal "is to increase the organization's effectiveness, service, and bottom line."

Be aware of the skills all employers are looking for, these days, regardless of the position you are seeking. They are looking for employees: *who are punctual, arriving at work on time or better yet, early; who stay until quitting time, or even leave late; who are dependable; who have a good attitude; who have drive, energy, and enthusiasm; who want more than a paycheck; who are self-disciplined, well-organized, highly motivated, and good at managing their time; who can handle people well; who can use language effectively; who can work on a computer; who are committed to teamwork; who are flexible, and can respond to novel situations, or adapt when circumstances at work change; who are trainable, and love to learn; who are project-oriented, and goal-oriented; who have creativity and are good at*

*problem solving; who have integrity; who are loyal to the organization; who are able to identify opportunities, markets, and coming trends.* Above all, they want to hire people who can bring in more money than they are paid. *So, plan on claiming all of these that you* **legitimately** *can, during the hiring-interview, with evidence (short short stories of your past achievements, such as the skills identification stories you will write in chapter 13).*

## TIP #7

Realize that the employer thinks the way you are doing your job-hunt is the way you will do the job. So, be sure that you illustrate throughout the interview what you want to claim will be true of you, once hired. For example, if you plan on claiming that you are very thorough in all your work, be sure to be thorough in the way you have researched the company or organization ahead of time. The manner in which you do your job-hunt and the manner in which you would do the job you are seeking, are not assumed by most employers to be two unrelated subjects, but one and the same. They can tell when you are doing a slipshod, half-hearted job-hunt (*"Uh, what do you guys do here?"*), and this is taken as a clear warning that you will do a slipshod, half-hearted job, were they foolish enough to hire you. Most people job-hunt the same way they live their lives, and do their work.

## TIP #8

Try to think of some way to bring evidence of your skills, to the hiring-interview. For example, if you are an artist, a craftsperson, or anyone who produces a product, try to bring a sample of what you have made or produced—in scrapbook or portfolio form, with photos, or even videos. (Just in case.) If you are a programmer, bring examples of your scripts. And so on.

## TIP #9

Do not bad-mouth your previous employer(s) during the interview, even if they were terrible bosses. Employers sometimes feel as though they are a fraternity or sorority. During the interview you want to come across as one who displays courtesy toward *all* members of that fraternity or sorority. Bad-mouthing a previous employer only makes this employer who is interviewing you, worry about what you would say about *them*, after they hire you.

*(I learned this in my own experience. I once spoke graciously about a previous employer during a job-interview. Unbeknownst to me, the interviewer already knew that my previous employer had badly mistreated me. He therefore thought very highly of me because I didn't bring it up. In fact, he never forgot this incident; talked about it for years afterward.)*

Plan on saying something nice about any previous employer, or if you are pretty sure that the fact you and they didn't get along will surely come out, then try to nullify this ahead of time, by saying something simple like, "I usually get along with everybody; but for some reason, my past employer and I just didn't get along. Don't know why. It's never happened to me before. Hope it never happens again."

## TIP #10

Naturally, the employer is going to ask you questions, as a way of helping them figure out whether or not they want to hire you. Books on *interviewing*, of which there are many, often publish long lists of these questions, with timeworn, semi-clever answers suggested, and the recommendation that you memorize the answers to all those questions. Their lists include such questions as:

- Tell me about yourself.
- What do you know about this company?
- Why are you applying for this job?
- How would you describe yourself?
- What are your major strengths?
- What is your greatest weakness?
- What type of work do you like to do best?
- What are your interests outside of work?
- What accomplishment gave you the greatest satisfaction?
- Why did you leave your last job?
- Why were you fired (if you were)?

- Where do you see yourself five years from now?
- What are your goals in life?
- How much did you make at your last job?

But really there are only *five basic questions* that you need pay attention to. The people-who-have-the-power-to-hire-you need to know the answers to these five, which they may ask directly or try to find out obliquely:

1. "Why are you here?" *This means "Why are you knocking on my door, rather than someone else's door?"*

2. "What can you do for us?" *This means "If I were to hire you, would you be part of the problems I already have, or would you be a part of the solution to those problems? What are your skills, and how much do you know about the subject or field that we are in?"*

3. "What kind of person are you?" *This means "Will you fit in? Do you have the kind of personality that makes it easy for people to work with you, and do you share the values that we have at this place?"*

4. "What distinguishes you from nineteen or nine hundred other people who are applying for this job?" *This means "Do you have better work habits than the others, do you show up earlier, stay later, work more thoroughly, work faster, maintain higher standards, go the extra mile, or . . . what?"*

5. "Can I afford you?" *This means "If we decide we want you here, how much will it take to get you, and are we willing and able to pay that amount—governed, as we are, by our budget, and by our inability to pay you as much as the person who would be next above you, on our organizational chart?"*

These are the five principal questions that employers need to know the answers to. *This is the case, even if the interview begins and ends with these five questions never once being mentioned explicitly by the employer.* The questions are still *floating* beneath the surface of the conversation, beneath all the things being discussed. Anything you can do, during the interview, to help the employer answer these five questions, will make the interview more helpful to the employer. And you can do a lot, if you'll just do the Flower Exercise (chapter 13) in this book. You will *know* the answers.

Of course, it's not just the employer who has questions. You have some too—inevitably. And—surprise—they are basically the same questions (in only slightly different form) *as the employer's.* Your questions come out sounding like this:

1. "What does this job involve?" *You want to understand exactly what tasks will be asked of you, so that you can determine if these are the kinds of tasks you would really like to do, and can do.*

2. "What are the skills a top employee in this job would have to have?" *You want to find out if your skills match those that the employer thinks a top employee in this job has to have, in order to do this job well; not just an average employee.*

3. "Are these the kinds of people I would like to work with, or not?" *Do not ignore your intuition if it tells you that you would not be comfortable working with these people!! You want to know if they have the kind of personalities that would enable you to accomplish your best work. If these people aren't it, keep looking! You don't want to be miserable at work. It pays to be picky here.*

4. "If we like each other, and both want to work together, can I persuade them there is something unique about me, that makes me different from nineteen or nine hundred other people who are applying for this job?" *You need to think out, way ahead of time, what does make you different from other people who can do the same job. For example, if you are good at analyzing problems, how do you do that? Painstakingly? Intuitively, in a flash? By consulting with greater authorities in the field? You see the point. You are trying to put your finger on the "style" or "manner" in which you do your work, that is distinctive and hopefully appealing, to* this *employer.*

5. "Can I persuade them to hire me at the salary I need or want?" *This requires some knowledge on your part of how to conduct salary negotiation. (Key things to know: it should always take place at the end of the interviews there, and whoever mentions a salary figure first, generally loses, in the negotiation.) That's covered in the next chapter.*

You will probably want to ask questions one and two, above, out loud. You will *observe* quietly the answer to question three. You will be prepared to make the case for questions four and five, when the *appropriate* time in the interview arises.

How do you first raise these questions of yours? If you initiated the interview, you might begin by reporting to them just exactly how you've been conducting your job-hunt, and what impressed you so much about *their* organization during your research, that you decided to come in and talk to them about a job. From there, and thereafter, you can fix your attention on these five questions—in the employer's form, and in yours.[4]

Incidentally, let's not leave this tip without observing that these five questions pop up (yet again), if you're there to talk *not* about a job that already exists, but rather, one that you hope they will *create* for you. In that case, these five questions change form slightly again. They get changed into six *statements*, that you make to the person-who-has-the-power-to-*create*-this-job:

1. What you like about this organization.
2. What sorts of needs you find intriguing in this field, in general, and in this organization, in particular (as mentioned earlier, unless you first hear the word coming out of their mouth, don't use the word "*problems*," as most employers prefer synonyms that sound gentler to their ears, such as "*challenges*" or "*needs*").
3. What skills seem to you to be necessary in order to meet such needs.
4. Evidence from your past experience that demonstrates you have those very skills. Employers, in these days of "behavioral interviews," are looking for *examples* from your past performance and achievement—your behavior—not just vague statements like: "I'm good at . . ." They want concrete examples, specifically of any transferable skills, work content skills, or self-management skills, i.e., traits., that you claim to have.

   You may be asked, or you can pose the question to yourself before you ever go in there: "What are *the three most important* competencies, for this job?" Then, of course, you need to demonstrate

---

4. To help you explore these five, ask:
   What significant changes has this company gone through in the past five years?
   What values are sacred to this company?
   What characterizes the most successful employees this company has?
   What future changes do you see in the work here?
   Who do you see as your allies, colleagues, or competitors in this business?

during the interview that you *have* those three—for the job that you want them to create.

5. What is unique about the way *you* perform those skills. Every prospective employer wants to know *what makes you different* from nineteen or nine hundred other people who can do the same kind of work as you. You *have* to know what that is. And then not merely talk about it, but actually demonstrate it by the way you conduct your side of the hiring-interview.

6. How the hiring of you will not cost them, in the long run. You need to be prepared to demonstrate that you will, in the long run, end up costing them nothing, as you will bring in more money than your salary costs.

## TIP #11

Throughout the interview, keep in mind: employers don't really care about your past; they only ask about it, in order to try to predict your future (behavior) with them, if they decide to hire you.

Legally, U.S. employers may only ask you questions that are related to the requirements and expectations of the job. They cannot ask about such things as your creed, religion, race, age, sexual orientation, or marital status. But, any other questions about your past are *fair game*. And they *will* ask them, if they know what they're doing. (Not always the case.)

Therefore, during the hiring-interview, before you answer any question the employer asks you about your past, you should pause to think out "What fear about the *future* caused them to ask this question about my past?" and then address that fear, obliquely or directly.

Here are some *examples*:

| Employer's Question | The Fear Behind the Question | The Point You Try to Get Across | Phrases You Might Use to Get This Across |
| --- | --- | --- | --- |
| "Tell me about yourself." | The employer is afraid he/she isn't going to conduct a very good interview, by failing to ask the right questions. Or is afraid there is something wrong with you, and is hoping you will blurt it out. | You are a good employee, as you have proved in the past at your other jobs. (Give the briefest history of who you are, where born and raised, interests, hobbies, and kind of work you have enjoyed the most to date.) *Keep it to two minutes, max.* | In describing your work history, use any *honest* phrases you can about your work history, that are self-complimentary: "Hard worker." "Came in early, left late." "Always did more than was expected of me." Etc. |
| "What kind of work are you looking for?" | The employer is afraid that you are looking for a different job than that which the employer is trying to fill. E.g., he/she wants an assistant, but you want to be an office supervisor, etc. | You are looking for precisely the kind of work the employer is offering (but don't say that, if it isn't true). Repeat back to the employer, in your own words, what he/she has said about the job, and emphasize the skills you have to do that. | If the employer hasn't described the job at all, say, "I'd be happy to answer that, but first I need to understand exactly what kind of work this job involves." *Then* answer, as at left. |
| "Have you ever done this kind of work before?" | The employer is afraid you don't possess the necessary skills and experience to do this job. | You have skills that are transferable, from whatever you used to do; and you did it well. | "I pick up stuff very quickly." "I have quickly mastered any job I have ever done." |

| Employer's Question | The Fear Behind the Question | The Point You Try to Get Across | Phrases You Might Use to Get This Across |
|---|---|---|---|
| "Why did you leave your last job?"—or "How did you get along with your former boss and co-workers?" | The employer is afraid you don't get along well with people, especially bosses, and is just waiting for you to "bad-mouth" your previous boss or co-workers, as proof of that. | Say whatever positive things you possibly can about your former boss and co-workers (without telling lies). Emphasize you usually get along very well with people—and then let your gracious attitude toward your previous boss(es) and co-workers prove it, right before this employer's very eyes (and ears). | If you left voluntarily: "My boss and I both felt I would be happier and more effective in a job where [here describe your strong points, such as] I would have more room to use my initiative and creativity." If you were fired: "Usually, I get along well with everyone, but in this particular case the boss and I just didn't get along with each other. Difficult to say why." You don't need to say anything more than that. If you were laid off and your job wasn't filled after you left: "My job was terminated." |
| "How is your health?"—or "How much were you absent from work during your last job?" | The employer is afraid you will be absent from work a lot, if they hire you. Unfortunately for them, and fortunately for you, this is a question they cannot legally ask you. | Just because the question is illegal, doesn't mean you can't address their hidden fear. Even if they never mention it, you can try to disarm that fear. | You can find a way to say, "My productivity always exceeded other workers, in my previous jobs." |
| "Can you explain why you've been out of work so long?"—or "Can you tell me why there are these gaps in your work history?" (Usually said after studying your resume.) | The employer is afraid that you are the kind of person who quits a job the minute he/she doesn't like something at it; in other words, that you have no "stick-to-it-iveness." | You love to work, and you regard times when things aren't going well as challenges, which you enjoy learning how to conquer. | "During the gaps in my work record, I was studying/doing volunteer work/doing some hard thinking about my mission in life/finding redirection." (Choose one.) |

| Employer's Question | The Fear Behind the Question | The Point You Try to Get Across | Phrases You Might Use to Get This Across |
|---|---|---|---|
| "Wouldn't this job represent a step down for you?"—or "I think this job would be way beneath your talents and experience."—or "Don't you think you would be underemployed if you took this job?" | The employer is afraid you could command a bigger salary, somewhere else, and will therefore leave him/her as soon as something better turns up. | You will stick with this job as long as you and the employer agree this is where you should be. | "This job isn't a step down for me. It's a step up—from welfare." "We have mutual fears; every employer is afraid a good employee will leave too soon, and every employee is afraid the employer might fire him/her, for no good reason." "I like to work, and I give my best to every job I've ever had." |
| And, last, "Tell me, what is your greatest weakness?" | The employer is afraid you have some character flaw, and hopes you will now rashly blurt it out, or confess it. | You have limitations just like anyone else, but you work constantly to improve yourself and be a more and more effective worker. | Mention a weakness and then stress its positive aspect, e.g., "I don't like to be over-supervised, because I have a great deal of initiative, and I like to anticipate problems before they even arise." |

## TIP #12

As the interview proceeds, you want to quietly notice the timeframe of the questions the employer is asking, because it's a way of measuring how the interview is going. If it's going favorably for you, the timeframe of the employer's questions will often move—*however slowly*—through the following stages.

1. Distant past: *e.g., "Where did you attend high school?"*
2. Immediate past: *e.g., "Tell me about your most recent job."*
3. Present: *e.g., "What kind of a job are you looking for?"*
4. Immediate future: *e.g., "Would you be able to come back for another interview next week?"*
5. Distant future: *e.g., "Where would you like to be five years from now?"*

Well, you get the point. The more the timeframe of the interviewer's questions moves from the past to the future, the more favorably you may assume the interview is going for you. On the other hand, if the interviewer's questions stay firmly in the past, the outlook is not so good. *Ah well, ya can't win them all!*

When the timeframe of the interviewer's questions moves firmly into the future, *then* is the time for you to get more specific about the job in question. Experts say it is essential for you to ask, at that point, these kinds of questions, *if* you don't already know the answers:

> What is the job, specifically, that I am being considered for?
>
> If I were hired, what duties would I be performing?
>
> What responsibilities would I have?
>
> What would you be hiring me to accomplish?
>
> Would I be working with a team, or group? To whom would I report?
>
> Whose responsibility is it to see that I get the training I need, here, to get up to speed?
>
> How would I be evaluated, how often, and by whom?
>
> What were the strengths and weaknesses of previous people in this position?
>
> If you don't mind my asking, I'm curious as to why *you* yourself decided to work at this organization?
>
> What do you wish you had known about this company before you started here?
>
> May I meet the persons I would be working with and for (if it isn't you)?

## TIP #13

After all this careful, rational approach, I hate to tell you but sometimes interviews are lost for the darnedest reasons, that would not occur to you in a million years. I think of this as losing to mosquitoes when you were prepared to fight dragons. And losing in the first two minutes (ouch)!

So let us look at *what* mosquitoes (*as it were*) can fly in, during the first thirty seconds to two minutes of your interview so that *the person-who-*

*Chapter 8*

has-the-power-to-hire-you starts muttering to themselves, *"I sure hope we have some other candidates besides this one"*:

1. Your appearance and personal habits. Interview after interview has revealed that *you are much more likely to get the job if*:

   - you have obviously freshly bathed; if a male that you have your face freshly shaved or your hair and beard freshly trimmed, have clean fingernails, and are using a deodorant; if a female that you have not got tons of makeup on your face, have had your hair newly cut or styled, have clean or nicely manicured fingernails, that don't stick out ten inches from your fingers, are using deodorant, and are not wearing clothes so daring that they call *a lot* of attention to themselves; *and in either case, that*

   - you have on freshly laundered clothes, pants, or pantsuits with a sharp crease, and shoes, not flip-flops, freshly polished; *and*

   - you do not have bad breath, do not dispense gallons of the odor of garlic, onion, stale tobacco, or strong drink, into the enclosed office air, but have brushed and flossed your teeth; *and equally*

   - you are not wafting tons of aftershave cologne or overwhelming perfume fifteen feet ahead of you, as you enter the room. Employers are super-sensitive these days to the fact that many of their employees are allergic to such things.

2. Nervous mannerisms. *It is a turnoff for employers if*:

   - you continually avoid eye contact with the employer (in fact, this is a *big, big* no-no), *or*

   - you give a limp handshake, *or*

   - you slouch in your chair, or endlessly fidget with your hands, or crack your knuckles, or constantly play with your hair during the interview.

3. Lack of self-confidence. *It is a turnoff for employers if*:

   - you are speaking so softly you cannot be heard, or so loudly you can be heard two rooms away, *or*

   - you are giving answers in an extremely hesitant fashion, *or*

   - you are giving one-word answers to all the employer's questions, *or*

   - you are constantly interrupting the employer, *or*

- you are downplaying your achievements or abilities, or are continuously being self-critical in comments you make about yourself during the interview.

4. The consideration you show to other people. *It is a turnoff for employers if:*
   - you show a lack of courtesy to the receptionist, secretary, and (if at lunch) to the waiter or waitress, *or*
   - you display extreme criticalness toward your previous employers and places of work, *or*
   - you drink strong stuff during the interview process. Ordering a drink if the employer takes you to lunch is *always* a no-no, as it raises the question in the employer's mind, *Do they normally stop with one, or do they normally keep on going?* Don't . . . do . . . it! even if they do;
   - you forget to thank the interviewer as you're leaving, or forget to send a thank-you note afterward. Says one human resources expert: "A prompt, brief, faxed business letter thanking me for my time along with a (brief!) synopsis of his/her unique qualities communicates to me that this person is an assertive, motivated, customer-service-oriented salesperson who utilizes technology and knows the rules of the 'game.' These are qualities I am looking for. . . . At the moment I receive approximately one such letter . . . for every fifteen candidates interviewed."
   - Incidentally, *many* an employer will watch to see if you smoke, either in the office or at lunch. *In a race between two equally qualified people, the nonsmoker will win out over the smoker 94 percent of the time, according to a study done by a professor of business at Seattle University.* Sorry to report this, but there it is;

5. Your values. *It is a complete turnoff for most employers, if they see in you:*
   - any sign of arrogance or excessive aggressiveness; any sign of tardiness or failure to keep appointments and commitments on time, including this hiring-interview; *or*
   - any sign of laziness or lack of motivation; *or*
   - any sign of constant complaining or blaming things on others; *or*

- any signs of dishonesty or lying—especially on your resume or during the interview; *or*
- any signs of irresponsibility or tendency to goof off; *or*
- any sign of not following instructions or obeying rules; *or*
- any sign of a lack of enthusiasm for this organization and what it is trying to do; *or*
- any sign of instability, inappropriate response, and the like; *or*
- the other ways in which you evidence your *values*, such as: what things impress you or don't impress you in their office; *or* what you are willing to sacrifice in order to get this job *and* what you are *not* willing to sacrifice in order to get this job; *or* your enthusiasm for work; *or* the carefulness with which you did or didn't research this company before you came in; and blah, blah, blah.

There you have it: the *mosquitoes* that can kill you, when you're on the watch only for dragons, during the hiring-interview. One favor I ask of you: do not write me, telling me how picayune or asinine some of this is. Believe me, I *know* that. I'm not reporting the world as it *should* be, and certainly not as I would like it to be. I'm only reporting what study after study has revealed about the hiring world as it *is*.

But here's the good news, when all is said and done: you can *kill* all these mosquitoes. Yes, you control and can change *every one* of these factors. Go back and read the list; you will see.

## TIP #14

Before you let the interview end, there are five questions you should *always* ask:

1. *"Can you offer me this job?"* I know this seems stupid, but it is astonishing (at least to me) how many job-hunters have secured a job simply by being bold enough to ask for it, at the end of the (final) interview, in language they feel comfortable with. I don't know *why* this is. I only know that it is. Anyway, if after hearing all about this job at this place, you decide you'd really like to have it, you must *ask for it*. The worst thing the employer can say

is "No," or "We need some time to think about all the interviews we're conducting."

2. *"When may I expect to hear from you?"* If the employer says, *"We need some time to think about this,"* or *"We will be calling you for a second interview,"* you don't want to leave this as a vague good intention on the employer's part. You want to nail it down.

3. *"Might I ask what would be the latest I can expect to hear from you?"* The employer has probably given you their best guess, in answer to your previous question. Now you want to know: *what is the worst-case scenario?* Incidentally, when I was job-hunting once, and I asked my interviewer when was the latest I might expect to hear from him, he replied, *"Never!"* I thought he had a great sense of humor. Turned out he was dead serious. I never heard from him again, despite repeated attempts at contact.

4. *"May I contact you after that date, if for any reason you haven't gotten back to me by that time?"* Some employers resent this question. You'll know that is the case if they snap at you. But most employers appreciate your offering them what is in essence a safety-net. They know they can get busy, become overwhelmed with other things, forget their promise to you. It's reassuring, in such a case, for you to offer to rescue them.

(Optional: #5. *"Can you think of anyone else who might be interested in hiring me?"* This question is invoked *only* if they replied *"No,"* to your first question, above.)

Jot down any answers they give you to the questions above, then stand up, thank them sincerely for their time, give a firm handshake, and leave.

In the following days, rigorously keep to all that you said, and don't contact them except with that mandatory thank-you note, until after the latest deadline you two agreed upon, in answer to question #4, above. If you do have to contact them after that date, and if they tell you things are still up in the air, you should gently ask questions #2, #3, and #4, all over again.

Incidentally, it is entirely appropriate for you to insert a thank-you note into the running stream, after *each* interview or telephone contact. Just keep it brief. Very brief.

# TIP #15

Every expert on interviewing will tell you two things:

(1) Thank-you notes *must* be sent after *every* interview, by every job-hunter; and (2) most job-hunters ignore this advice.

Indeed, it is safe to say that it is the most overlooked step in the entire job-hunting process.

If you want to stand out from the others applying for the same job, send thank-you notes—to *everyone* you met there, that day. Ask if they have a business card, and if not, ask them to write out their name and address. Do this with secretaries (who often hold the keys to the kingdom) as well as with your interviewer.

If you need any additional encouragement to send thank-you letters (*besides the fact that it may get you the job*), here are six more reasons for sending a thank-you note, especially to the one who interviewed you:

First, you were presenting yourself as one who has good skills with people. Your actions with respect to the job-interview must back this claim up. Sending a thank-you note does that. The employer can see you are good with people; you remembered to thank them.

Second, it helps the employer recall who you are. Very helpful if they've seen a dozen people that day.

Third, if a committee is involved in the hiring process, the man or woman who first interviewed you has something to show the others on the committee.

Fourth, if the interview went rather well, and the employer seemed to show an interest in further talks, the thank-you letter can reiterate *your* interest in further talks.

Fifth, the thank-you note gives you an opportunity to correct any wrong impression you left behind. You can add anything you forgot to tell them, that you want them to know. And from among all the things you two discussed, you can underline the two or three points that you most want to stand out in their minds.

Lastly, if the interview did not go well, or you lost all interest in working there, and this thank-you note is sort of "*goodbye, and thanks,*" keep in mind that they may hear of openings, elsewhere, that would be of interest to you. In the thank-you note, you can mention this, and ask them to please let you know if they hear of anything anywhere. If this was a kind man or woman who interviewed you, you may hear of additional leads.

## TIP #16

Remember, despite all your careful preparation, and all your thoughtful questions, you may not be offered the job. I remind you of what I said at the beginning of this chapter: *the hiring process is more like choosing a mate, than it is like deciding whether or not to buy a new car.* "Choosing a mate" here is a metaphor. To elaborate upon the metaphor just a bit, it means that *the mechanisms* by which human nature decides to hire someone, are *similar* to the mechanisms by which human nature decides whether or not to marry someone. Those mechanisms, of course, are often impulsive, intuitional, nonrational, unfathomable, and made on the spur of the moment.

There is no magic in job-hunting. No techniques work all the time. I hear regularly from job-hunters who report that they paid attention to all the tips I have mentioned in this chapter and book, and are quite successful at securing interviews—but they never get hired. And they want to know what they're doing wrong.

Well, unfortunately, the answer *sometimes* is: "Maybe you're doing nothing wrong." I don't know *how often* this happens, but I know it *does* happen: namely, *some* employers play despicable tricks on job-hunters, whereby they invite you in for an interview despite the fact that they have already hired someone for the position in question, and they know from the beginning that they have absolutely no intention of hiring you—not in a million years!

You are cheered, of course, by the ease with which you get these interviews. But unbeknownst to you, the manager who is interviewing you (we'll say it's a *he*) has a personal friend he already agreed to give the job to. Only one small problem remains: the state or the federal government gives funds to this organization, and has mandated that this position be opened to all. So this manager must *pretend* to interview ten candidates, including his favorite, *as though* the job opening were still available. But, he intended, from the beginning, to reject the other nine and give the job to his favorite. You were selected for the honor of being among those nine *rejectees*.

You will, of course, be baffled as to *why* you got turned down. Trouble is, they will *never* confess it to you.

On the other hand, there is always the chance that no games are being played. You are getting rejected, at place after place, because there is something really wrong with the way you are coming across, during these hiring-interviews.

Employers will rarely ever tell you this. You will never hear them say something like, "You came across as just too cocky and arrogant during the interview." You will almost always be left in the dark as to *what* it is you're doing wrong.

If you've been interviewed by a whole bunch of employers, one way around this deadly silence, is to ask for *generalized* feedback from whoever was the *friendliest* employer that you saw. You can always try phoning, reminding them of who you are, and then asking the following question—deliberately kept generalized, vague, unrelated to just *that* place, and above all, future-directed. Something like: *"You know, I've been on several interviews at several different places now, where I've gotten turned down. From what you've seen, is there something about me in an interview, that you think might be causing me not to get hired at those places? If so, I'd really appreciate your giving me some pointers so I can do better in my future hiring-interviews."*

Most of the time they'll *still* duck saying anything hurtful or helpful. Their legal advisor, if they have one, will certainly advise against it. First of all, they're afraid of lawsuits. Second, they don't know how you will use what they might have to say. (Said an old military veteran to me one day, "I used to think it was my duty to tell everyone the truth. Now I only give it to those who can use it.")

But *occasionally* you will run into an employer who is willing to risk giving you the truth, because they think you will know how to use it wisely. If so, thank them from the bottom of your heart, no matter how painful their feedback is. Such advice, seriously heeded, can bring about just the changes in your interviewing strategy that you most need, in order to win the interview.

In the absence of any such help from employers who interviewed you, you might want to get a good business friend of yours to role-play a mock hiring-interview with you, in case they immediately see something glaringly wrong with how you're "coming across."

When all else fails, I would recommend you go to a career coach who charges by the hour, and put yourself in their tender knowledgeable hands. Role-play an interview with them, and take their advice seriously (you've just paid for it, after all).

## CONCLUSION

I have left out the subject of salary negotiation in this chapter. It requires a chapter of its own (next!).

Hopefully, however, with these tips you will do well in your interviews. And if you do get hired, make one resolution to yourself right there on the spot: plan to keep track of your accomplishments at this new job, on a weekly basis—jotting them down, every weekend, in your own private log. Career experts recommend you do this without fail. You can then summarize these accomplishments annually on a one-page sheet, for your boss's eyes, when the question of a raise or promotion comes up.[5]

> *How wonderful it is that nobody need wait a single moment before starting to improve the world.*
>
> ANNE FRANK

---

5. In any good-size organization, you will often be amazed at how little attention your superiors pay to your noteworthy accomplishments, and how little they are aware at the end of the year that you really are entitled to a raise, based on the profits you have brought in. Noteworthy your accomplishments may be, but no one is taking notes . . . unless you do. You may even need to be the one who brings up the subject of a raise or promotion. Waiting for the employer to bring this up may never happen.

# THE TEN COMMANDMENTS
# FOR JOB-INTERVIEWS

*Whereby Your Chances of Finding a Job Are Vastly Increased*

I. Go after new small organizations with twenty or fewer employees, since they create two-thirds of all new jobs. Only if you turn up nothing should you broaden the search to slightly larger organizations.

II. Hunt for places to interview using the aid of, say, eighty friends and acquaintances—because a job-hunt requires eighty pairs of eyes and ears. But first do homework on yourself so you can tell them exactly what you are looking for.

III. As for who to interview, once you've identified a place that interests you, you really need to find out who has the power to hire you there, for the position you want, and use "bridge-people" (those who know you and also know them) to get an introduction to that person. Employ LinkedIn.com and similar, to find these people.

IV. Do thorough homework on an organization before going there, using Informational Interviews plus the Internet to find out as much about them as you possibly can. If you have a public library in town, ask there too.

V. Then prepare for the interview with your own agenda, your own questions and curiosities about whether or not this job fits you. This will always impress employers.

VI. If you initiated the appointment, ask for just twenty minutes of their time; and keep to your word strictly. Watch your watch.

VII. When answering a question of theirs, talk only between twenty seconds to two minutes, at any one time. Try to be succinct. Don't keep rattling on, out of nervousness.

VIII. Basically approach them not as a "job-beggar" but humbly as a resource person, able to produce better work for that organization than any of the people who worked in that position, previously.

IX. At the end of the interviewing process, ask for the job: "Given all that we have discussed, can you offer me this job?" Salary negotiation should only happen when they have definitely said they want you; prior to that, it's pointless.

X. Always write a thank-you note the same evening as the interview, and mail it at the latest by early next morning. You may also e-mail it.

*According to our faith, so is the world to each of us. I dare to give my pity to some man who seems to me to live a meagre life. . . . But who am I that I should give him pity? Let me know that it is not what he has but what he is that makes the poverty or richness of his life.*

PHILLIPS BROOKS (1835–1893)

# Chapter 9. The Six Secrets of Salary Negotiation

We have come now to the tail end of an interview for hire. We covered that in the previous chapter. Now it's time to discuss salary. I hope you know that it *must* be discussed.

I remember once talking to a breathless high school graduate, who was elated at having just landed her first job. "How much are they going to pay you?" I asked. She looked startled. "I don't know," she said, "I never asked. I just assume they will pay me a fair wage." *Boy!* did she get a rude awakening when she received her first paycheck. It was so miserably *low*, she couldn't believe her eyes. And thus did she learn, painfully, what you must learn too: *Before accepting a job offer, always ask about salary.* Indeed, *ask and then negotiate.*

It's the "negotiate" that throws fear into our hearts. We feel ill prepared to do this. Well, set your mind at ease; it's not all that difficult. While whole books can be—and have been—written on this subject, there are basically just six secrets to keep in mind.

## THE FIRST SECRET OF SALARY NEGOTIATION

### NEVER DISCUSS SALARY UNTIL THE END OF THE INTERVIEWING PROCESS WHEN (AND IF) THEY HAVE DEFINITELY SAID THEY WANT YOU

*"The end of the interviewing process"* is difficult to define. It's the point at which the employer says, or thinks, "We've got to get this person!" That may be at the end of the first (and therefore the last) interview; or it may be at the end of a whole series of interviews, often with different people within the same company or organization. But assuming things

are going favorably for you, whether after the first, or second, or third, or fourth interview, if *you* like them and *they* increasingly like you, a job offer *will* be made. Then, and only then, is it time to deal with the question that is inevitably on any employer's mind: *how much is this person going to cost me?* And the question that is on *your* mind: *how much does this job pay?*

If the employer raises the salary question earlier, say near the beginning of the interview, innocently asking, "What kind of salary are you looking for?" you should have three responses ready at your fingertips.

Response #1: If the employer seems like a kindly man or woman, your best and most tactful reply might be: "Until you've decided you definitely want me, and I've decided I definitely could help you with your tasks here, I feel any discussion of salary is premature."

*That will work, in most cases. There are instances, however, where that doesn't work. Then you need:*

Response #2: You may be face-to-face with an employer who will not be put off so easily, and demands within the first two minutes of the interview to know what salary you are looking for. At this point, you may need your second response: "I'll gladly answer that, but could you first help me understand what this job involves?"

*That is a good response, in most cases. But what if it doesn't work? Then you need:*

Response #3: The employer with rising voice says, "Come, come, don't play games with me. I want to know what salary you're looking for." You have your third response ready at hand for *this very eventuality.* You answer in terms of a *range.* For example, "I'm looking for a salary in the range of $35,000 to $45,000 a year."

If that still doesn't satisfy them, then consider what this means. Clearly, you are being interviewed by an employer who has no range in mind. Their beginning figure is their ending figure. No negotiation is possible.[1] This happens, when it happens, because many employers in this post-Recessionary period of history are making salary their major

---

1. One job-hunter said his interviews *always* began with the salary question, and no matter what he answered, that ended the interview. Turned out, this job-hunter was doing all the interviewing over the phone. That was the problem. Once he went face to face, salary was no longer the first thing discussed in the interview.

criterion for deciding who to hire, and who not to hire. *It's an old game, now played with new determination by many employers, which runs,* "among two equally qualified candidates, the one who is willing to work for the least pay, *wins.*"

If you run into this situation, and if you want that job badly enough, you will have no choice but to give in. Ask what salary they have in mind, and make your decision. (Of course you can always postpone announcing your decision by saying, "*I need a little time, to think about this.*")

However, all the foregoing is merely the *worst-case scenario.* Usually, things won't go this badly. In most interviews these days, the employer *will* be willing to save salary negotiation until they've finally decided they want you (and you've decided you want them). And at that point, the salary *will be* negotiable.

## When You Should be Willing to Discuss Salary

*Not until all of the following conditions have been fulfilled—*

- *Not until they've gotten to know you, at your best, so they can see how you stand out above the other applicants.*
- *Not until you've gotten to know them, as completely as you can, so you can tell when they're being firm, or when they're flexible.*
- *Not until you've found out exactly what the job entails.*
- *Not until they've had a chance to find out how well you match the job requirements.*
- *Not until you're in the final interview at that place, for that job.*
- *Not until you've decided, "I'd really like to work here."*
- *Not until they've said, "We want you."*
- *Not until they've said, "We've got to have you."*

*—should you get into salary discussion with any employer.*
If you'd prefer this to be put in the form of a diagram, here it is:

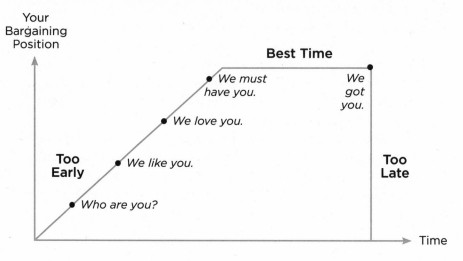

Why is it to your advantage to delay salary discussion? Because, if you really *shine* during the hiring-interview, they may—at the end—offer you a higher salary than they originally had in mind when the interview started—and this is particularly the case when the interview has gone so well, that they're now *determined* to obtain your services.

## THE SECOND SECRET OF SALARY NEGOTIATION

### THE PURPOSE OF SALARY NEGOTIATION IS TO UNCOVER THE MOST THAT AN EMPLOYER IS WILLING TO PAY TO GET YOU

Salary negotiation would never happen if *every* employer in *every* hiring-interview were to mention, right from the start, the top figure they are willing to pay for that position. *Some* employers do, as I mentioned. And that's the end of any salary negotiation. But, of course, most employers don't. Hoping they'll be able to get you for less, they start *lower* than

*Chapter 9*

they're ultimately willing to go. **This creates *a range*. And that range is what salary negotiation is all about.**

For example, if the employer wants to hire somebody for no more than $20 an hour, they may start *the bidding* at $12 an hour. In which case, their *range* runs between $12 and $20 an hour.

So, why do you want to negotiate? Because, if a range *is* thus involved, you have every right to try to discover the highest salary that employer is willing to pay you *within that range.*

The employer's goal is to save money, if possible. Your goal is to bring home to your family, your partner, or your own household the most money that you can, for the work you will be doing. Nothing's wrong with the goals of either of you. But it does mean that, where the employer starts lower, salary negotiation is legitimate, and expected.

## THE THIRD SECRET OF SALARY NEGOTIATION

### DURING SALARY DISCUSSION, NEVER BE THE FIRST ONE TO MENTION A SALARY FIGURE

Where salary negotiation has been kept *offstage* for much of the interview process, when it finally does come *onstage* you want the employer to be the first one to mention *a figure*, if you possibly can.

Nobody knows why, but it has been observed over the years that where the goals are opposite, as in this case—you are trying to get the employer to pay the most they can, and the employer is trying to pay the least they can—whoever mentions a salary *figure* first, generally loses. You can speculate from now until the cows come home, as to *why* this is; all we know is *that* it is.

Inexperienced employer/interviewers often don't know this quirky rule. But experienced ones are very aware of it; that's why they will *always* toss the ball to you first, with some innocent-sounding question, such as: "What kind of salary are you looking for?" *Well, how kind of them to ask me what I want*—you may be thinking. No, no, no. Kindness has nothing to do with it. They are hoping *you* will be the first to mention a figure, because they know this strange and funny truth: *whoever mentions a salary figure first, generally loses salary negotiation, at the end.*

Accordingly, if they ask you to name a figure, the *countermove* on your part should be: "Well, you created this position, so you must have some figure in mind, and I'd be interested in knowing what that figure is."

## THE FOURTH SECRET OF SALARY NEGOTIATION

### BEFORE YOU GO TO THE INTERVIEW, DO SOME CAREFUL RESEARCH ON TYPICAL SALARIES FOR YOUR FIELD AND IN THAT ORGANIZATION

As I said, salary negotiation is possible *anytime* the employer does not open discussion of salary by naming the top figure they have in mind, but starts instead with a lower figure.

Okay, so here is our $64,000 question: how do you tell whether the figure the employer first offers you is only their *starting bid*, or is their *final final offer*? The answer is: by doing some research on the field *and* that organization, before you go to the interview.

*Oh, come on!* I can hear you say. *Isn't this more trouble than it's worth?* No, not if you want to win the salary negotiation.

Trust me, salary research pays off *handsomely*. Let's say it takes you from one to three days to run down this sort of information on the three or four organizations that interest you the most. And let us say that because you've done this research, when you finally go in for the hiring-interview you are able to ask for and obtain a salary that is $15,000 a year higher than you would otherwise have gotten. In just the next three years, you will be earning $45,000 extra, because of your salary research. *Not bad pay, for one to three days' work!* And it can be even more. I know *many* job-hunters and career-changers to whom this has happened.

There is a financial penalty exacted from those who are too lazy, or in too much of a hurry, to go gather this information. In plain language: *if you don't do this research, it'll cost ya!*

Okay, then, how do you do this research? Well, there are two ways to go: on the Internet, and off the Internet. Let's look at each, in turn:

## Salary Research on the Internet

If you have access to the Internet, and you want to research salaries for particular geographical regions, positions, occupations, or industries, or even (sometimes) organizations, here are some free sites that may give you just what you're looking for:

- http://jobstar.org/tools/salary/index.cfm: This site is a treasure trove. It links to 300 different sites that maintain salary lists, and joy, joy, it is kept updated. It's one of the largest and most complete lists of salary reviews on the Web, maintained by a genius named Mary Ellen Mort.

- www.salary.com: The most visited of all the salary-specific job-sites, with a wide variety of information about salaries. It was started by Kent Plunkett, and acquired by Kenexa Corporation, in August 2010. It has expanded a lot, over the years, and has a multitude of resources.

- www.bls.gov/oco: The Bureau of Labor Statistics' survey of salaries in individual **occupations**, from *The Occupational Outlook Handbook 2010–2011*.

- http://stats.bls.gov/oes/oes_emp.htm: The Bureau of Labor Statistics' survey of salaries in individual industries (it's a companion piece to *The Occupational Outlook Handbook*). This site is up-to-date as of December 2010.

- http://stats.bls.gov/opub/ooq/1999/fall/art02.pdf: If you Google "High Earning Workers Who Don't Have a Bachelor's Degree" because you want to know how to earn *a lot* without having to go to college first, you'll find a bunch of references, but they're all referring to one article written back in 1999, by Matthew Mariani at the Bureau of Labor Statistics. So, if you want current figures, I think you're out of luck. Nonetheless, you may want to browse this article anyway, to get some *ideas* about what kinds of jobs—at least of those available in 1999—pay better than most, if you didn't ever go to or finish college.

- www.salaryexpert.com: When you need a salary expert, it makes sense to go to "the Salary Expert." Lots of stuff on the subject of salaries here, including a free "Salary Report" for hundreds of job-titles, varying by area, skill level, and experience. Also has some salary calculators.

If you "strike out" on all the above sites, then you're going to have to get a little more clever, and work a little harder, and pound the pavement, as I shall describe below.

## Salary Research off the Internet

Offline, how do you go about doing salary research? Well, there's a simple rule: generally speaking, abandon **books**, and go talk to **people**. Use books and libraries only as a *second*, or *last*, resort. Their information is often just way too outdated.

You can get much more complete and up-to-date information from people who are doing the kind of job you're interested in, but *at another company or organization.* If you don't know where to find them, talk to people at a nearby university or college who *train* such people, whatever their department may be. Teachers and professors will usually know what their graduates are making.

How to you research salaries at particular places? Let's look at some concrete examples:

*First Example:* Working at your first entry-level job, say at a fast-food place. You may not need to do any salary research. They pay what they pay. You can walk in, ask for a job application, and interview with the manager. He or she will usually tell you the pay, outright. It's usually set in concrete. But at least it's easy to discover what the pay is. *(Incidentally, filling out an application, or having an interview there, doesn't force you to take the job—but you probably already know that. You can always decline an offer from any place. That's what makes this approach harmless.)*

*Second Example:* Working at a place where you can't discover what the pay is, say, at a construction company. If that construction company where you would *hope* to get a job is difficult to research, go visit a *different* construction company in the same town—one that isn't of much interest to you—and ask what they make *there*. Or, if you don't know who to talk to there, fill out one of *their* applications, and talk to the hiring person about what kinds of jobs they have (or might have in the future), at which time prospective wages you would be paid, is a legitimate subject of discussion. Then, having done this research on a place you don't care about, go back to the place that *really* interests you, and apply. You still don't know *exactly* what they pay, but you do know what their competitor pays—which will usually be *close* to what you're trying to find out.

*Third Example:* Working in a one-person office, say *as an adminis-trative assistant.* Here you can often find useful salary information by perusing the Help Wanted ads in the local newspaper for a week or two, assuming you still have a local paper! Most of the ads won't mention a salary figure, but a few may. Among those that do, note what the lowest salary offering is, and what the highest is, and see if the ad reveals any reasons for the difference. It's interesting how much you can learn about administrative assistants' salaries, with this approach. I know, because I was an administrative assistant myself, once upon a time.

There's a lot you can find out by talking to people. But another way to do salary research—if you're out of work and have time on your hands— is to find a *Temporary Work Agency* that places different kinds of workers, and let yourself be farmed out to various organizations: the more, the merrier. It's relatively easy to do salary research when you're *inside* a place. *(Study what that place pays the agency, not what the agency pays you after they've taken their "cut.")* If you're working temporarily at a place where the other workers *like* you, you'll be able to ask questions about a lot of things, including salary.

## THE FIFTH SECRET OF SALARY NEGOTIATION

### RESEARCH THE RANGE THAT THE EMPLOYER LIKELY HAS IN MIND, AND THEN DEFINE AN INTERRELATED RANGE FOR YOUR-SELF, RELATIVE TO THE EMPLOYER'S RANGE

Before you go into any organization for your final interview, you want more than just *one* salary figure at your fingertips. You want *a range:* what's the *least* the employer may offer you, and what's the *most* the employer may be willing to offer you. In any organization that has more than five employees, that range is comparatively easy to figure out. It will be less than what the person who would be above you makes, **and** more than what the person who would be below you makes. Examples:

| If the Person Who Would Be Below You Makes | And the Person Who Would Be Above You Makes | The Range for Your Job Would Be |
| --- | --- | --- |
| $45,000 | $55,000 | $47,000–$53,000 |
| $30,000 | $35,500 | $32,500–$34,000 |

One teensy-tiny little problem here: *how* do you find out the salary of those who would be above and below you? Well, first you have to find out their **names** or the names of their **positions**. If it is a small, small organization you are going after—one with twenty or fewer employees—finding out this information should be *duck soup*. Any employee who works there is likely to know the answer, and you can usually get in touch with one of those employees, or even an ex-employee, through your own personal "bridge-people"—people who know you and also know them. Since up to two-thirds of all new jobs are created by small companies of that size, that's the size organization you are likely to be researching, anyway.

If you are going after a larger organization, then you fall back on that familiar life preserver, namely **every person you know** (family, friend, relative, business, or spiritual acquaintance) and ask them who they know that might know the company in question, and therefore, the information you seek. LinkedIn should prove immensely helpful to you here, in locating such people. If you're not already on it, get on it. (LinkedIn.com.)

If, in the end, you absolutely run into a blank wall at a particular organization (everyone who works there is pledged to secrecy, and they have shipped all their ex-employees to Siberia), then seek out information on their nearest *competitor* in the same geographic area. *For example,* let us say you were trying to find out managerial salaries at Bank X, and that place was proving to be inscrutable about what they pay their managers. You would then turn to Bank Y as your research base, to see if the information were easier to come by, there. And if it were, you can then assume the two are basically similar in their pay scales, and that what you learned about Bank Y is probably applicable to Bank X.

Experts say that in researching salaries, you should also take note of the fact that most governmental agencies have civil service positions paralleling those in private industry—and government job descriptions and pay ranges are available to the public. Go to the nearest city, county, regional, state, or federal civil service office, find the job description nearest what you are seeking in private industry, and then ask the starting salary.

Once you've made a guess at what the employer's range might be, for the job you have in mind, you then define your own range *accordingly*. Let me give an example. Suppose you guess that the employer's range is $36,500 to $47,200. Accordingly, you now *invent* an "asking" range for yourself, where your *minimum* "hooks in" just below that employer's *maximum*.

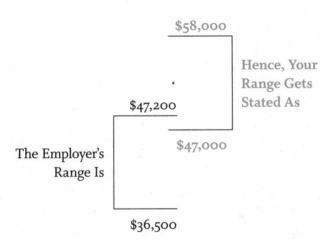

And so, when the employer has stated a figure (probably around his or her *lowest*—i.e., $36,500), you will be ready to respond with something along these lines: "I understand, of course, the constraints under which all organizations are operating these days, but I am confident that my productivity is going to be such, that it will *justify* a salary"—*and here you mention a* range *whose bottom figure hooks in just below the top of their range, and goes up from there, as shown on the diagram above*—"in the **range** of $47,000 to $58,000."

It will help a lot during this discussion, if you are prepared to show in what ways you will *make money* or in what ways you will *save money* for that organization, such as would justify the higher salary you are seeking. Hopefully, this will get you at least near the salary you want.

What if this just doesn't work? The employer has a ceiling they *have to* work with, it's above what you're asking, and you are unwilling to lower your definition of what you're worth? Daniel Porot, the job-expert in Europe, suggests that if you're *dying* to work there, but they cannot afford the salary you need and deserve, consider offering them part of your time. If you need, and believe you deserve, say $50,000 annually, but they can only afford $30,000, you might consider offering them three days a week of your time for that $30,000 (30/50 = 3/5). This leaves you free to take work elsewhere during those other two days. You will *of course* determine to produce so much work during those three days per week you are there, that they will be ecstatic about this bargain—won't you?

## THE SIXTH SECRET OF SALARY NEGOTIATION

### KNOW HOW TO BRING THE SALARY NEGOTIATION TO A CLOSE; DON'T LEAVE IT "JUST HANGING"

Salary negotiation with this employer is not finished until you've addressed both salary and so-called fringe benefits. "Fringes" such as life insurance, health benefits or health plans, vacation or holiday plans, and retirement programs typically add anywhere from 15 to 28 percent to many workers' salaries. That is to say, if an employee receives $3,000 salary per week, the fringe benefits are worth another $450 to $840 per week.

Before you walk into the interview, you should decide what benefits are particularly important to you, so after the basic salary discussion, when you ask them what benefits are on offer, you can negotiate for the benefits you particularly care about. Thinking this out ahead of time makes that negotiating easier, by far.

Finally, under the subject of closing the interview, you want to get *everything they're offering* summarized, in writing. Always request a letter of agreement—or employment contract.

Many executives unfortunately "forget" what they told you during the hiring-interview, or even deny they ever said such a thing.

Also, many executives leave a company abruptly and unexpectedly, and their successor or the top boss may disown any *unwritten* promises:

*"I don't know what caused them to say that to you, but they clearly exceeded their authority, and of course we can't be held to that."*

## CONCLUSION: THE GREATEST SECRET

We are hoping, of course, that your interview and salary negotiation end up well. There are times, however, when all seems to be going well, and then without any warning it suddenly comes totally unraveled. You're hired, told to report next Monday, and then get a phone call on Friday telling you that all hiring has been put, mysteriously, "on hold." You're therefore back out "on the street." Having seen this happen so many times, over the years, I remind you of the truth we began with, in chapter 1: *successful* job-hunters and career-changers *always have alternatives.*

Alternative ideas of what they could do with their life.

Alternative ways of describing what they want to do right now.

Alternative ways of going about the job-hunt (not just the Internet, not just resumes, agencies, and ads).

Alternative job prospects.

Alternative "target" organizations that they go after.

Alternative ways of approaching employers.

And, of course, alternative job offers. Make sure you are continuing to pursue more than just one employer, until after that new job starts.

Remember, job-hunting always involves luck, to some degree. But with a little bit of luck, and a lot of hard work, and determination, these instructions about how to get hired and negotiate a salary, should work for you, as they have worked for so many hundreds of thousands before you.

Take heart from those who have gone before you, such as this determined job-hunter, who wrote me this heartfelt letter, with which I close this chapter:

*Before I read this book, I was depressed and lost in the futile job-hunt using Want Ads only. I did not receive even one phone call from any ad I answered, over a total of four months. I felt that I was the most useless person on earth. I am female, with a two-and-a-half-year-old daughter, a former professor in China, with no working experience at all in the U.S. We came here seven months ago because my husband had a job offer here.*

*Then, on June 11th of last year, I saw your book in a local book-store. Subsequently, I spent three weeks, ten hours a day except Sunday, reading every single word of your book and doing all of the flower petals in the Flower Exercise. After getting to know myself much better, I felt I was ready to try the job-hunt again. I used* Parachute *throughout as my guide, from the very beginning to the very end, namely, salary negotiation.*

*In just two weeks I secured (you guessed it) two job offers, one of which I am taking, as it is an excellent job, with very good pay. It is (you guessed it again) a small company, with twenty or so employees. It is also a career-change: I was a professor of English; now I am to be a controller!*

*I am so glad I believed your advice: there are jobs out there, and there are two types of employers out there, and truly there are!*

*I hope you will be happy to hear my story.*

# THE FIVE PARTS OF JOB-HUNTING AS A SURVIVAL SKILL:

# III.

# ADVANCED JOB-*CREATION* TECHNIQUES

*You've got to be careful
if you don't know where you're going,
because you might not get there.*

*YOGI BERRA (b. 1925)*

# Chapter 10. Starting Your Own Business

If you're unemployed, and just can't find any job-openings, no matter how hard you try, you're going to need to consider the possibility of creating a job. That is the third of the job-hunting skills required to survive in these times. And in this day and age that requires *advanced* job-creating skills. "Advanced" means learning two different ways to do job-creating.

Let us illuminate those two ways with a tale of two shoes. The first shoe is Cinderella's. In Charles Perrault's 1697 version of the classic fairy tale, you recall, the Prince went through the kingdom, house by house, trying to find who fit a shoe—a glass slipper, in fact—that he already had.

The other shoe belongs to Edward Green, a famous shoemaker, who in 1890 started handcrafting men's shoes, in Northampton, north of London. He had no shoe, but he fashioned a shoe from the start. He made the shoe to fit a particular client. It might turn out to be a shoe that no one had ever seen before.

You get the point: one shoe already existed; the charge was to find who fitted it. The other shoe didn't exist; the charge was to create it from scratch, after taking the measure of a particular client.

So it is with job-creation. Analogous to the Cinderella shoe, you can create a job by starting with a career that already exists, some model that research can find for you—a franchise, perhaps—and see if it fits you.

Or, analogous to the Edward Green shoe, you can create a job by taking the measure of yourself, and then trying to design a career or job that fits you. It may turn out to be a job that no one has ever seen before. At least not in your neighborhood or city.

The first method, creating a job by finding a fit, is the subject of this chapter. The second method, creating a job by inventing something new, is the subject of the next chapter, on inventiveness.

I want to do two things in this chapter. I want to tell you about the existing business opportunties there are, which you may want to look at, to see if there is a fit. But I also want to sound warning notes about each of them, so that you will go in with your eyes wide open, if you decide it might be a fit. We live in a world of spams and scams these days, and consequently the pathway to creating your own job has its perils, as well as its rewards. Anyway, here are three ideas for creating your own job:

Finding a Fit, Idea #1: Consider a business already existing that you could start a branch of. Franchises, as they are called, exist because some people want to start their own business, but don't want to go through the agony of starting from scratch. They want to *buy in* on an already established business, and they have some money in their savings with which to do that. Fortunately for them, there are a lot of such franchises. To find the range of possibilities, to decide if any one of them might be a fit for you, start with the following sites:

www.franchiseopportunities.com

www.franchisedirect.com

www.franchisegenius.com

Now, here's the rub. Franchises require you, generally speaking, to have a bundle of cash, if you wish to buy in. And you may not be able to take much money out, the first year. And they are highly risky businesses. Their failure rate is high, particularly in these difficult economic times. You have to guess what kind of services or products the public wants. And the public is tremendously fickle.

So, if you start out thinking that maybe, just maybe, a franchise might fit you—not only creating a job for you, but also for others—you owe it to yourself to investigate the whole idea, and that particular franchise, thoroughly. That's: thoroughly. *Thoroughly.*

Start that homework with these sites:

http://tinyurl.com/64gda2: Interesting checklist from *Entrepreneur Magazine* on "Are You Suited to be a Franchisee?"

http://tinyurl.com/4286yju: The best franchises in 2011 according to their owners' ratings.

http://tinyurl.com/23kuwp: The Ten Riskiest Businesses to Start, according to Fair Isaac Corporation, popularly known as FICO.

http://thefranchisehound.com/2011/01/25/the-best-and-worst-franchises-to-own: This has very current data on the best and the worst, plus news items about retirement as a vanishing dream, etc. Good stuff.

www.bbb.org/us/article/4580: An article by the Better Business Bureau on the things you should beware of when considering a franchise.

http://tinyurl.com/97zy3a: You want specifics about home business offers that are scams? The government will be glad to help you. Here they list the business offers to avoid like the plague.

http://tinyurl.com/3vv97lw: This site goes over all the things you need to know the answers to, if you're going to come up with a business plan.

www.bestfranchise.org: A site so new they haven't posted their data yet, as of this writing, but it promises to be helpful once that data is up.

http://tinyurl.com/3bzbrxw: This site cleverly lists franchises whose owners have defaulted most frequently on their SBA (Small Business Administration) loans, as well as those franchises whose owners have defaulted the least frequently.

http://tinyurl.com/44yxdvh: Nolo Press has a good article here about *fit*, called "Starting the Right Business for You."

After doing this homework please note that there isn't a franchising book, or site, that doesn't warn you eighteen times to go talk to people who have *already* bought that same franchise, before you ever decide to go with them. And I mean *several* people, not just one. Most experts also warn you to go talk to *other* franchises in the same field, not just the kind you're thinking about signing up with. Maybe there's something better, which your research can uncover.

You want to keep in mind that some *types* of franchises have a failure rate *far* greater than others.

And you want to keep in mind also that some individual franchises are *terrible*—and that includes well-known names. They charge too much for you to *get on board*, and often they don't do the advertising or other commitments that they promised they would.

If you are in a hurry, and you don't want to do this homework first, *'cause it's just too much trouble*, you will deserve what you get, believe me. You will rue the day.

Finding a Fit, Idea #2: Starting a Home Business. A home seems like an excellent place to create your own job. Low rent (ha!). Short commute! Low overhead. That's the vision. Sounds like it might be a fit, for you.

So let's start out with a dose of reality. It *can* be a great idea (I have a home business myself). But be aware that there are three major problems with home businesses:

1. The first major problem of home businesses is that this is a rich playground for scams, that can cost you lots of money but never give any back. A lot of people like the idea of a home business, so vultures have taken advantage of that. You will run into ads on TV and on the Web and in your e-mail, offering you a home business "buy-in." They sound enticing. But, as AARP's Bulletin of March 23, 2009, pointed out: of the more than 3 million Web entries that surface from a Google search on the terms "work at home," more than 95 percent of the results are scams, links to scams, or other dead ends. Even the sites that claim to be scam-free often feature ads that link to scams. The statistic is: a 48 to 1 scam ratio among ads offering you a nice home business. That's 48 scams for every one true ad. *The swamp is filled with alligators!*

2. The second major problem of home businesses is that even if you start a legitimate one, be it writer, artist, business expert, lawyer, accountant (doing people's taxes), consultant, childcare, or the like, out of your home, it's often difficult to maintain a balance between business and family time. Sometimes the *family* time gets

shortchanged, while in other cases the demands of family (particularly with small children) may become so interruptive, that the *business* gets shortchanged. So, do think out thoroughly, ahead of time, *how* you would go about doing this *well*.

3. The third major problem of home businesses is that it puts you into a perpetual job-hunt. Yes, I know. You liked the idea of a home business because you *hate* job-hunting. You were attracted to the idea of a home business because this seems like an ideal way to cut short your job-hunt, by creating your own job.

   The irony is, that a home business makes you in a very real sense a *perpetual* job-hunter—because you have to be *always* seeking new clients or customers—which is to say, new *employers*. Yes, they are *employers* because they *pay* you for the work you are doing. The only difference between this and a full-time job is that here *the contract is limited*. But if you are running your own business, you will have to *continually* beat the bushes for new clients or customers. Some of us have absolutely no appetite for that aspect of home businesses. *Forewarned is forearmed.*

Of course, the dream of most budding home business people is that you will become so well known, and so in demand, that clients or customers will be literally beating down your doors, and you will be able to stop this endless job-hunt. But that only happens to a relative minority, sorry to report. The greater likelihood is that you will *always* have to beat the bushes for employers/clients. It may get easier as you get better at it, or it may get harder, if the economy goes further south. But you must learn to make your peace with it—however grudgingly. Otherwise, you're probably going to find *a home business* is just a glamorous synonym for "*starving*." I know *many* home business people to whom this has happened, and it happened precisely because they couldn't stomach going out to beat the bushes for clients or customers. If that's true for you, but you're still determined to start a home business, then for heaven's sake start out by *hiring* someone part-time, who is willing to do this for you—one who, in fact, "eats it up."

Anyway, there are a bunch of resources on the Web, to help you make a home business succeed, such as:

www.ahbbo.com; www.ahbbo.com/articles.html: This is a great site, with lots of information for you if you want to learn more about a home-based business. There are more than a hundred articles at the second URL.

Finding a Fit, Idea #3: Starting Your Own Business, Outside the Home. It may be that, in thinking about creating your own job, you know exactly *what* business you'd like to start, because you've been thinking about it for *years*, and may even have been *doing* it for years— but in the employ of someone else.

But now, you're thinking about doing this kind of work for yourself, whether it be business services, consultancy, or repair work, or some kind of craft, or some kind of product, or service. Maybe your dream is: *I want to run a bed-and-breakfast place.* Or *I want a horse ranch, where I can raise and sell horses.* Or *I want to grow lavender and sell soap and perfume made from it.* Stuff like that.

The first thing you should do is to read up on all the virtues and perils of running your own business. The Internet has lots of stuff about this. For example:

### Business Owner's Toolkit

www.toolkit.com/small_business_guide/index.aspx

Yikes, there is a lot of information here for the small business owner. Everything about your business: starting, planning, financing, marketing, hiring, managing, getting government contracts, taxes—all that stuff.

### Small Business Administration

www.sba.gov

The SBA has endured some bad press in the face of the multiple natural catastrophes that have been striking the U.S. in the past five years, from hurricanes to tornadoes to floods. But keep in mind that it was established to help start, manage, and grow small businesses. Lots of useful articles and advice are online, here. Also, check out its *Starting a Business* resources at http://tinyurl.com/24h59yy.

### The Business Owner's Idea Café

www.businessownersideacafe.com

Great, fun site for the small business owner.

### Small Business Marketing

http://online.wsj.com/public/page/news-small-business-marketing.html

(If you want a shorter version of this url, try http://tinyurl.com/6nvox9.) The *Wall Street Journal* brings its considerable resources to bear on this site for the entrepreneur. Many articles, how-tos, advice, and resources for the business owner, with some focus on women business owners.

### Free Agent Nation

www.fastcompany.com/online/12/freeagent.html

Daniel Pink, before he became famous for such books as *Drive* and *A Whole New Mind*, was the first to call attention to how many people were refusing to work for any employer. This is his classic work, written in 1997, on the site of the popular magazine *Fast Company*. It's still regarded as timeless, though of course its statistics *are* outdated. His basic thesis: self-employment has become a broader concept than it was in another age. The concept now includes not only those who own their own business but also free agents: independent contractors who work for several clients; temps and contract employees who work each day through temporary agencies; limited-timeframe workers who work only for a set time, as on a project, then move on to another company; consultants; and so on. This is a fascinating article to help you decide if you want to be a "free agent."

### Working Solo

www.workingsolo.com/faqstarting.html
www.workingsolo.com/resources/resources.html

Working Solo is a good site for the small business worker. The first url, above, is a series of questions to help you determine if you have it in you to be an entrepreneur. The second url gives you a whole bunch of resources if you decide *Yes*.

### Nolo's Business, LLCs & Corporations

www.nolo.com/legal-encyclopedia/business-llcs-corporations

Lots of helpful legal stuff here, about how to form an LLC, and other stuff you'll really need to know.

### Entrepreneur

www.entrepreneurmag.com

*Entrepreneur* magazine's website. It has lists of home-based businesses, start-up ideas, how to raise money, shoestring start-ups, small business myths, a franchise and business opportunity site-seeing guide, how to research a business opportunity—and more.

### World Wide Web Tax

www.wwwebtax.com/miscellaneous/self_employment_tax.htm

Wow. If you're going to be self-employed, you *really really* want this site. One of the banes of being self-employed is dealing with taxes; this site has more than 1,300 pages to help you handle all of that: articles, resources, links, downloadable tax forms (going back ten years!), in PDF format, of course. The site is selling something (e-filing tax returns), but it has a lot of free information about what self-employed people have to do vis-à-vis taxes, in the United States at least.

## WHEN YOU'RE OPERATING
## ON A SHOESTRING

**Finding clients or customers**: With the Internet came globalization. And this changed everything for the self-employed. You now have a much larger market at your disposal where you can sell your skills, knowledge, services, and products, worldwide.

**Finding employees or vendors**: In this global age if you're operating on a shoestring, and you need, let us say, to have something printed or produced as inexpensively as possible, you can search for an inexpensive printer, vendor, or manufacturer anywhere in the world, and solicit bids. All you have to do is type in the name of the skill-set you need, plus the word "overseas," and the word "jobs"—and see what you can find. For example, if you try "overseas cartoonist jobs" this will turn up a list of sites to try.

There are lots of books and magazines that are filled with ideas for home businesses. The best books on home businesses are written by Paul Edwards and Sarah Edwards. Their most recent one (2010) is called *Home-Based Business for Dummies*. Earlier works include (2008) *Middle-Class Lifeboat: Careers and Life Choices for Navigating a Changing Economy*; (2004) *Best Home Businesses for People 50+*; and (2001) *The Best Home Businesses for the Twenty-First Century*. For other titles, browse the business shelves in your local independent bookstore or Barnes & Noble, or go online at Amazon.com.

## DOING YOUR HOMEWORK, DOING YOUR HOMEWORK

With this research behind you, if you still want to go ahead with the idea of your own business, then the next step would be this: once you've decided what kind of business you want to start, you *must* go talk to other people who have already done what you are thinking of doing. You *must* pick their brains for everything they're worth. You *must* avoid stepping on the same *land mines* that they did.

One job-hunter told me she started a home-based soap business, without ever talking to anyone who had started a similar endeavor, before her. Not surprisingly, her business went belly-up within a year and a half. She falsely then concluded: no one should go into such a business. Ah, but Paula Gibbons created "Paula's Soaps" very successfully twenty-two years ago in Seattle, Washington.[1] *Someone is already doing the work you are dreaming of. The key to your success, is go talk to them.*

Starting up your own business outside the home without first listening to the experience of those who have gone before you, and profiting from their mistakes, is just nuts. Yet millions of people do just that, every

---

1. http://paulassoap.com

year. And then they wonder why it didn't work out. As one woman said to me, "Yes, I knew I was being foolish, but I thought I'd get lucky." P.S. She didn't.

But you are wiser. And you intend to do the research I am recommending, I know. All you want is just some guidance as to how to go about picking other people's brains. Okay, here it is: the key lies in a simple formula:

$$A - B = C$$

You have a great idea for starting your own business. But you want to interview others who have started the same kind of business, so you don't make the same mistakes they did. Your interviewing, then, should have three steps to it:

1. Finding out what skills, knowledge, or experience it takes to make this kind of business idea work, from several business owners. *This is "A."*

2. Then making a list of the skills, knowledge, or experience that you have. *This is "B."*

3. Then subtracting "B" from "A," we arrive at a list of skills, etc., required for success in such a business, that you *don't* have. And you must go out and hire someone with those missing skills. *This is "C."*

Let me explain this in a little more detail:

1. You first write out *in as much detail as you can* just exactly what kind of business you are thinking about starting. Do you want to be a freelance writer, or a craftsperson, or a consultant, independent screenwriter, copywriter, digital artist, songwriter, photographer, illustrator, interior designer, video person, videographer, film person, filmmaker, counselor, therapist, plumber, electrician, agent, soap maker, bicycle repairer, public speaker, or *what?*

2. You then identify towns or cities that are at least fifty to seventy-five miles away (so they won't feel you are in competition with them directly down the block, as it were) and by using the Yellow Pages or the chamber of commerce, or some smartphone apps, try

to identify at least three businesses in those towns, that are identical or at least similar to the business you are thinking of starting. You drive to that town or city, and talk to the founder or owner of each such business.

3. When you talk to them, you explain that you're exploring the possibility of starting your own business, similar to theirs, but seventy-five miles away. You ask them if they would mind sharing something of their own history, so you can better understand what pitfalls or obstacles one runs into, when starting this kind of business. You ask them what skills, knowledge, or experience they think are necessary to making this kind of business successful.

   Will they give you such information? Yes, most of the time. People love to help others get started in their same business, *if* they love the way their business turned out—although, let's face it, occasionally you may run into owners who are of an ungenerous nature. But if that happens, thank them politely for their time, and go on to the next name on your list. When you've found three people willing to help you by relating their own history, you should now know enough to make a list of the necessary skills, knowledge, and experience they all agree are essential. If not, go visit another city and find some more fellow business owners. When you have a list you're satisfied with, give this list a name. Call it "A" of course.

4. Back home you sit down and inventory your own skills, knowledge, and experience, by doing the self-inventory described in chapter 13, the Flower Exercise. Give this list a name, also. Call it "B."

5. Having done this, subtract "B" from "A." This gives you another new list, which you should name "C." "C" is by definition a list of the skills or knowledge that you *don't* have, but *must* find—either by taking courses yourself, or by hiring someone with those skills, or by getting a friend or family member (who has those skills) to volunteer to help you for a while.

6. For example, if your investigation revealed that it takes good accounting practices in order to turn a profit, and you don't know a thing about accounting, you now know enough to go out and hire a part-time accountant *immediately*—or, if you absolutely have no money, maybe you can talk an accountant friend of yours into giv-

ing you some volunteer time, for a while.

I can illustrate this whole process with a case history. Our job-hunter is a woman who has been making harps for some employer, but now is thinking about going into business for herself, not only *making* harps at home, but also *designing* harps, with the aid of a computer. After interviewing several home-based harp makers and harp designers, and finishing her own self-assessment, her chart of A − B = C came out looking like the next page.

If she decides she does indeed want to try her hand at becoming an independent harp maker and harp designer, she now knows what she needs *but lacks*: computer programming, knowledge of the principles of electronics, and accounting. In other words, List C. These she must either go to school to acquire for herself, OR enlist from some friends of hers in those fields, on a volunteer basis, OR go out and hire, part-time.

It is *always* possible—with a little blood, sweat, and imagination—to find out what A − B = C is, for any business you're dreaming of doing.

But let's say you've come up with a business idea that you're just sure no one else has ever thought of. Who do you go interview, then? *Parallel businesses.* Let's take a ridiculous example. You want to start a business of using computers to monitor the growth of plants at the Antarctic (!?). A parallel business, in this case, would be:

> someone who's *used computers with plants here in the States,*
>
> *or* someone who's *used computers in the Antarctic,*
>
> *or* someone who has *worked with plants in the Antarctic,* etc.

You would get names of these people, go talk to them, and along the way you might even discover that there *is* actually someone who has used computers to monitor the growth of plants at the South Pole. Then again, you might not.

But what you *would* get, for certain, is an awareness of most of the pitfalls that wait for you, by learning from the experience of those who are in these *parallel* businesses or careers.

| Skills and Knowledge Needed to Run This Kind of Business Successfully | Skills and Knowledge That I Have | Skills and Knowledge Needed, Which I Don't Have, So I'm Going to Go Out and Hire Someone Who Has Them |
|---|---|---|
| Precision-working with tools and instruments | Precision-working with tools and instruments | |
| Planning and directing an entire project | Planning and directing an entire project | |
| Programming computers, inventing programs that solve physical problems | | Programming computers, inventing programs that solve physical problems |
| Problem solving: evaluating why a particular design or process isn't working | Problem solving: evaluating why a particular design or process isn't working | |
| Being self-motivated, resourceful, patient, persevering, accurate, methodical, and thorough | Being self-motivated, resourceful, patient, persevering, accurate, methodical, and thorough | |
| *Thorough knowledge of:* Principles of electronics | | *Thorough knowledge of:* Principles of electronics |
| Physics of strings | Physics of strings | |
| Principles of vibration | Principles of vibration | |
| Properties of woods | Properties of woods | |
| Accounting | | Accounting |

"YES, THE BUSINESS HAS BECOME BIGGER, BUT FRED STILL LIKES TO WORK AT HOME."

## CONCLUSION: "CAN I CREATE MY OWN JOB BY CREATING MY OWN BUSINESS?"

It takes a lot of guts to try ANYTHING new (*to you*) in today's brutal economy. It's easier, however, if you keep these things in mind:

1. There is always some risk, in trying something new. Your goal, I hope, is not to avoid risk—there is no way to do that—but to make sure ahead of time that the risks are *manageable*.

2. You find this out before you start, by first talking to others who have already done what you are thinking of doing; then you evaluate whether or not you still want to go ahead and try it.

*Chapter 10*

3. Have a Plan B, laid out, *before you start,* as to what you will do if it doesn't work out; i.e., know where you are going to go, next. Don't wait, *puh-leaze!* Write it out, now. *This is what I'm going to do, if this doesn't work out.*

4. If you're sharing your life with someone, be sure to sit down with that partner or spouse and ask what the implications are *for them* if you try this new thing. Will they have to give up things? If so, what? Are they willing to make those sacrifices? And so on. You have a responsibility to make them full partners in any decision you're facing. Love demands it!

It is up to you to do your research thoroughly, weigh the risks, decide if they're *manageable* risks, count the costs, get counsel from those intimately involved with you, and then if you decide you still want to create your own job by starting this kind of business, go ahead and try—no matter what your well-meaning but cautious friends or family may say. They love you, they're concerned for you, and you should thank them for that; but come on, you only have one life here on this Earth, and that life is *yours* (under God) to say how it will be spent, or not spent. Parents, well-meaning friends, etc., can give loving advice, but in the end they get no vote. Just you . . . and God.

*I do not think there is any thrill that can go through the human heart like that felt by the inventor as he sees some creation of the brain unfolding to success . . . such emotions make a man forget food, sleep, friends, love, everything.*

NIKOLA TESLA (1856–1943)

# Chapter 11. Being Inventive Is Key to Survival

It's lovely to be able to find a job. Even lovelier to create a job that somebody else has thought of, and then make a success of it—as in the previous chapter. But what if we have to absolutely start from scratch?

What if we were a stranger riding into town in the Old West of 1870? No employment agencies are there. No government assistance is there. We're on our own. Gonna have to mosey around town, and see what kind of work we can put together for ourselves.

Or, never mind 1870. What if we were riding into a town or city like Joplin, Missouri, this year, just after it was torn apart by the worst tornado to hit the U.S. since 1947, and we need work. Where would we begin?

Well, we would begin by *inventing*. I know the popular phrases are *being creative*, or *innovating*. But I like *inventing*. It's more meaningful to say we are inventors, than it does to say we are *creative*, or *innovative*. Those words have been overworked to death. Let's go back to good old-fashioned *inventive*.

I think everybody is by nature *inventive*. Maybe in small ways. Maybe in big. But we all have it in us. After high school I worked on a grass-cutting crew for the Board of Education. We were dropped off at a school in the morning with our lawnmowers and surrey, and then picked up again, later in the day. I figured out a way to do the job more elegantly, and everyone noticed. I was just being *inventive*.

In the film and TV series, *Mildred Pierce*, the heroine needs to support herself, so she looks around town to see what is needed, and she becomes inventive. One answer that occurs to her is: apple pies. People hunger for apple pies. And Mildred, it turns out, makes very good apple pies, not to mention other kinds of pies. Thus she creates her own job in that place. She was just being inventive.

Jack K. Wolf was a real-life theorist (he died May 12, 2011). He figured out a way to store more data in less space, say on a magnetic disk. This formed the heart of computers and other devices we all know. He was just being inventive.

A cook is working in her kitchen, off a standard recipe. Suddenly she gets an idea for putting some different ingredients into the mix—and her new recipe is saluted by everyone. But she was just being inventive.

Yes, we all have it in us, to one degree or another. And we need it, if we look for jobs and just can't find one. And then try to create a job from the menu of typical options in our society, but come up empty. What is left? We have to become inventive.

## THE INGREDIENTS OF INVENTIVENESS

Inventiveness depends upon two habits of mind, which we can adopt and develop: attention and curiosity.

Attention means *paying attention*. Go downtown, to a familiar street. Walk down that street and see what is there that you never noticed before. Make a list. Notice how often we are blind to things that are right in front of us. *Could I possibly have walked by "that" all this time, and never noticed it?* Yes, you could and you did. We all do. Especially in this age in which we live, we've been encouraged to develop *continuous partial attention*, as Linda Stone (formerly of Microsoft) puts it.

Curiosity means just that. Endlessly curious. Endlessly asking questions. Endlessly wanting to know *how*, and *why*? Anyone who watched Katherine Bigelow's masterpiece, *The Hurt Locker*, saw this kind of relentless curiosity in the restless mind of the hero. *Why does this wire lead here, and not there? What is the reason people are staring so intently from their windows at this point?*

Walk into any town or city. You can't find a job, and you can't create a job from the options offered you. So, now, you're going to have to figure out how to create a job for yourself, from scratch. What are the tools at your command? Powerful ones: Attention. And curiosity.

What does this place need, and is willing to pay money for? What is there that is not being done? Or what is there that is being done, but you could invent a way to do it better? Or quicker? Or more thoroughly? It may be as simple as *they need apple pies.*

It may also turn out that the need is not just in that place. It's more universal, and you have the wit and the wherewithal to put something up on the Web, that could attract ads and make you money.

## CONCLUSION

There is no limit to ways that you could put together work that meets somebody's need, for which they will pay you money. In other words, *a job.* All you have to do is stop thinking of inventors as someone *over there.* And realize that you are an inventor, too. We all are. So, use and encourage that strain in yourself. Notice the ways in which you are inventive already, in your daily life. Read the daily obituaries in the *New York Times,* and notice what inventive thing each person did while yet they lived.

As our economy worldwide grows harsher, as jobs are harder to find, we all need to become job creators. We need at least to know how, even if it is a survival skill that we never have to use. We can at least teach it to others.

As you go about your daily business, buying stuff, or getting repairs, or whatever, just think to yourself: *every job is somebody's invention.* Somebody invented this job, and made it work. You have the same ability.

*Two roads diverged in a yellow wood,*
*And sorry I could not travel both*
*And be one traveler, long I stood*
*And looked down one as far as I could*
*To where it bent in the undergrowth;*

*Then took the other, as just as fair,*
*And having perhaps the better claim,*
*Because it was grassy and wanted wear;*
*Though as for that the passing there*
*Had worn them really about the same,*

*And both that morning equally lay*
*In leaves no step had trodden black.*
*Oh, I kept the first for another day!*
*Yet knowing how way leads on to way,*
*I doubted if I should ever come back.*

*I shall be telling this with a sigh*
*Somewhere ages and ages hence:*
*Two roads diverged in a wood, and I—*
*I took the one less traveled by,*
*And that has made all the difference.*

ROBERT FROST (1874–1963)[1]

---

1. The title of this poem is "The Road Not Taken," from *The Poetry of Robert Frost,* edited by Edward Connery Lathem, published by Holt, Rinehart & Winston, 1916, 1969. Incidentally, the late M. Scott Peck's classic, *The Road Less Traveled,* took its title from this poem.

# Chapter 12. How to Choose a New Career

## THE THREE WAYS OF CREATING YOUR OWN JOB

Once you've decided you need the advanced survival skill of being able to *create* a job, rather than just *find* one, you have three choices.

One is, you can invent a job. We just covered that in chapter 11.

The second is you can work with the things *you already know*, and start your own business. We covered that in chapter 10.

And the third is to start with things *you don't know*. Instead of contemplating a lake, you can contemplate an ocean. You can survey the whole field of careers, and consider ones you may never have ever even thought of, up to now. That is the subject of this chapter.

So, how do we begin, in looking at careers we never thought of? Left to our own instincts, most of us will opt for taking a test of one kind or another.

Easy enough to do.

In the U.S. 82 percent of all job-hunters or career-changers have access to the Internet. And tests are everywhere on the Internet.

Except, "tests" are not really "tests." "Instruments" or "assessments" would be a more accurate description. Nonetheless, everyone loves to call them "tests." "Vocational tests." "Psychological tests." Whatever. You can take them all by yourself. That's their virtue.

Or, if you don't want to tackle them all by yourself, you can pay a career coach or career counselor to give them to you (*see the back of this book, beginning on page 313*). Some make *testing* the cornerstone of everything they do with a client. So, they're experienced. One way or another, take a test, and voilà! The test will tell you what you should do, or what you should become.

*Or will it?*

## Six Warnings About Testing

1. You are absolutely unique. There is no person in the world like you. It follows from this that no test can measure YOU; it can only describe the family to which you belong.

*Tests tend to divide the population into what we might call groups, tribes, or families—made up of all those people who answered the test the same way. After you've taken any test, don't ever say to yourself, "This must be who I am." (No, no, this must be who your family am.[2])*

*I grew up in the Bolles family (surprise!), and they were all very "left-brained." I was a maverick in that family. I was right-brained. Fortunately, my father was an immensely loving man, who found this endearing. When I told him the convoluted way by which I went about figuring out something, he would respond with a hearty affectionate laugh, and a big hug, as he said: "Dick, I will never understand you." Tests are about families, not individuals. The results of any test are descriptors—not of you, but of your family—i.e., all those who answered the test the same way you did. The SAI family. Or the blue family. Or the INTJ family. Or whatever. The results are an accurate description of that family of people, in general; but are they descriptors also of you? Depends on whether or not you are a maverick in that family, the same way I was in mine. These family characteristics may or may not be true in every respect of you. You may be exactly like that group, or you may be different in important ways.*

2. Don't try to figure out ahead of time how you want the test to come out. Stay loose and open to new ideas.

*It's easy to develop an emotional investment that the test should come out a certain way. I remember a job-hunting workshop where I asked everyone to list the factors they liked about any place where they had ever lived, and*

---

2. Yes, I know that is bad grammar. But press on: if you want to explore testing in any more depth, there is an excellent course online, from S. Mark Pancer, at Wilfred Laurier University in Waterloo, Ontario, Canada, at www.wlu.ca/page.php?grp_id=265&p=2941. Pay special attention to Lectures 1 and 19.

*then prioritize those factors, to get the name of a new place to live. We had this immensely lovable woman from Texas in the workshop, and when we all got back together after a "break" I asked her how she was doing. With a glint in her eye she said, "I'm prioritizing, and I'm gonna keep on prioritizin', until it comes out: Texas!" That was amusing, as she intended it to be; it's not so amusing when you try to make the test results come out a certain way. If you're gonna take tests, you need to be open to new ideas. If you find yourself always trying to outguess the test, so it will confirm you on a path you've already decided upon, then testing is not for you.*

3. In taking a test, you should just be looking for clues, hunches, or suggestions, rather than for a definitive answer that says "this is what you must choose to do with your life."

*And bear in mind that an online test isn't likely to be as insightful as one administered by an experienced psychologist or counselor, who may see things that you can't. But keep saying this mantra to yourself, as you read or hear the test results: "Clues. Clues, I'm only looking for clues."*

4. Take several tests and not just one. One can easily send you down the wrong path.

*People who do a masters or doctorate program in "Testing and Measurement" know that tests are notoriously flawed, unscientific, and inaccurate. Sometimes tests are more like parlor games than anything else. Basing your future on tests' outcomes is like putting your trust in the man behind the curtain in* The Wizard of Oz.

5. In good career planning, you're trying, in the first instance, to broaden your horizons, and only later narrow your options down; you are *not* trying to narrow them down from the outset.

*Bad career planning looks like this:*

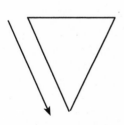
*Most computerized tests embody the idea of starting with a wide range of options, and narrowing them down. So, each time you answer a question, you narrow down the number of options. For example, if you say, "I don't like to work outdoors," immediately all outdoor jobs are eliminated from your consideration, etc., etc.*

*A model of good career planning looks like this, instead:*

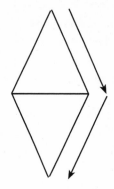

*Good career-choice or career planning postpones the "narrowing down," until it has first broadened your horizons, and expanded the number of options you are thinking about. For example, you're in the newspaper business; but have you ever thought of teaching, or drawing, or doing fashion? You first expand your mental horizons, to see all the possibilities, and only then do you start to narrow them down to the particular two or three that interest you the most.*

So, *what's a good test? All together now: a test that broadens to show you new possibilities for your life.*

And, *what's a bad test? Again, all together: a test that narrows the possibilities for your life. Often this is the result of a counselor's interpretation of a test, or rather misinterpretation.*

*I'll give you an example: I met a man who, many years before, had taken the Strong Inventory.[3] He was told, by his counselor, that this inventory measured that man's native gifts or aptitudes. And, in his particular case, the counselor said, the inventory revealed he had no mechanical aptitude whatsoever. For years thereafter, this man told me, "I was afraid to even pick up a hammer, for fear of maiming myself. But there finally came a time in my life when my house needed aluminum siding, desperately, and I was too poor to hire anyone else to do it for me. So I decided I had to do it myself, regardless of what the test said. I climbed the ladder, and expected to fail. Instead, it was a glorious experience! I had never enjoyed myself so much in my whole life. I later found out that the counselor was wrong. The inventory didn't measure aptitudes; it only measured current interests. Now, today, if I could find that counselor, I would wring his neck with my own bare hands, as I think of how much of my life he ruined with his misinterpretation of that test."*

6. Testing will always have "mixed reviews." On the one hand, you can run into successful men and women who will tell you they took this or that test twenty years ago, and it made all the difference in their career direction and ultimate success.

---

3. See www.personalitydesk.com and similar websites.

Other men and women, however, will tell you a horror story about their encounter with testing, like the one just mentioned.

*So, it's up to you. If you like tests, help yourself. There are lots of them on the Internet. Counselors can also give them to you, for a fee; if you want one, shop around.*

*If you want to know where to start, you might try these tests, which are the ones I personally like the best:*

- *Dr. John Holland's Self-Directed Search*
  www.self-directed-search.com

- *Carolyn Kalil's True Colors Test*
  www.truecolorscareer.com/quiz.asp

- *Supplemented by the University of Missouri's Career Interests Game*
  http://career.missouri.edu/students/majors-careers/skills-interests/career-interest-game

- *If you want further suggestions, you can type "career tests" or "personality tests" into Google, and/or you can go to my website,* www.jobhuntersbible.com, *for suggestions.*

If you don't like tests, what can you do? Well, there's a nice process for determining what to do with your life, later in this book. It's called the Flower Exercise (in chapter 13). It is in a test-free zone.

## SEVEN RULES FOR CHOOSING OR CHANGING CAREERS

When you have to choose or change a career, here are seven rules to keep in mind:

Rule #1 about choosing or changing a career: go for *any* career that seems interesting or even fascinating to you. But *first* talk to people who are already doing that work, to find out if the career or job is as great as it seems at first impression. Ask them: *what do you like best about this work? What do you like least about this work? And, how did you get into this work?* This last question, which sounds like mere cheeky curiosity, actually can give you important job-hunting clues about how you could get into this line of work or career.

Rule #2 about choosing or changing a career: make sure that you preserve constancy as well as change, during this transition. In other words, don't change *everything*. Remember the words of Archimedes with his long lever,[4] loosely paraphrased as: *Give me a fulcrum and a place to stand, and with a lever I will move the Earth.* You need a place to stand, when you move your life around, and that place is provided by the things that stay constant about you: your transferable skills, your values, your character, your faith.

We can illustrate this principle about maintaining *some* constancy with a simple diagram of creative career change, below. Let us say you are an accountant, in the television industry, and you want to become

THREE TYPES OF CAREER-CHANGE, VISUALIZED

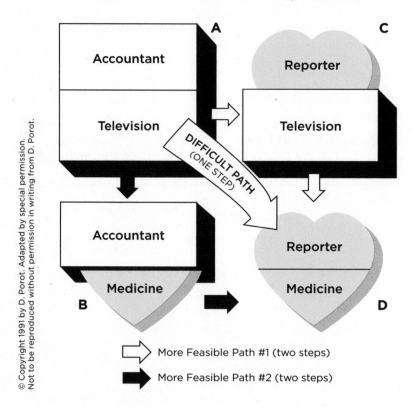

---

4. Archimedes (ca. 235 BCE), Greek inventor, mathematician, and physicist.

a reporter, covering medicine. You can, of course, try to change everything in one big leap (labeled *the difficult path* in this diagram), but that's all change and no constancy. To preserve some constancy, you can first change just your job-title and only later your field. Or you can first change just your field, and only later your job-title (*two steps*). This two-step plan for career-change preserves *some* constancy at every turn, some continuity with the past, and allows you to always claim some past experience and expertise, each time you make a move.

Rule #3 about choosing or changing a career: you do better to start with yourself and what *you* want, rather than with the job-market, and what's "hot." The difference is "enthusiasm" or "passion."

Rule #4 about choosing or changing a career: the best *work*, the best career, for you is going to be one that uses: your *favorite* transferable skills, in your *favorite* subjects, fields, or special knowledges, in a job that offers you your *preferred* people-environments, your *preferred* working conditions, with your *preferred* salary or other rewards, working toward your *preferred* goals and values. This requires thorough self-inventory. Detailed instructions are to be found in chapter 13.

Rule #5 about choosing or changing a career: the more time you give to the choosing, the better your choice is going to be. There is a penalty for seeking "quick and dirty" fixes.

Rule #6 about choosing or changing a career: if you are a young adult, you don't have to get it right, the first time; it's okay to make a mistake, in your choice. You'll have time to correct it, down the road. Most of us have three to five *careers* during our lifetime, and heaven only knows how many jobs.

Rule #7 about choosing or changing a career: this should be fun, as much fun as possible. The more fun you're having, the more you can be sure you're doing it right.

## DEVELOPING A PICTURE

This builds upon a little-known truth in career-counseling or job-hunting: *"The clearer your vision of what you seek, the closer you are to finding it. For, what you are seeking is also seeking you."* Sounds kooky, but I've seen it happen too many times, not to believe it. Okay, so how do you make your vision clearer?

Take a large piece of white paper, with some colored pencils or pens, and draw a picture of your ideal life: where you live, who's with you, what you do, what your dwelling looks like, what your ideal vacation looks like, etc. Don't let *reality* get in the way. Pretend a magic wand has been waved over your life, and it gives you everything you think your ideal life would be.

Now, *of course* you're going to tell me you can't draw. Okay, then make symbols for things, or create little "doodads" or symbols, with labels—anything so that you can *see* all together on one page your vision of your ideal life—however haltingly expressed.

The power of this exercise is sometimes amazing. Reason? By avoiding words and using pictures or symbols as much as possible, it bypasses the left side of the brain ("the safekeeping self," as George Prince calls it) and speaks directly to the right side of your brain ("the experimental self"), whose job it is to engineer change.

Oh, and apropos of Rule #7, this exercise is *fun!*

This done, let's look at the Internet for further clues. In my opinion, the single most useful website with regard to careers is Susan Joyce's www.job-hunt.org; the volume of information on her site is stunning. The second most useful would be business sites that you can uncover by typing "careers" into a search engine like Google. One that will turn up, if you do this, is CNNMoney's (http://money.cnn.com). This site is home to CNN, *Money* magazine, and *Fortune*. The site has a fascinating article, about Warren Farrell's research on salaries and careers, at http://tinyurl.com/qcys5. It's called "Where Women's Pay Trumps Men's," and it is chock-full of brilliant ideas about how to make a career choice, where money is the issue. It is based on Warren's blockbuster book (*my opinion*): *Why Men Earn More*. Warren is a brilliant, meticulous, highly ethical researcher, but his book is more *news* than it is just another research tome. If I had my way, I would give this book to every female career-chooser or career-changer on the planet.

I suppose somewhere along the way you want lists of "hot jobs" or such. Try CareerCast.com's list of "Best Jobs for 2011," at http://tinyurl.com/3atala3.

## Try on the Suit First

Well, these may be "Best Jobs" but that doesn't *necessarily* mean they're the best *for you*. Just as you would when buying a suit, test it, try it on first, then make up your own mind. *Puh-leeze.*

How? It's our old familiar tenets of Informational Interviewing (pages 105–12 and 252–68):

Talk to at least three people who are actually *doing* this career that looks appealing, and ask them these questions:

*How did you get into this field?*

*What do you like best about it?*

*What do you like least about it?*

*How do I get into this career, and how much of a demand is there for people who can do this work?*

*Is it easy to find a job in this career, or is it hard?*

*Who else would you recommend or suggest I go talk to, to learn more about this career?*

## Don't Get a Job by Degrees

One final word of caution, here: if you're just graduating from high school, don't go get a college degree in some career field just because you think that will guarantee you a job! It will not.

I wish you could see my mail, filled with bitter letters from people who believed this myth, went and got a degree in a field that looked just great, thought it would be a snap to find a job, but are still unemployed two years later. Even in good times. They are bitter (often), angry (always), and disappointed in a society that they feel lied to them. Now that they have that costly worthless degree, and still can't find a job, they find a certain irony in the phrase, *"Our country believes in getting a job by degrees."*

If you already made this costly mistake, you know what I mean. It is sad.

Choose a career, explore it to death, find out if you love it, and *then* go get your degree. Not because it guarantees a job, but because it inspires in you passion, enthusiasm, and energy.

# THE FIVE PARTS OF JOB-HUNTING AS A SURVIVAL SKILL:

# IV.

# INVENTORY OF WHAT YOU HAVE TO OFFER THE WORLD

*Frequently the real health care problem arises from failure to discover one's life mission . . .*
*Attention must be given to helping individuals discover their own life mission as an integral aspect of health care . . .*

PROFESSOR BRIAN COSTELLO (b. 1943)

# Chapter 13. Self-Inventory (The Flower Exercise)

Why are we doing this inventory? I can best answer by referring to something I said about Survival Job-Hunting, in chapter 2:

Sometimes our problem is we do not realize all the richness of what we each have to offer to the world. So, a fourth essential part of Survival Job-Hunting is: **You must do a fresh inventory** of what you have to offer the world: what transferable skills, what knowledges, and what preferences. The purpose of this research is to discover **alternative ways** of describing who you are. You can no longer restrict your definition of yourself to just your old job-title. No longer: *"I am a construction worker (or whatever)*," but *"I am a person who . . ."* Maybe, after you inventory yourself, you will decide to go train for a whole new career or direction for your life. *Maybe.* But first, you should inventory what you already have. It's broader, deeper, richer, than you think. Maybe you can put together a new career just using what you already know.

Why do you need to do a self-inventory, besides the reasons above? Well, a life well lived is a *journey*. A journey with some Emerald City beckoning in the far distance, as in *The Wonderful Wizard of Oz*.

So, it's useful to recall what travel experts teach about *taking a journey*: before you go, they say, lay out on your bed two piles. In one pile, put all the clothes (plus toiletries, and stuff) that you think you'll need to take. In the other pile, put all the money you think you'll need to take.

Then, they say, pack only half the clothes, but twice the money.

A parallel ratio occurs in the journey you are taking, called *Life*.

That is: for this journey, you will need only half the information you initially thought you would need about *the job-market*, but twice the amount of information you initially thought you would need about *yourself*.

And some Emerald City beckons, which in our culture we describe alternately as *what we want to do with our life*, or *our purpose in life*, or *our mission in life*, or *our dream job*.

"Dream job" is the phrase on our lips most often. So, let's define what we mean by that. You can describe yourself under seven headings—vis-à-vis the world of work, at least.

You can describe yourself in terms of what you can do—your favorite functional/transferable skills.

Or you can describe yourself in terms of what you know—your favorite knowledges or fields of interest.

Or you can describe yourself in terms of the kinds of people you like to be surrounded by, or the kinds of people you like to help.

Or you can describe yourself in terms of where you are most effective—the surroundings or working conditions that enable you to do your best work.

And so on.

Now suppose when all this inventorying is done, you find some kind of work out there that matches you in only one particular: let us say it lets you use your favorite knowledges. But it doesn't let you use your favorite skills, nor does it have you working with the kinds of people you most enjoy, nor does it give you the surroundings where you can do your best work. What would you call such a job? I think you would call it *boring*.

But now let us suppose you find another kind of work out there that matches you in all seven particulars. What would you call *that* kind of job? You would call it *your dream job*.

Precisely! A dream job by definition is one that *matches* you. Do an inventory of yourself, and of course you end up with a description of you—free of job-title, as yet. But equally you end up with a description of what would be a dream job for you. It's dreamy because it would be a perfect match in all seven arenas.

So we may paraphrase (massacre?) Alexander Pope, here:

*Know then thyself,*
*Do not the Market scan*
*Until you've surveyed all You are—*
*Then you will have your plan.*

Most job-hunters who fail to find their dream job, fail not because they lack sufficient information about the job-market, but because they lack sufficient information about themselves.

## WHO ARE YOU?

At this point—being human—our first instinct is to protest that we already know loads of information about ourselves. After all, we've lived with ourselves all these years. We *surely* know who we are, by now, don't we?

Maybe. Maybe not. So, let's test that premise. How well *do* you know yourself? Let's do a little exercise:

1. Take ten sheets of blank paper. Write, at the top of each one, just these three words: Who Am I?

2. Then write, on each sheet in turn, just one answer to that question. And only one.

3. When you're done, go back over all ten sheets and expand now upon what you have written on each sheet. Looking at each answer, write below it, *why* you said that, and *what turns you on* about that answer.

4. When finished with all ten sheets, go back over them and arrange them in order of priority. That is, which identity is the most important to you? That page goes on top. Then, which is next? That goes immediately underneath the top one. Continue arranging the rest of the sheets in order, until what you think is your least important identity is at the bottom of the pile.

5. Finally, go back over the ten sheets, in order, and look particularly at your answer, on each sheet, to *What Turns Me On About This?* See if there are any common denominators, or themes, among the ten answers you gave. If so, jot them down on a separate piece of paper. Voilà! You have begun to put your finger on some things that your dream job or career, vocation, mission, or whatever, needs to give you if you are to feel truly excited, fulfilled, useful, effective, and operating at the height of your powers.

Here is how one woman did this exercise:

**Who am I?**

1. A woman
2. Esoteric
3. Nature dweller
4. People person
5. Creative
6. A traveler
7. Worldly wise
8. Inquisitive/investigative
9. Troubleshooter
10. Manager/leader

**What turns you on about the above?**

1. Ever-changing, emotion, caring, warm, loving and giving. Strong stock, independent, sexy, magnetic. Mother and teacher. Survivor, activist, unique, and creative.
2. For the love of the mystical, healing of self and the spirit, human sciences and Mother Nature.
3. Where I am happiest for the peace and wondrous beauty of the world and miracles created each and every day. Seasons change, colors, and aromas. Joy of knowing the healing powers of a peaceful and idyllic universe, pure and unsolved.
4. The love of humor and socializing. Being a friend, sharing wisdoms, and helping when in need. Where we can teach and be taught as reflections of each other. To be carried and carry on our journey as we are all one.
5. The appreciation of art, music, literature. To play with your imagination, relaxing and shutting off. To create with different mediums that are fun, exciting, and produce an unknown outcome.
6. Comfortable in facing the unknown with acceptance before I arrive.
7. Knowledge of own wisdom through tragedy, love, travel.
8. Gaining knowledge and understanding through intense questioning and action.
9. To be able to assess a situation, take the bull by the horns, and turn it around. Self-satisfaction and passion seeing the momentum turn to the positive. Mother Theresa.
10. Being an example to others in whatever you do. When good is not good enough and pushing forward. Individual and creative.

**Any common denominators?** Various creative situations that are new to gain knowledge of the unknown through travel, esoteric/nature, arts, people.

**What must my career use (and include) for me to be truly happy, useful, and effective?** Investigation using creativity in an esoteric or environment field with people of like-mindedness. Human sciences/Environmental studies/Journalist/Presenter/Traveling/People.

Now, if this exercise was easy for you, then you do indeed know a lot about yourself. *But* if it was harder than you thought it would be, then you see there is work to be done.

You need to know more about who you are.

## The Three Secrets to Finding Out More About Who You Are

The late Barbara B. Brown, who was the first to bring *biofeedback* to the public's awareness back in 1974, with her groundbreaking book (at the time) *New Mind, New Body*, once said, at a public lecture I attended, that *brain scientists* like herself had discovered there were three things you can do, that greatly facilitate such decision making.

1. Put everything you know about yourself, on one piece of paper. Jot down anything and everything that occurs to you about yourself. Write small. Very small. Or use a big sheet of paper. Call it "That One Piece of Paper."

2. Also, put some kind of graphic on that piece of paper, in order to organize the information *about yourself.* A graphic—any graphic—keeps "That One Piece of Paper" interesting, and not just a cloud of words and spaces.

3. Prioritize all this information, when you have finished gathering it. Put it in its order of importance to you.

Select out the top ten things about yourself that you consider most important; not "marketable"—just *important*, to you.

Over the years the people I have been trying to help have invented various graphics for "That One Piece of Paper:" a parachutist and his/her parachute, a Grecian temple, a clown holding a bunch of round balloons, a tree with several branches, etc., etc. The common denominator has been that each graphic has had seven parts, as you might guess.

Ultimately we settled on a diagram of *a flower*, with seven petals, because readers preferred it above all other graphics. Why? I don't know. Maybe because a flower is a living entity, beautiful and growing, and therefore a reflection of them more than graphics of inanimate objects can be.

It's been refined over the years, of course. Here's what it's come out looking like:

# The Flower

"That One Piece of Paper"

**Step 1:**
In organizations using THESE **special knowledges:**
(in order of priority for me)

**Step 2:**
In organizations having THESE **people-environments:**
(in order of priority for me)

**Step 7:**
**USING THESE TRANSFERABLE SKILLS:**
(in order of priority for me)

1
2
3

**Step 6:**
Serving THESE **goals/purposes/values:**
(in order of priority for me)

**Step 5: Where**
Geography-wise?
(in order of priority for me)

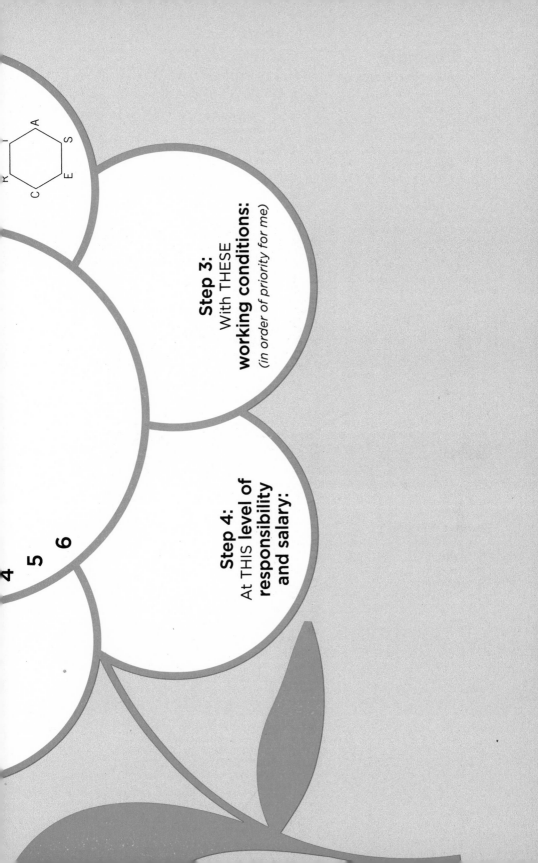

R I A
C E S

4 5 6

**Step 3:**
With THESE
**working conditions:**
*(in order of priority for me)*

**Step 4:**
At THIS level of
**responsibility
and salary:**

# Example
### (Rich Feller's Flower)

## Salary and Level of Responsibility

1. Can determine 9/12 month contract 2. Can determine own projects 3. Considerable clout in organization's direction without administrative responsibilities 4. Able to select colleagues 5. 3 to 5 assistants 6. $35K to $50K 7. Serve on various important boards 8. Can defer clerical and budget decisions and tasks 9. Speak before large groups 10. Can run for elected office

## Favorite Interests

1. Large conference planning 2. Regional geography & culture 3. Traveling on $20/day 4. Career planning seminars 5. Counseling techniques / theories 6. American policies 7. Fundamentals of sports 8. Fighting sexism 9. NASCAR auto racing 10. Interior design

## Geography

1. Close to major city 2. Mild winters / low humidity 3. Change in seasons 4. Clean and green 5. 100,000 people 6. Nice shopping malls 7. Wide range of athletic options 8. Diverse economic base 9. Ample local culture 10. Sense of community (pride)

## Favorite Skills

1. Observational / learning skills • continually expose self to new experiences • perceptive in identifying and assessing potential of others 2. Leadership skills • continually searches for more resonsibility • sees a problem / acts to solve it 3. Instructing / interpreting / guiding • committed to learning as a lifelong process • create atmosphere of acceptance 4. Serving / helping / human relations skills • shapes atmosphere of particular place • relates well in dealing with public 5. Detail / follow-through skills • handle great variety of tasks • resource broker 6. Influencing / persuading skills • recruiting talent / leadership • inspiring trust 7. Performing skills • getting up in front of a group (if I'm in control) • addressing small and large groups 8. Intuitional / innovative skills • continually develop / generate new ideas 9. Develop / plan / organize / execute • designing projects • utilizing skills of others 10. Language / read / write • communicate effectively • can think quickly on my feet

## Favorite People-Environment

1. Strong social, perceptual skills 2. Emotionally and physically healthy 3. Enthusiastically include others 4. Heterogeneous in interests and skills 5. Social changers, innovators 6. Politically, economically astute 7. Confident enough to confront / cry and be foolish 8. Sensitive to nontraditional issues 9. I and R (see page 204) 10. Nonmaterialistic

## Favorite Working Conditions

1. Receive clinical supervision 2. Mentor relationship 3. Excellent secretary 4. Part of larger, highly respected organization with clear direction 5. Near gourmet and health food specialty shops 6. Heterogeneous colleagues (race, sex, age) 7. Flexible dress code 8. Merit system 9. Can bike / bus / walk to work 10. Private office with window

## Favorite Values

1. Improve the human condition 2. Promote interdependence and futuristic principles 3. Maximize productive use of human / material resources 4. Teach people to be self-directed / self-responsible 5. Free people from self-defeating controls (thoughts, rules, barriers) 6. Promote capitalistic principles 7. Reduce exploitation 8. Promote political participation 9. Acknowledge those who give to the community 10. Give away ideas

Readers have asked to see an example of "That One Piece of Paper" all filled out. Rich W. Feller—a student of mine back in 1982, now a world-famous professor and expert in the national career development field—filled out his flower as you see, on the facing page. He said "That One Piece of Paper" has been his lifelong companion ever since, and his guiding star.

*Rich Feller, a University Distinguished Teaching Scholar and Professor at Colorado State University, whose own personal "Flower Diagram" is on the facing page, first put his personal "picture" together almost thirty years ago. Here are his comments about its usefulness since, and how "That One Piece of Paper" helped him, how he's used it, and how it's changed.*

### What the Parachute Flower Has Meant to Me

More than anything I've gained from an academic life, my Flower has given me hope, direction, and a lens to satisfaction. Using it to assess my life direction during crisis, career moves, and stretch assignments, it helps me define and hold to personal commitments. In many ways it's my "guiding light." Data within my Flower became and remain the core of any success and satisfaction I have achieved.

After I first filled out my own Flower Diagram in a two-week workshop with Dick Bolles back in 1982, I decided to teach the Flower to others. My academic position has allowed me to do this, abundantly. Having now taught the Flower to thousands of counselors, career development, and human resource specialists, I continually use it with clients, and in my own transitional retirement planning.

I'm overwhelmed with how little has changed within my Flower, over the years. My Flower is the best of what I am. Its petals are my compass, and using my "favorite skills" are the mirror to a joyful day. I trust the wisdom within "That One Piece of Paper." It has guided my work and my life, ever since 1982, and it has helped my wife and I define our hopes for our son.

The process of filling out and acting on "That One Piece of Paper" taught me a lot. Specifically, it taught me **the importance of the following ten things, often running contrary to what my studies and doctoral work had taught me previously.**
**I learned from my Flower the importance of:**
   1. Chasing after passions, honoring strengths, and respecting skill identification

continued

2. Challenging societal definitions of balance and success
3. Committing to something bigger than oneself
4. Living authentically and with joy
5. Being good at what matters to oneself and its relationship to opportunity
6. Finding pleasure in all that one does
7. Staying focused on well-being and life satisfaction
8. Personal clarity and responsibility for designing "possible selves"
9. Letting the world know, humbly but clearly, what we want
10. "Coaching" people amidst a world of abundance where individuals yearn for individual meaning and purpose more than they hunger for possessions, abject compliance with society's expectations, or simply fitting in

This technologically enhanced, global workplace we now face in the twenty-first century certainly challenges all we thought we knew about our life roles. Maintaining clarity, learning agility, and identifying development plans have become elevated to new and critical importance, if we are to maintain choice. As a result I've added the following four emphases to "Rich's Flower": *Have, do, learn,* and *give.* That is to say, I try to keep a running list (constantly updated) of ten things that I want to:

1. Have
2. Do
3. Learn
4. Give

Through the practice of answering the four questions listed above, I can measure change in my growth and development.

I feel so fortunate to have the opportunity to share with others how much I gained from the wisdom and hope embedded within "Rich's Flower."

I humbly offer my resume, home location and design, and family commitments on my website at www.mycahs.colostate.edu/Rich .Feller. I'd be honored to share my journey, and encourage others to nurture and shine light on their garden as well. I believe you'll find about 90 percent of the Flower's items influence our daily experience.

Rich Feller
Professor of Counseling and Career Development
University Distinguished Teaching Scholar
Colorado State University
Fort Collins, CO

Okay, now to get to work:

The flower is essentially designed to answer three questions:

1. WHAT skills do you most enjoy using?

2. WHERE do you want to use these skills?

3. HOW do you find the name of that kind of job (or jobs)?

That's the logical order of things. But we don't do the Flower in its logical order. We do the petals that are easiest first, then work our way toward the more difficult exercises (because they require more thought) for those other petals.

So, our order will be:

1. WHERE do you want to use your skills?
   Step 1: Favorite Special Knowledges
   Step 2: Preferred People-Environments
   Step 3: Preferred Working Conditions
   Step 4: Desired Responsibility (and Salary)
   Step 5: Preferred Geographical factors
   Step 6: With these Goals and Purposes (and Values) in mind

2. WHAT skills do you most enjoy using?
   Step 7: Your favorite Transferable Skills, in order of their priority for you

3. HOW do you find the name of that kind of job (or jobs)?
   Following the completion of the Flower, there'll be a detailed explanation of the exercises you use to find out this information.

Now, to the petals.

# THE FLOWER'S PETALS
## WHERE Do You Want to Use Your Skills?

---

### Step 1: What Knowledges That You Already Have in Your Head, Do You Most Want to Use in Your Life and Work?

---

You have a whole filing cabinet up there in your head. The number of things that you know *something* about, by this time in your life, is awesome.

You, in fact, have doubtless lost track of all you know. What files are up there in your head? What do you know something, or a lot, about, anyway? Football? Skiing? Antiques? Gardening? Computers? Cars? Knitting? Scrapbooking? Information technology? Management practices? How to raise children? Design? Career counseling?

Let's do an inventory of all that you know, and then pick your favorite subjects.

In order for you to do this, it is helpful to fill out the following chart; *you may first copy it onto a larger piece of paper, if you wish, in order to have more room to write.*

Please note that this chart is asking you what subjects you know *anything* about, not whether you *like* the subject or not. (*Later,* you will ask yourself which of these you like or even *love.*) For now, the task facing you is merely *inventory.* That is a task similar to inventorying what clothes you've got in your closet, before you decide which ones to give away. Only, here, *the closet is your head,* and you're inventorying all the stuff that's in *there.* Don't try to evaluate your degree of mastery of a particular subject. Put down something you've only read a few articles about (*if it interests you*) side by side with a subject you studied for three semesters in school.

Throwaway comes later (*though, obviously, if there's a subject you hate so much you can barely stand to write it down, then . . . don't . . . write . . . it . . . down*).

## THE SUBJECTS CHART

### Subjects I Know Something About

Which column you decide to put a subject in, below, doesn't matter at all. The columns are only a series of pegs, to hang your memories on. Which peg is of no concern. Jot down a subject anywhere you like.

| Column 1 | Column 2 | Column 3 | Column 4 | Column 5 |
|----------|----------|----------|----------|----------|
| Studied in High School or College or Graduate School | Learned on the Job | Learned from Conferences, Workshops, Training, Seminars | Learned at Home: Reading, TV, Tape Programs, Study Courses | Learned in My Leisure Time: Volunteer Work, Hobbies, etc. |
| *Examples: Spanish, Typing, Accounting, Computer Literacy, Psychology, Geography* | *Examples: Publishing, Computer Graphics, How an Organization Works, How to Operate Various Machines* | *Examples: Welfare Rules, Job-Hunting, Painting, How to Use the Internet* | *Examples: Art Appreciation, History, Speed Reading, a Language* | *Examples: Landscaping, How to Sew, Antiques, Camping, Stamps* |
| | | | | |

*Self-Inventory (The Flower Exercise)*

# THE SUBJECTS CHART

You want an example, of course, of what kind of things you might put in these columns; here is how a reader from South Africa filled out her chart:

| Column 1 | Column 2 | Column 3 | Column 4 | Column 5 |
| --- | --- | --- | --- | --- |
| Studied in High School / College | Learned on the Job | Workshops / Seminars | Learned at Home | Hobbies |
| Sports/teamwork | Banking | Human Pin Code | Love | Art |
| Public speaking | Waitressing | Paganism | Relationships | Writing |
| German | Bar work | Think and Grow (TAG) | Gardening | Esoteric arts |
| French | Stock accounting | Firewalking | Cooking | Meditation |
| English lit | Computers | NLP | Household duties | Diving |
| English language | Service | Basic coaching | Budgeting | Hiking |
| Typing | Organizing | Relationship management | Decorating | Gardening |
| Hairdressing | Accounting | Toastmasters | Moving | Reading about eso- teric arts |
| Home economics | Dealing with money | Public speaking | Animals | Magazines |
| Woodwork | E-mail | Events management | Driving | Pottery |
| Art | Document completion | Taking minutes | General knowledge | The unusual |
| Geography | Working under pressure | Enviromental (various) | Rainbow home | Investigating the unknown |
| Music | Politics | Photography | Reading crime novels | |
| Acting | Leadership | Yoga | Witchcraft | |
| Eviromental studies | Tour leader | Science of the souls | Herbs | |
| Playing | Building bookings | Business entrepeneur | Entertaining | |
| Social interactivity | Traveling | Shaman course | | |
| Changing enviro- ments/schools and places | Problem solving | High performance management | | |
| Budgeting | Excel | | | |
| | Word | | | |
| | Powerpoint presentations | | | |
| | Operations manger | | | |
| | Relationship management | | | |
| | Reports | | | |
| | Team building | | | |
| | Event management | | | |
| | Working as a team | | | |
| | Cultures | | | |
| | Advancing people | | | |
| | Teaching | | | |
| | Fare courses | | | |
| | Human resourcing | | | |
| | Retail manager— Clothes | | | |
| | Displaying goods | | | |
| | Communication | | | |

© ScienceCartoonsPlus.com

"I CAN REMEMBER WHEN ALL WE NEEDED WAS SOMEONE WHO COULD CARVE AND SOMEONE WHO COULD SEW."

When filling this chart out, do not forget to list those things you've learned—no matter how—about *Organizations* (*including volunteer organizations*), and what it takes to make them work.

It is not necessary that you should have ever taken a course in management or business. Examples of things you may know something about (and should list here) are: *accounting or book-keeping; administration; applications; credit collection of overdue bills; customer relations and service; data analysis; distribution; fiscal analysis, controls, reductions; government contracts; group dynamics or work with groups in general; hiring, human resources, or manpower; international business; management; marketing, sales; merchandising; packaging; performance specifications; planning; policy development; problem solving or other types of troubleshooting with operations or management systems; production; public speaking/ addressing people; R & D program management; recruiting; show or conference planning, organization, and management; systems analysis; travel or travel planning, especially international travel; etc.*

When you're done, you may want to let this chart just sit around for a few days, to see if any other items occur to you. But when you're sure you've listed all you want to, then draw the matrix found on the next page on a large sheet of paper, and sort the knowledges on the chart into the four boxes.

## YOUR FAVORITE SUBJECTS MATRIX

HIGH

| | |
|---|---|
| **3.** Subjects for Which You Have Little Enthusiasm but in Which You Have Lots of Expertise | **1.** Subjects for Which You Have Lots of Enthusiasm and in Which You Have Lots of Expertise BINGO! |
| **4.** Subjects for Which You Have Little Enthusiasm and in Which you Have Little Expertise | **2.** Subjects for Which You Have Lots of Enthusiasm but in Which You Have Little Expertise |

E X P E R T I S E

LOW    **ENTHUSIASM**    HIGH

Then, choose your three favorite knowledges, from any of these boxes. You want to pay particular attention to the knowledges you put in box 1 above. And next, those you put in box 2. Last of all, those in box 3.

Let us say it turns out your three favorite knowledges are gardening and carpentry in box 1, and your knowledge of psychiatry in box 2.

What you want to be able to do is to use all three expertises, not just one of them—if you possibly can.

So, put your three favorite knowledges on a series of overlapping circles, as follows:

Now, to figure out how to combine these three, imagine that each circle is a person; that is, in this case, Psychiatrist, Carpenter, and Gardener.

You ask yourself which person took the longest to get trained in their specialty. The answer, here, is the psychiatrist. The reason you ask yourself this question, is that the person with the longest training is most likely to have the largest overview of things. So, you go to see a psychiatrist, either at a private clinic or at a university or hospital. You ask for fifteen minutes of his or her time, and pay them if necessary.

Then you ask the psychiatrist if he or she knows how to combine psychiatry with *one*—just one, initially—of your other two favorite knowledges. Let's say you choose gardening, here. "Doctor, do you know anyone who combines a knowledge of psychiatry with a knowledge of gardening or plants?"

Since I'm talking about a true story here, I can tell you what the psychiatrist said: "Yes, in working with catatonic patients, we often give them a plant to take care of, so they know there is something that is depending on them for its future, and its survival."

"And how would I also employ a knowledge of carpentry?"

"Well, in building the planters, wouldn't you?"

(Parenthetically, healers also use pets as they do plants. See www .sniksnak.com/therapy.html.)

This is the way you explore how to combine your three favorite knowledges, all at once, no matter what those three may be. The Internet can also be useful in this regard.

Put these three on your Knowledges petal of the Flower, on pages 194–95.

With the great emphasis upon the importance of the environment, in recent years, and global warming in particular, it has become increasingly realized that jobs are environments, too. The most important environmental factor always turns out to be people, since every job, except possibly that of a full-fledged hermit, surrounds us with people to one degree or another.

Indeed, many a good job has been ruined by the people one is surrounded by. Many a mundane job has been made delightful, by the people one is surrounded by. Therefore, it is important to think out what kinds of people you want to be surrounded by.

The late Dr. John L. Holland offered the best description of people-environments. He said there are six principal ones:

1. The **Realistic** People-Environment: filled with people who prefer activities involving "the explicit, ordered, or systematic manipulation of objects, tools, machines, and animals." "Realistic," incidentally, refers to Plato's conception of "the real" as that which one can apprehend through the senses.

I summarize this as: R = people who like nature, or athletics, or tools and machinery.

2. The **Investigative** People-Environment: filled with people who prefer activities involving "the observation and symbolic, systematic, creative investigation of physical, biological, or cultural phenomena."

I summarize this as: I = people who are very curious, liking to investigate or analyze things.

3. The **Artistic** People-Environment: filled with people who prefer activities involving "ambiguous, free, unsystematized activities and competencies to create art forms or products."

I summarize this as: A = people who are very artistic, imaginative, and innovative.

4. The **Social** People-Environment: filled with people who prefer activities involving "the manipulation of others to inform, train, develop, cure, or enlighten."

I summarize this as: S = people who are bent on trying to help, teach, or serve people.

5. The **Enterprising** People-Environment: filled with people who prefer activities involving "the manipulation of others to attain organizational or self-interest goals."

I summarize this as: E = people who like to start up projects or organizations, and/or influence or persuade people.

6. The **Conventional** People-Environment: filled with people who prefer activities involving "the explicit, ordered, systematic manipulation of data, such as keeping records, filing materials, reproducing materials, organizing written and numerical data according to a prescribed plan, operating business and data processing machines." "Conventional," incidentally, refers to the "values" that people in this environment usually hold—representing the broad mainstream of the culture.

I summarize this as: C = people who like detailed work, and like to complete tasks or projects.

> There is, incidentally, a relationship between the people you like to be surrounded by *and* your skills *and* your values. See John Holland's book, *Making Vocational Choices* (3rd ed., 1997). You can procure it by going to the Psychological Assessment Resources, Inc., website at www3.parinc.com or calling 1-800-331-8378. *The book is $56.00 at this writing.* PAR also has John Holland's instrument, called *The Self-Directed Search* (or SDS, for short), for discovering what your Holland Code is. PAR lets you take the test online for a small fee ($4.95) at www.self-directed-search.com.

According to John's theory and findings, everyone has three preferred people-environments, from among these six. The letters for your three preferred people-environments gives you what is called your "Holland Code."

For those who don't have Internet access (or are in a hurry), I invented (many years ago) a quick and easy way to get an *approximation* of your "Holland Code," as it's called. I call it "The Party Exercise." Here is how the exercise goes (do it!):

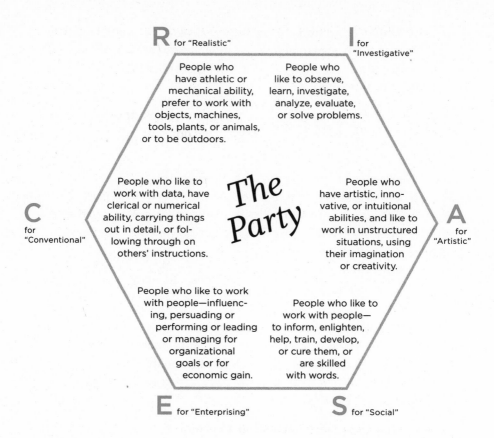

R for "Realistic"

People who have athletic or mechanical ability, prefer to work with objects, machines, tools, plants, or animals, or to be outdoors.

I for "Investigative"

People who like to observe, learn, investigate, analyze, evaluate, or solve problems.

*The Party*

C for "Conventional"

People who like to work with data, have clerical or numerical ability, carrying things out in detail, or following through on others' instructions.

A for "Artistic"

People who have artistic, innovative, or intuitional abilities, and like to work in unstructured situations, using their imagination or creativity.

E for "Enterprising"

People who like to work with people—influencing, persuading or performing or leading or managing for organizational goals or for economic gain.

S for "Social"

People who like to work with people—to inform, enlighten, help, train, develop, or cure them, or are skilled with words.

Below is an aerial view of a room in which a party is taking place. At this party, people with the same or similar interests have (for some reason) all gathered in the same corner of the room.

1) Which corner of the room would you instinctively be drawn to, as the group of people you would most enjoy being with for the longest time? (Leave aside any question of shyness, or whether you would have to talk to them.) Write the letter for that corner here:

2) After fifteen minutes, everyone in the corner you have chosen leaves for another party crosstown, except you. Of the groups that still remain now, which corner or group would you be drawn to the most, as the people you would most enjoy being with for the longest time? Write the letter for that corner here:

3) After fifteen minutes, this group too leaves for another party, except you. Of the corners, and groups, which remain now, which one would you most enjoy being with for the longest time? Write the letter for that corner here: ☐

The three letters you just chose, in the three steps, are called your "Holland Code." Here is what you should now do:

**1. Circle them on the People petal, on your Flower Diagram.**

Put three circles around your favorite corner; two circles around your next favorite; and one circle around your third favorite.

**2. Once the corners are circled, you may wish to write (for yourself and your eyes only) a temporary statement about your future job or career, using the descriptors on the Party Exercise, previous.**

> *If your "Code" turned out to be IAS, for example, you might write: "I would like a job or career best if I were surrounded by people who are very curious, and like to investigate or analyze things (I); who are also very innovative (A); and who are bent on trying to help or serve people (S)."*

**3. See what clues the Internet has to offer.**

Back in April 1977, I conducted a workshop at the University of Missouri-Columbia, introducing "The Party Exercise." Subsequently, some unknown genius there did a rhapsody on this, calling it "The Career Interests Game." It is brilliant, and can be found on that University's Career Center's website, at: http://career.missouri.edu/students/majors-careers/skills-interests/career-interest-game. You play the "Game" the same way, but afterward you can click on each letter of RIASEC (in color!) and find out which skills, interests, hobbies, and career possibilities go with each letter. For a complete *Holland Code*, of course, you need the *combination* of all three letters in your Code; but this at least offers a good beginning, taking one letter at a time. It is free.

Another Holland website is Lawrence Jones's *Career Key*, found at http://careerkey.org/asp/your_personality/take_test.asp. It costs $9.95 to take it, but offers suggestions as to related college majors, possible careers, etc., when you are done. Great test!

The final *Holland*-related site I want to mention is CareerPlanner .com's *Career Test*, invented by Michael T. Robinson, and found at http://careerplanner.com. I recommend it; it will cost you $24.95 to take this test, so you must decide if it's worth the cost. You get a listing of thirty to one hundred careers related to the results of your test. As in all test results, treat these as starting points, only, for your subsequent research and Informational Interviewing. Please.

## Step 3: What Working Conditions Do You Like Best, Because They Enable You to Do Your Most Effective Work?

### DISTASTEFUL WORKING CONDITIONS

| | Column A — Distasteful Working Conditions | Column B — Distasteful Working Conditions Ranked | Column C + The Keys to My Effectiveness at Work |
|---|---|---|---|
| Places I Have Worked Thus Far in My Life | I Have Learned from the Past That My Effectiveness at Work Is Decreased When I Have to Work Under These Conditions | Among the Factors or Qualities Listed in Column A, These Are the Ones I Dislike Absolutely the Most (in Order of Decreasing Dislike) | The Opposite of These Qualities, in Order:<br><br>I Believe My Effectiveness Would Be at an Absolute Maximum, If I Could Work Under These Conditions |

Plants that grow beautifully at sea level, often perish if they're taken ten thousand feet up the mountain. Likewise, we do our best work under certain conditions, but not under others. Thus, the question: "What are your favorite working conditions?" actually is a question about "Under what circumstances do you do your most effective work?"

The best way to approach this is by starting with the things you *disliked* about all your previous jobs, using the chart on the facing page to list these. You may copy this chart onto a larger piece of paper if you wish, before you begin filling it out. *Column A may begin with such factors as: "too noisy," "too much supervision," "no windows in my workplace," "having to be at work by 6 a.m.," etc.*

If you are baffled as to how to prioritize your list in Column A, I recommend you use a little invention of mine called the Prioritizing Grid. It's on page 212. Rather than trying to guess about ten or more items all at once, it asks you to compare just two items at a time.

Instructions:

A. In Section A write down ten factors you are trying to prioritize, in any random order you choose.

B. Then in Section B, start to compare just two items; in the little box to the left of factor 1 and factor 2, you will see the numbers 1 and 2. The question you would frame for yourself, here, would be as follows: "If I were offered two jobs, and in the first job offer I would be rid of my first distasteful working condition (1) but not the second (2), while in the second job offer I would be rid of my second distasteful working condition (2), but not the first (1), which job offer would I take?

C. Then in that little box you circle either 1 or 2, depending on which distasteful working condition you are *more anxious* to get rid of, (1) or (2).

D. Now you work your way down the boxes nearest Section A, which as you can see lie in a diagonal running from northwest to southeast. So the next little box has 2 and 3 in it. Same question, except

# PRIORITIZING GRID FOR 10 ITEMS OR LESS

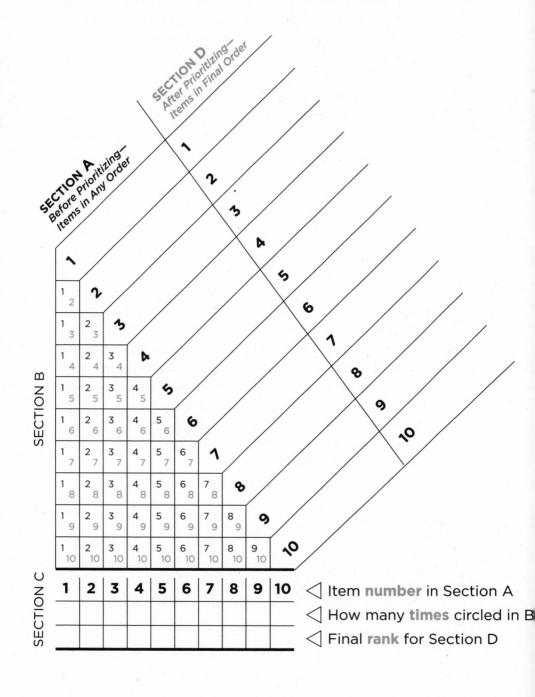

◁ Item **number** in Section A

◁ How many **times** circled in B

◁ Final **rank** for Section D

now you have to determine which working condition you hate the worst, between those two (2) or (3). Circle the appropriate number.

E. When you've reached the little box at the bottom of that first diagonal (containing the little numbers 9 and 10), go back up to the top and work down the next diagonal (first the little box containing 1 and 3; then the little box containing 2 and 4; then the one containing 3 and 5, etc.

F. When you've reached the box at the bottom of *that* diagonal, go back up to the top, and work down the next diagonal (the little box containing 1 and 4, then the box containing 2 and 5, and so on, down to box containing 7 and 10).

G. Back up to the top to the next diagonal (to the left of those you've already used), namely, the box containing 1 and 5, then the box containing 2 and 6, and so on.

H. Keep this up until you've used every little box (the final one being 1 and 10).

I. Now you turn to Section C, at the bottom of the grid. First row is the numbers of the items you randomly listed in Section A, at the beginning. Second row is how many times each got circled. So, you count how many times the number 1 got circled in all of Section B. Let's say item 1 got circled 3 times. In the second row at the bottom, right below the number 1, you put 3. Next, count how many times item 2 got circled; let's say it was five times, so you put the number 5 right below 2. And so on, up to item 10.

J. Look at the counts in the second row. Let's suppose you have two items that each got circled 5 times. How do you resolve the tie? Well, let's suppose they were item #2 and item #7. You look back at Section B, to find the little box that had 2 and 7 in it. See which one you circled; let's say it was 2. Then give 2 an extra half point. Now its "count" is 5 1/2.

K. Let's say you have a three-way tie in your "times circled" line. That means you contradicted yourself somewhere in Section B. For example, you said 1 was more important to you than 2, and 2 was more important to you than 3. So far so good; but then, you contradicted yourself. You said 3 was more important than 1. That can't be. Figure out some way to resolve it, even by comparing those three items to each other, and assigning an extra three-quarters point to the distasteful working condition you hated the most, extra one-half point to the condition you hated the next most, and leave the count for the third one as it is. Now, no two factors or items have the same count.

L. Now down on the bottom line in Section C, rank the items, according to their count. The one that got circled the most, let's say it was item 2, gets a final rank of #1. Write that down beneath item number 2 in the third row. Let's say item 5 got the next most circles or points on line 2; write down a 2 beneath the 5. Let's say item 10 got the next most circles; write the number 3 on the final rank line. And so forth.

M. Finally, recopy your list in Section D—now in the exact order the grid ranked them. In terms of our examples above, copy item 2 in Section A onto line 1 in Section D. Copy item 5 onto line 2 in Section D, etc., until you've copied all ten factors or items, in exactly the order of priority for you.

N. What have you ended up with, in Section D? The exact list you copy into Column B of your Distasteful Working Conditions chart, page 210.

Now that you have that list in Column B, ranked in terms of most distasteful down to least distasteful working conditions, turn to Column C in that chart and write *the opposite*, or something near *the opposite*, directly opposite each item in Column B.

Copy the top 5 items in Column C, onto the Working Conditions petal of your Flower Diagram, pages 194–195.

## Step 4: What Level (of Responsibility) Do You Most Enjoy Working at, and at What Salary?

Salary is something you must think out ahead of time, when you're contemplating your ideal job or career. Level goes hand in hand with salary, of course.

**1. The first question here is at what level would you like to work, in your ideal job?**

Level is a matter of how much responsibility you want, in an organization:

- ❑ Boss or CEO (this may mean you'll have to form your own business)
- ❑ Manager or someone under the boss who carries out orders
- ❑ The head of a team
- ❑ A member of a team of equals
- ❑ One who works in tandem with one other partner
- ❑ One who works alone, either as an employee or as a consultant to an organization, or as a one-person business

Enter a two- or three-word summary of your answer, on the Level of Responsibility and Salary petal of your Flower Diagram, pages 194–95.

**2. The second question here is what salary would you like to be aiming for?**

Here you have to think in terms of minimum or maximum. **Minimum** is what you would need to make, if you were just barely "getting by." And you need to know this *before* you go in for a job interview with anyone (*or before you form your own business, and need to know how much profit you must make, just to survive*).

**Maximum** could be any astronomical figure you can think of, but it is more useful here to put down the salary you realistically think you could make, with your present competency and experience, were you working for a real, *but generous*, boss. (If this maximum figure is still depressingly low, then put down the salary you would like to be making five years from now.)

Make out a detailed outline of your estimated expenses *now*, listing what you need *monthly* in the following categories:[2]

Housing
    Rent or mortgage payments. . . . . . . . . . . . . . . . . $ _____
    Electricity/gas. . . . . . . . . . . . . . . . . . . . . . . . . . . . . $ _____
    Water. . . . . . . . . . . . . . . . . . . . . . . . . . . . . . . . . . . . . $ _____
    Phone/Internet. . . . . . . . . . . . . . . . . . . . . . . . . . . . $ _____
    Garbage removal. . . . . . . . . . . . . . . . . . . . . . . . . . . $ _____
    Cleaning, maintenance, repairs[3] . . . . . . . . . . . . $ _____
Food
    What you spend at the supermarket
    and/or farmer's market, etc. . . . . . . . . . . . . . . . $ _____
    Eating out . . . . . . . . . . . . . . . . . . . . . . . . . . . . . . . $ _____
Clothing
    Purchase of new or used clothing . . . . . . . . . . . $ _____
    Cleaning, dry cleaning, laundry. . . . . . . . . . . . . $ _____
Automobile/transportation
    Car payments . . . . . . . . . . . . . . . . . . . . . . . . . . . . . $ _____
    Gas (who knows?)[4]. . . . . . . . . . . . . . . . . . . . . . . . $ _____
    Repairs . . . . . . . . . . . . . . . . . . . . . . . . . . . . . . . . . . $ _____
    Public transportation (*bus, train, plane*) . . . . . . $ _____
Insurance
    Car. . . . . . . . . . . . . . . . . . . . . . . . . . . . . . . . . . . . . . $ _____
    Medical or health care . . . . . . . . . . . . . . . . . . . . . $ _____
    House and personal possessions . . . . . . . . . . . . . $ _____
    Life . . . . . . . . . . . . . . . . . . . . . . . . . . . . . . . . . . . . . $ _____

---

2. If this kind of financial figuring is not your cup of tea, find a buddy, friend, relative, family member, or anyone, who can help you do this. If you don't know anyone who could do this, go to your local church, synagogue, religious center, social club, gym, or wherever you hang out, and ask the leader or manager there, to help you find someone. If there's a bulletin board, put up a notice on the bulletin board.

3. If you have extra household expenses, such as a security system, be sure to include the quarterly (or whatever) expenses here, divided by three.

4. Your checkbook stubs and/or online banking records will tell you a lot of this stuff. But you may be vague about your cash or credit card expenditures. For example, you may not know how much you spend at the supermarket, or how much you spend on gas, etc. But there is a simple way to find out. Just carry a little notepad and pen around with you for two weeks or more, and jot down everything you pay cash (or use credit cards) for—on the spot, right after you pay it. At the end of those two weeks, you'll be able to take that notepad and make a realistic guess of what should be put down in these categories that now puzzle you. (Multiply the two-week figure by two, and you'll have the monthly figure.)

Medical expenses
  Doctors' visits . . . . . . . . . . . . . . . . . . . . . . . . . . . . . $ _____
  Prescriptions. . . . . . . . . . . . . . . . . . . . . . . . . . . . . $ _____
  Fitness costs . . . . . . . . . . . . . . . . . . . . . . . . . . . . . $ _____
Support for other family members
  Child-care costs (*if you have children*) . . . . . . . . . $ _____
  Child-support (*if you're paying that*). . . . . . . . . . . $ _____
  Support for your parents (*if you're helping out*) . . $ _____
Charity giving/tithe (*to help others*) . . . . . . . . . . . . . $ _____
School/learning
  Children's costs (*if you have children in school*) . . $ _____
  Your learning costs (*adult education,*
  *job-hunting classes, etc.*) . . . . . . . . . . . . . . . . . . . . $ _____
Pet care (*if you have pets*) . . . . . . . . . . . . . . . . . . . . . $ _____
Bills and debts (*usual monthly payments*)
  Credit cards . . . . . . . . . . . . . . . . . . . . . . . . . . . . . $ _____
  Local stores. . . . . . . . . . . . . . . . . . . . . . . . . . . . . . $ _____
  Other obligations you pay off monthly . . . . . . . . $ _____
Taxes
  Federal[5] (*next April's due, divided by*
  *months remaining until then*). . . . . . . . . . . . . . . . . $ _____
  State (*likewise*) . . . . . . . . . . . . . . . . . . . . . . . . . . $ _____
  Local/property (*next amount due, divided by*
  *months remaining until then*). . . . . . . . . . . . . . . . . $ _____
  Tax-help (*if you ever use an accountant,*
  *pay a friend to help you with taxes, etc.*). . . . . . . . $ _____
Savings . . . . . . . . . . . . . . . . . . . . . . . . . . . . . . . . . . . $ _____
Retirement (Keogh, IRA, SEP, etc.). . . . . . . . . . . . . $ _____
Amusement/discretionary spending
  Movies, video rentals, etc. . . . . . . . . . . . . . . . . . . . $ _____
  Other kinds of entertainment . . . . . . . . . . . . . . . $ _____
  Reading, newspapers, magazines, books . . . . . . . $ _____

---

5. Incidentally, for U.S. citizens, looking ahead to next April 15, be sure to check with your local IRS office or a reputable accountant to find out if you can deduct the expenses of your job-hunt on your federal (and state) income tax returns. At this writing, some job-hunters can, if—big IF—this is not your first job that you're looking for, if you haven't been unemployed too long, and if you aren't making a career-change. Do go find out what the latest "ifs" are. If the IRS says you are eligible, keep careful receipts of everything related to your job-hunt, as you go along: telephone calls, stationery, printing, postage, travel, etc.

Gifts (birthday, Christmas, etc.) . . . . . . . . . . . . . $ _____

Vacations . . . . . . . . . . . . . . . . . . . . . . . . . . . . . . $ _____

Total Amount You Need Each Month . . . . . . . . . . $ _____

Multiply the total amount you need each month by 12, to get the yearly figure. Divide the yearly figure by 2,000, and you will be reasonably near the *minimum* hourly wage that you need. Thus, if you need $3,333 per month, multiplied by 12 that's $40,000 a year, and then divided by 2,000, that's $20 an hour.

Parenthetically, you may want to prepare two different versions of the above budget: one with the expenses you'd ideally *like* to make, and the other a minimum budget, which will give you what you are looking for, here: the floor, below which you simply cannot afford to go.

Enter the maximum, and minimum, on your Level of Responsibility and Salary petal on the Flower Diagram, pages 194–95.

---

**Optional Exercise:** You may wish to put down other rewards, besides money, that you would hope for, from your next job or career. These might be:

❏ Adventure ❏ Challenge ❏ Respect ❏ Influence
❏ Popularity ❏ Fame ❏ Power
❏ Intellectual stimulation from the other workers there
❏ A chance to be creative
❏ A chance to help others
❏ A chance to exercise leadership
❏ A chance to make decisions
❏ A chance to use your expertise
❏ A chance to bring others closer to God
❏ Other: _____

If you do check off things on this list, arrange your answers in order of importance to you, and then add them to the Level of Responsibility and Salary petal.

---

## Step 5: What Geographical Factors Are Most Important to You, and in What Places Do You Think You Would Do Your Best Work?

**The Point of This Step:** To answer this question: *to the degree you have a choice—now or down the line—where would you most like to live?*

**Why This Is Important for You to Know:** Human beings are like flowers. Our soul flourishes in some environs, but withers and dies—or at least becomes extremely unhappy—in others.

**What You Want to Beware Of:** Thinking that where you live is not important. Or thinking, if you have a partner, and you each want to live in different places, that one of you can get their way, but the other is going to have to give up *their* dream. Nonsense! If this were part of a course about Thinking, what would the Lesson be? The subject of the Lesson would be: how can two partners, who initially disagree, learn to agree on a place where both get what they want?

In case you haven't got a clue, there is an interesting exercise you can do. It begins with your past *(the places where you used to live)*, and extracts from it some information that is tremendously useful in plotting your future.

It is particularly useful when you have a partner, and the two of you haven't yet been able to agree on where you want to live.

DIRECTIONS FOR DOING THIS EXERCISE:

1. Copy the chart that is on the next two pages, onto a larger (*e.g.*, 24 by 36-inch) piece of paper or cardboard, which you can obtain from any arts and crafts store or supermarket, in your town or city. If you are doing this exercise with a partner, make a copy for them too, so that each of you is working on a clean copy of your own, and can follow these instructions independently.

2. In *Column 1*, each of you should list all the places where you have ever lived.

3. In *Column 2*, each of you should list all the factors you disliked (and still dislike) about each place. The factors do not have to be

## My Geographical Preferences
### Decision Making for Just You

| Column 1
Names of Places
I Have Lived | Column 2
From the Past:
Negatives | Column 3
Translating the
Negatives into Positives | Column 4
Ranking of
My Positives |
|---|---|---|---|
| | Factors I Disliked and
Still Dislike about
Any Place | | 1.

2.

3.

4.

5.

6.

7.

8.

9.

10.

11.

12.

13.

14.

15. |
| | Factors I Liked and
Still Like about
Any Place | | |

| Column 5 | | Column 6 | Column 7 | Column 8 |
|---|---|---|---|---|
| **Column 5**<br>Places That Fit<br>These Criteria | | **Our Geographical Preferences**<br>Decision Making for You and a Partner | | |
| | | **Column 6**<br>Ranking of<br>His/Her<br>Preferences | **Column 7**<br>Combining Our<br>Two Lists<br>(Columns 4 & 6) | **Column 8**<br>Places That<br>Fit These<br>Criteria |
| | | a. | a.<br>1. | |
| | | b. | b.<br>2. | |
| | | c. | c.<br>3. | |
| | | d. | d.<br>4. | |
| | | e. | e.<br>5. | |
| | | f. | f.<br>6. | |
| | | g. | g.<br>7. | |
| | | h. | h.<br>8. | |
| | | i. | i.<br>9. | |
| | | j. | j.<br>10. | |
| | | k. | k.<br>11. | |
| | | l. | l.<br>12. | |
| | | m. | m.<br>13. | |
| | | n. | n.<br>14. | |
| | | o. | o.<br>15. | |

put exactly opposite the name in *Column 1*. The names in *Column 1* exist simply to jog your memory.

If, as you go, you remember some good things about any place, put *those* factors at the bottom of the next column, *Column 3*.

If the same factors keep repeating, just put a checkmark after the first listing of that factor, every time it repeats.

Keep going until you have listed all the factors you disliked or hated about each and every place you named in *Column 1*. Now, in effect, throw away *Column 1;* discard it from your thoughts. The negative factors were what you were after. *Column 1* has served its purpose.

4. Look at *Column 2*, now, your list of negative factors, and in *Column 3* try to list each one's opposite (or near opposite). For example, "the sun never shone, there" would, in *Column 3*, be turned into "mostly sunny, all year 'round." It will not always be *the exact opposite.* For example, the negative factor "rains all the time" does not necessarily translate into the positive "sunny all the time." It might be something like "sunny at least 200 days a year." It's your call. Keep going, until every negative factor in *Column 2* is turned into its opposite, a positive factor, in *Column 3*. At the bottom, note the positive factors you already listed there, when you were working on *Column 2*.

5. In *Column 4*, now, list the positive factors in *Column 3*, in the order of most important (to you), down to least important (to you). For example, if you were looking at, and trying to name a new town, city, or place where you could be happy and flourish, what is the first thing you would look for? Would it be, good weather? or lack of crime? or good schools? or access to cultural opportunities, such as music, art, museums, or whatever? or would it be inexpensive housing? etc., etc. Rank all the factors in *Column 4*. Use a clean photocopy of the Prioritzing Grid on page 212 if you need to.

6. If you are doing this by yourself, list on a *scribble sheet* the top ten factors, in order of importance to you, and show it to everyone you meet for the next ten days, with the ultimate question: "Can you think of places that have these ten factors, or at least the top five?" Jot down their suggestions on the back of the *scribble sheet.* When the ten days are up, look at the back of your sheet and circle

the three places that seem the most interesting to you. If there is only a partial overlap between your dream factors and the places your friends and acquaintances suggested, *make sure the overlap is in the factors that count the most.* Now you have some names that you will want to find out more about, until you are sure which is your absolute favorite place to live, and then your second, and third, as backups.

Put the names of the three places, and/or your top five geographical factors, on the Flower Diagram, on the Where petal, pages 194–95.

7. If you are doing this with a partner, skip *Column 5.* Instead, when you have finished your *Column 4,* look at your partner's *Column 4,* and copy it into *Column 6.* The numbering of *your* list in *Column 4* was 1, 2, 3, 4, etc. Number your partner's list, as you copy it into *Column 6,* as a, b, c, d, etc.

8. Now, in *Column 7,* combine your *Column 4* with *Column 6* (your partner's old *Column 4,* renumbered). Both of you can work now from just one person's chart. Combine the two lists as illustrated on the chart. First your partner's top favorite geographical factor ("a"), then *your* top favorite geographical factor ("1"), then your partner's second most important favorite geographical factor ("b"), then *yours* ("2"), etc., until you have ten or fifteen favorite geographical factors (*yours and your partner's*) listed, in order, in *Column 7.*

9. List on a *scribble sheet* the top ten factors, and both of you should show it to everyone you meet, for the next ten days, with the same question as above: "Can you think of any places that have these ten factors, or at least the top five?" Jot down their suggestions on the back of the *scribble sheet.* When the ten days are up, you and your partner should look at the back of your sheet and circle the three places that look the most interesting to the two of you. If there is only a partial overlap between your dream factors and the places your friends and acquaintances suggested, make sure the overlap is in the factors that matter the most to the two of you, i.e., the ones that are at the top of your list in *Column 7.* Now you have some names of places that you will want to find out more about,

until you are sure which is the absolute favorite place to live for both of you, and then your second, and third, as backups.

Put the names of the top three places, and/or your top five geographical factors, on the Flower Diagram, on the Where petal, pages 194–95.

Conclusion: Was all of this too much work? Then do what one family did: they put a map of the U.S. up on a corkboard, and then they each threw a dart at the map from across the room, and when they were done they asked themselves where the most darts landed. It turned out to be around "Denver." So, *Denver* it was!

## Step 6: What Goals or Purposes Would You Most Enjoy Setting Your Energies To?

## WHAT DID YOU COME INTO THE WORLD TO DO?

There is a name for this moment in your life; in fact, there are several names.

We call it "at last going after your dreams."
We call it "finding more purpose and meaning for your life."
We call it "making a career-change."
We call it "deciding to try something new."
We call it "setting out in a different direction in your life."
We call it "getting out of the rat race."
We call it "going after your dream job."
We call it "finding your mission in life, at last."

But what you call it doesn't really matter. It is instantly recognizable as that moment when you decide that *this time* you're not going to do just a traditional job-hunt; you're going to do a life-changing job-hunt or career-change: one that begins with you and what it is that you want out of life.

This time it's all about: *Your* agenda. *Your* wishes. *Your* dreams. *Your* mission in life, given you by the Great God, our Creator.

## Not a Selfish Activity

You may think that this is a selfish activity—because it deals with You, you, you. But it is not. It is concerned with what *the world* most needs from you. That world currently is *filled* with workers whose weeklong question is, *When is the weekend going to be here?* And, then, *Thank God It's Friday!* Their work puts bread on the table *but* . . . they are bored out of their minds. They've never taken the time to think out what they uniquely can do, and what they uniquely have to offer to the world.

You've got talent, no doubt about that. You have special gifts, and skills. The question is: what do you want to accomplish with that talent, those skills, and those gifts? What values do you want your life, ultimately, to serve?

That is the question with which you must begin. Even before you inventory your skills. They can be made to serve any goal or value you choose. By way of example, the movie credits that roll at the end of a movie show us how many talents and skills it took to produce that movie. You will see such talents listed as: *researcher (especially for movies set in another historical period), travel expert (to scout locations), interior designer (to design sets), carpenter (ditto), painter (ditto), costume designer, hair stylist, makeup artist, lighting technician, sound editor and sound mixer, computer graphics people, singer, conductor, musicians, composer, sound recordist, stunt artists, animal trainer, talent coordinator, camera operator and cinematographer, special effects people, continuity editor, director, art director, casting director, actor, actress, producer, accountant, personal assistants, drivers, first aid people, secretaries, publicists,* and many others, depending on the type of movie it is.

The point is: if what you most want to do is to make movies, it doesn't matter what your skills are, because almost any skills you have can be put to use there.

And so it is, with all goals, fields, and values.

Figure out what cause, what problem, what values, you want your life to serve. Then, almost any talent, skill, or gift you later discover you have, or already know you have, can be put into its service.

The word "values" can refer to almost anything. Do you value chocolate over broccoli? Or do you value broccoli over chocolate? That's a matter of your values.

But "values" in the sense I'm using it here, refers to the broad outcome of your life. What kind of footprint do you want to leave on this Earth, after your journey here is done? Figure *that* out, and you're well on your way to finding a life that has purpose and meaning.

I will list nine broad outcomes here; all of them are important, in this life; the question is, which one (or ones) grips you the most?

1. **Mind.** Is the human mind your major concern? When you are gone, do you want there to be more knowledge, truth, or clarity in the world, because you were here? If so, knowledge, truth, or clarity concerning what, in particular?

2. **Body.** Is the human body your major concern? When you are gone, do you want there to be more wholeness, fitness, or health in the world, more binding up of the body's wounds and strength, more feeding of the hungry, and clothing of the poor, because you were here? If so, what issue in particular—concerning the human body—do you want to work on?

3. **Eyes and Other Senses.** Are the human senses your major concern? When you are gone, do you want there to be more beauty in the world, because you were here? If so, what kind of beauty entrances you? Is it art, music, flowers, photography, painting, staging, crafts, clothing, jewelry, or what—that you want your life to contribute toward?

4. **Heart.** Is the human heart your major concern? When you are gone, do you want there to be more love and compassion in the world, because you were here? If so, love or compassion for whom? Or for what?

5. **The Will or Conscience.** Is the human will or conscience your major concern? When you are gone, do you want there to be more morality, more justice, more righteousness, more honesty in the world, because you were here? If so, in what areas of human life or history, in particular? And in what geographical area?

6. **The Human Spirit.** Is the human spirit your major concern? When you are gone, do you want there to be more spirituality in the world, more faith, more compassion, more forgiveness, more love for God, and the human family in all its diversity, because you were here? If so, with what ages, people, or with what parts of human life?

7. **Entertainment.** When you are gone, do you want there to be more lightening of people's loads, more giving them perspective, more helping them to forget their cares for a spell, do you want there to be more laughter in the world, and joy, because you were here? If so, what particular kind of entertainment do you want to contribute to the world?

8. **Possessions.** Is the often false love of possessions your major concern? When you are gone, do you want there to be better stewardship of what we possess—as individuals, as a community, as a nation—in the world, because you were here? Do you want to see simplicity, savings, and a broader emphasis on the word *enough*, rather than on the word *more, more*? If so, in what areas of human life in particular?

9. **The Earth.** Is the planet on which we stand, your major concern? When you are gone, do you want there to be more protection of this fragile planet, more exploration of the world or the universe—*exploration*, not *exploitation*—more dealing with its problems and its energy, because you were here? If so, which problems or challenges in particular, draw your heart and soul?

In sum, remember that all of these are worthwhile values and outcomes, all of these are necessary and needed, in this life. The question is, which one in particular do you most want to bend your energies, your skills and gifts, your life, to serve, while you are here?

## The Prioritizing Grid

Here is our old friend, the Prioritizing Grid, again, on page 229; it looks familiar except that this time I have already entered the nine Values in random order in Section A. We need a new way here of posing the question, instead of the question we used when we were dealing with the Working Conditions petal. Here, let's try this:

Looking at the list in Section A in this sample grid, 1 and 2 would recall MIND and BODY. You can, of course, flesh these items out further, in your mind, any way you want, so that they are your own definition. So you might phrase "1 vs. 2" to mean:

"Would I like my life to be primarily remembered for

1. MIND. Bringing more knowledge, truth, or clarity to the world?"

OR

"Would I like my life to be primarily remembered for

2. BODY. Bringing more wholeness, fitness, or health to the world, more binding up of the body's wounds and strength, more feeding of the hungry, and clothing of the poor?"

Choose one of these. Even if it's hard, and you only prefer one just an eensy-teensy bit more.

Let's say you choose (2). Then, on the grid in Section B, in the little box where you see just the numbers 1 and 2, you circle the 2. You only have to decide between two Values at a time, never more than that.

Next, you compare just 2 and 3, or more specifically the Values that those numbers stand for. Choose which one is more important to you, and circle that number in the box that contains only a 2 and a 3.

Etc., etc.

When you're finished choosing just one number (i.e., just one Value) from every box with two numbers in it, in Section B, you then count how many times each number got circled, in the whole grid, and enter that count in the first empty horizontal row in Section C, right under the number in question. Continue doing this until every number has a count.

Study this ranked list, in Section D, thoughtfully. By definition, now, #1 is the most important to you *in determining what you want to do with your life*, and #9 in final rank is the least important—not necessarily in the overall scheme of things, *but certainly in determining what you want to do with your life.*

Look at your top three Values. Now you know which Value you most want your life to serve, which outcome you most want your life to produce; plus which one is next and which one is third.

You will need not just one of those Values, but the top three. Mark what they are. Those three top Values, together, determine what will be a Life that has meaning and purpose, for you.

# PRIORITIZING GRID FOR 10 ITEMS OR LESS

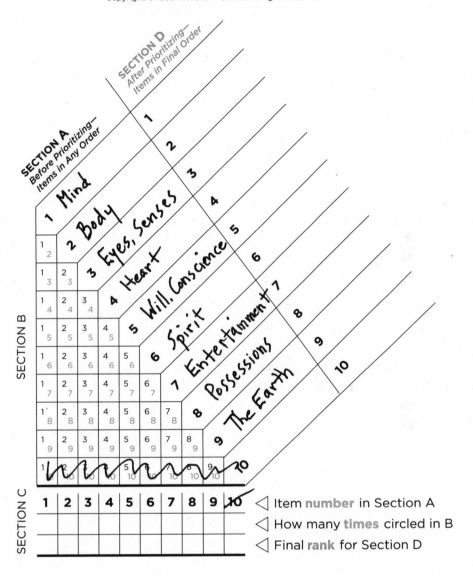

SECTION D—
After Prioritizing—
Items in Final Order

SECTION A—
Before Prioritizing—
Items in Any Order

SECTION B

SECTION C

1 Mind
2 Body
3 Eyes, Senses
4 Heart
5 Will, Conscience
6 Spirit
7 Entertainment
8 Possessions
9 The Earth

◁ Item **number** in Section A

◁ How many **times** circled in B

◁ Final **rank** for Section D

The three of them, put together in order of priority, should be entered now on your Flower Diagram, on the Values petal (pages 194–95). Put the top three in your own words, whatever makes the most sense to you.

And if you want to burrow under the headings of your top three, if you have a computer, go to the Internet, choose a browser (like Google), and type into it all the key words that occur to you—on the same line. For example, "work, beauty, gardens"—or any series of words that point toward the Values or issues you would like your life and your talents, skills, and experience, to serve.

## WHAT SKILLS DO YOU MOST ENJOY USING?

---

### Step 7: What Skills That You Already Have Do You Most Love to Use, Nevermind Your Skill *Level* in Each?

---

You are looking here for what you may think of as the basic building-blocks of your work. So, if you're going to identify your dream job, and/or attempt a thorough career-change, you must, above all else, identify your functional, transferable skills. And while you may think you know what your best and favorite skills are, in most cases your self-knowledge could probably use a little work.

A weekend should do it! In a weekend, you can inventory your *past* sufficiently so that you have a good picture of the *kind* of work you would love to be doing *in the future. (You can, of course, stretch the inventory over a number of weeks, maybe doing an hour or two one night a week, if you prefer. It's up to you as to how fast you do it.)*

## A Crash Course on "Transferable Skills"

Many people just "freeze" when they hear the word "skills."

It begins with high school job-hunters: "I haven't really got any skills," they say.

It continues with college students: "I've spent four years in college. I haven't had time to pick up any skills."

And it lasts through the middle years, especially when a person is thinking of changing his or her career: "I'll have to go back to college, and get retrained, because otherwise I won't have any skills in my new field." Or: "Well, if I claim any skills, I'll start at a very entry kind of level."

All of this fright about the word "skills" is very common, and stems from a total misunderstanding of what the word means. A misunderstanding that is shared, we might add, by altogether too many employers, or human resources departments, and other so-called "vocational experts."

By understanding the word, you will automatically put yourself way ahead of most job-hunters. And, especially if you are weighing a change of career, you can save yourself much waste of time on the adult folly called "I must go back to school." I've said it before, and I'll say it again: *maybe* you need some further schooling, but very often it is possible to make a dramatic career-change without any retraining. It all depends. And you won't really *know* whether or not you need further schooling, until you have finished all the exercises in this section of the book.

All right, then, if transferable skills are the heart of your vision and your destiny, let's see just exactly what transferable skills *are.*

Here are the most important truths you need to keep in mind about transferable, functional skills:

**1** Your transferable (functional) skills are the most basic unit—the atoms—of whatever career you may choose.

You can see this from this diagram:

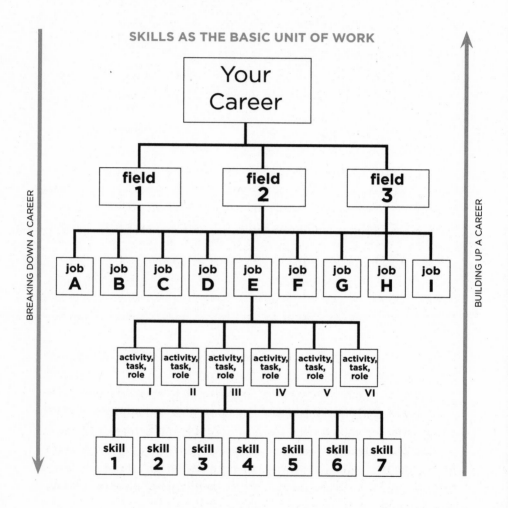

SKILLS AS THE BASIC UNIT OF WORK

Now, let's look at the very bottom level of the preceding diagram. It says "skill." That means "transferable skills." Below is a famous diagram of them, invented by the late Sidney A. Fine (reprinted by his permission).

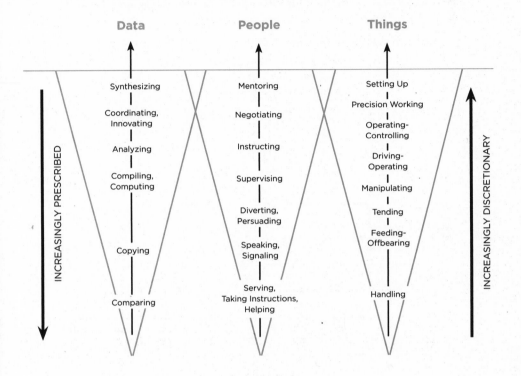

**2** You should always claim the highest skills you legitimately can, on the basis of your past performance.

As we see in the functional/transferable skills diagram above, your transferable skills break down into three *families,* according to whether you use them with **Data/Information, People,** or **Things.** And again, as this diagram makes clear, within each family there are *simple* skills, and there are higher, or *more complex* skills, so that these all can be diagrammed as inverted pyramids, with the simpler skills at the bottom, and the more complex ones in order above it.

Incidentally, as a general rule—to which there are exceptions—each *higher* skill requires you to be able also to do all those skills listed below it. So of course you can claim *those,* as well. But you want to especially claim the highest skill you legitimately can, on each pyramid, based on what you have already proven you can do, in the past.

**3** The higher your transferable skills, the more freedom you will have on the job.

Simpler skills can be, and usually are, heavily *prescribed* (by the employer), so if you claim *only* the simpler skills, you will have to *"fit in"*—following the instructions of your supervisor, and doing exactly what you are told to do. The *higher* the skills you can legitimately claim, the more you will be given discretion to carve out the job the way you want to—so that it truly fits *you.*

**4** The higher your transferable skills, the less competition you will face for whatever job you are seeking, because jobs that use such skills will rarely be advertised through normal channels.

Not for you the way of classified ads, resumes, and agencies, that we spoke of in earlier chapters. No, if you can legitimately claim higher skills, then to find such jobs you *must* follow the step-by-step process I am describing here.

The essence of this approach to job-hunting or career-change is that once you have identified your favorite transferable skills, and your favorite special knowledges, you may then approach *any organization that interests you, whether they have a known vacancy or not.* Naturally, whatever places you visit—and particularly those that have not advertised any vacancy—you will find far fewer job-hunters that you have to compete with.

In fact, if the employers you visit happen to like you well enough, they may be willing to create for you a job that does not presently exist. *In which case, you will be competing with no one, since you will be the sole applicant for that newly created job.* While this doesn't happen all the time, it is astounding to me how many times it *does* happen. *The reason* it does is that the employers often have been *thinking* about creating a new job within their organization, for quite some time—but with this and that, they just have never gotten around to *doing* it. Until you walked in.

Then they decided they didn't want to let you get away, since *good employees are as hard to find as are good employers.* And they suddenly remember that job they have been thinking about creating for many weeks or months, now. So they dust off their *intention*, create the job on the spot, and offer it to you! And if that new job is not only what *they* need, but is exactly what *you* were looking for, then you have a dream job. Match-match. Win-win.

*From our country's perspective, it is also interesting to note this: by this job-hunting initiative of yours, you have helped accelerate the creation of more jobs in your country, which is so much on everybody's mind here in the new millennium. How nice to help your country, as well as yourself!*

**5** Don't confuse transferable skills with traits.

Functional/transferable skills are often confused with **traits, temperaments**, or **type**.[6] People think transferable skills are such things as: *has lots of energy, gives attention to details, gets along well with people, shows determination, works well under pressure, is sympathetic, intuitive, persistent, dynamic, dependable,* etc. Despite popular misconceptions, these are **not** functional/transferable skills, but traits, or the *style* with which you do your transferable skills. For example, take *"gives attention to details."* If one of your *transferable skills* is *"conducting research"* then *"gives attention to details"* describes the manner or style with which you do the transferable skill called *conducting research.* If you want to know what your traits are, popular tests such as the *Myers-Briggs Type Indicator* measure that sort of thing, as we just saw in chapter 12.

---

6. The Myers-Briggs Type Indicator, or "MBTI®," measures what is called *psychological type.* For further reading about this, see:

Paul D. Tieger and Barbara Barron-Tieger, *Do What You Are: Discover the Perfect Career for You Through the Secrets of Personality Type* (Revised and Updated). Fourth Edition. 2007. Little, Brown & Company, Inc. For those who cannot obtain the MBTI®, this book includes a method for readers to identify their personality types. This is one of the most popular career books in the world. It's easy to see why. Many have found great help from the concept of personality type, and the Tiegers are masters in explaining this approach to career-choice. Highly recommended.

Donna Dunning, *What's Your Type of Career? Unlock the Secrets of Your Personality to Find Your Perfect Career Path.* 2010. Nicholas Brealey Publishing. This is a dynamite book on personality type. Donna Dunning's knowledge of "Type" is encyclopedic!

David Keirsey and Marilyn Bates, *Please Understand Me: Character & Temperament Types.* 1984. Includes the Keirsey Temperament Sorter—again, for those who cannot obtain the MBTI® (Myers-Briggs Type Indicator)—registered trademark of Consulting Psychologists Press.

If you have access to the Internet, there are clues, at least, about your traits or "type":

### Working Out Your Myers-Briggs Type

www.teamtechnology.co.uk/mb-intro/mb-intro.htm

An informative article about the Myers-Briggs

### The 16 Personality Types

www.personalitypage.com/high-level.html

A helpful site about Myers types

### What Is Your Myers-Briggs Personality Type?

www.personalitypathways.com/type_inventory.html

www.personalitypathways.com

Another article about personality types; also, there's a Myers-Briggs Applications page, with links to test resources

### Myers-Briggs Foundation home page

www.myersbriggs.org

The official website of the Foundation; lots of testing resources

### Human Metrics Test (Jung Typology)

www.humanmetrics.com/cgi-win/JTypes2.asp

Free test, loosely based on the Myers-Briggs

### Myers-Briggs Type Indicator Online

www.discoveryourpersonality.com/MBTI.html

On this site you can find the official Myers-Briggs test, $60

### The Keirsey Temperament Sorter

http://keirsey.com

Free test, similar to the Myers-Briggs

## "I Wouldn't Recognize My Skills If They Came Up and Shook Hands with Me"

Now that you know what transferable skills technically *are*, the problem that awaits you now, is figuring out your own. If you are one of the few lucky people who already know what your transferable skills are, blessed are you. Write them down, and put them in the order of preference, for you, on the Flower Diagram (pages 194–95).

If, however, you don't know what your skills are (and 95 percent of all workers *don't*), then you will need some help. Fortunately, there is an exercise to help.

It involves the following steps:

### 1. Write a Story (The First of Seven)

Yes, I know, I know. You can't do this exercise because you don't like to write. *Writers are a very rare breed.* That's what thousands of job-hunters have told me, over the years. And for years I kind of believed them—until "blogging" came along. Let's face it: we human beings are "a writing people," and we only need a topic we have a real passion for, or interest in, for the writing genie to spring forth from within each of us, pen or keyboard in hand.

So, call the *Seven Stories* you're about to write your personal *offline blog*, if you prefer. But start writing. Please.

Here is a specific example:

> "A number of years ago, I wanted to be able to take a summer trip with my wife and four children. I had a very limited budget, and could not afford to put my family up in motels. I decided to rig our station wagon as a camper.
>
> "First I went to the library to get some books on campers. I read those books. Next I designed a plan of what I had to build, so that I could outfit the inside of the station wagon, as well as topside. Then I went and purchased the necessary wood. On weekends, over a period of six weeks, I first constructed, in my driveway, the shell for the 'second story' on my station wagon. Then I cut doors, windows, and placed a six-drawer bureau within that shell.

*I mounted it on top of the wagon, and pinioned it in place by driving two-by-fours under the station wagon's rack on top. I then outfitted the inside of the station wagon, back in the wheel-well, with a table and a bench on either side, that I made.*

"The result was a complete homemade camper, which I put together when we were about to start our trip, and then disassembled after we got back home. When we went on our summer trip, we were able to be on the road for four weeks, yet stayed within our budget, since we didn't have to stay at motels. I estimate I saved $1,900 on motel bills, during that summer's vacation."

Ideally, each story you write should have the following parts, as illustrated above:

## I.

Your goal: what you wanted to accomplish: *"I wanted to be able to take a summer trip with my wife and four children."*

## II.

Some kind of hurdle, obstacle, or constraint that you faced (self-imposed or otherwise): *"I had a very limited budget, and could not afford to put my family up in motels."*

A description of what you did, step by step (how you set about to ultimately achieve your goal, above, in spite of this hurdle or constraint): *"I decided to rig our station wagon as a camper. First I went to the library to get some books on campers. I read those books. Next I designed a plan of what I had to build, so that I could outfit the inside of the station wagon, as well as topside. Then I went and purchased the necessary wood. On weekends, over a period of six weeks, I . . ."* etc., etc.

### IV.

A description of the outcome or result: *"When we went on our summer trip, we were able to be on the road for four weeks, yet stayed within our budget, since we didn't have to stay at motels."*

### V.

Any measurable/quantifiable statement of that outcome, that you can think of: *"I estimate I saved $1,900 on motel bills, during that summer's vacation."*

Now write *your* story, using the sample on the next page as a guide.

*Don't* pick a story where you achieved something *big.* At least to begin with, write a story about a time when you had fun!

Do not try to be too brief. This isn't Twitter.

If you absolutely can't think of any experiences you've had where you enjoyed yourself, and accomplished something, then try this: describe the seven most enjoyable jobs that you've had; or seven roles you've had so far in your life, such as: wife, mother, cook, homemaker, volunteer in the community, citizen, dressmaker, student, etc. Tell us something you did or accomplished, in each role.

**2. Analyze Your Story, to See What Transferable Skills You Used**

On page 241, write the title of your first story *above* the number 1. Then work your way down the column *below* that number 1, asking yourself in each case: "Did I use this skill in *this story*?"

**SAMPLE**

"The Halloween Experience. I won a prize on Halloween for dressing up as a horse."

THIS WON'T DO

THIS WILL DO

**SAMPLE**

"My Halloween Experience When I Was Seven Years Old. Details: When I was seven, I decided I wanted to go out on Halloween dressed as a horse. I wanted to be the front end of the horse, and I talked a friend of mine into being the back end of the horse. But, at the last moment he backed out, and I was faced with the prospect of not being able to go out on Halloween. At this point, I decided to figure out some way of getting dressed up as the whole horse, myself. I took a fruit basket, and tied some string to both sides of the basket's rim, so that I could tie the basket around my rear end. This filled me out enough so that the costume fit me, by myself. I then fixed some strong thread to the tail so that I could make it wag by moving my hands. When Halloween came I not only went out and had a ball, but I won a prize as well."

If the answer is "Yes," color the little square in, with a red pen or whatever you choose.

Example: "Did I use my hands, assembling something, in *this* story?" If so, color in the square under Column 1, and opposite A, 1. If not, leave it blank.

Next: "Did I use my hands constructing something, in *this* story?" If so, color in the square under Column 1, and opposite A, 2. If not, leave it blank.

Work your way through the entire Transferable Skills Inventory that way, with your first story.

# TRANSFERABLE
# SKILLS
## INVENTORY

| 1 | 2 | 3 | 4 | 5 | 6 | 7 | Name of Skill | Example of a Situation Where That Skill Is Used |
|---|---|---|---|---|---|---|---|---|
| | | | | | | | **A. Using My Hands** | |
| | | | | | | | 1. assembling | as with kits, etc. |
| | | | | | | | 2. constructing | as with carpentry, etc. |
| | | | | | | | 3. or building | |
| | | | | | | | 4. operating tools | as with drills, mixers, etc. |
| | | | | | | | 5. or machinery | as with sewing machines, etc. |
| | | | | | | | 6. or equipment | as with trucks, station wagons, etc. |
| | | | | | | | 7. showing manual or finger dexterity | as with throwing, sewing, etc. |
| | | | | | | | 8. handling with precision and/or speed | as with an assembly line, etc. |
| | | | | | | | 9. fixing or repairing | as with autos or mending, etc. |
| | | | | | | | 10. other | |
| | | | | | | | **B. Using My Body** | |
| | | | | | | | 11. muscular coordination | as in skiing, gymnastics, etc. |
| | | | | | | | 12. being physically active | as in exercising, hiking, etc. |
| | | | | | | | 13. doing outdoor activities | as in camping, etc. |
| | | | | | | | 14. other | |
| | | | | | | | **C. Using Words** | |
| | | | | | | | 15. reading | as with books; with understanding |
| | | | | | | | 16. copying | as with manuscripts; skillfully |
| | | | | | | | 17. writing or communicating | as with letters; interestingly |
| | | | | | | | 18. talking or speaking | as on the telephone; interestingly |
| | | | | | | | 19. teaching, training | as in front of groups; with animation |
| | | | | | | | 20. editing | as in improving a child's sentences in an essay, etc. |
| | | | | | | | 21. memory for words | as in remembering people's names, book titles, etc. |
| | | | | | | | 22. other | |

continued

*Self-Inventory (The Flower Exercise)*

| Sample Halloween | 1 | 2 | 3 | 4 | 5 | 6 | 7 | Name of Skill | Example of a Situation Where That Skill Is Used |
|---|---|---|---|---|---|---|---|---|---|
| | | | | | | | | **D. Using My Senses (Eyes, Ears, Nose, Taste, or Touch)** | |
| ▓ | | | | | | | | 23. observing, surveying | as in watching something with the eyes, etc. |
| | | | | | | | | 24. examining or inspecting | as in looking at a child's bumps, etc. |
| ▨ | | | | | | | | 25. diagnosing, determining | as in deciding if food is cooked yet |
| | | | | | | | | 26. showing attention to detail | as in shop, in sewing, etc. |
| | | | | | | | | 27. other | |
| | | | | | | | | **E. Using Numbers** | |
| | | | | | | | | 28. taking inventory | as in the pantry, shop, etc. |
| | | | | | | | | 29. counting | as in a classroom, bureau drawers |
| | | | | | | | | 30. calculating, computing | as in a checkbook, arithmetic |
| | | | | | | | | 31. keeping financial records, bookkeeping | as with a budget, etc. |
| | | | | | | | | 32. managing money | as in a checking account, bank, store, etc. |
| | | | | | | | | 33. developing a budget | as for a family, etc. |
| | | | | | | | | 34. number memory | as with telephone numbers, etc. |
| | | | | | | | | 35. rapid manipulation of numbers | as with doing arithmetic in the head |
| | | | | | | | | 36. other | |
| | | | | | | | | **F. Using Intuition** | |
| ▨ | | | | | | | | 37. showing foresight | as in planning ahead, predicting consequences, etc. |
| ▨ | | | | | | | | 38. quickly sizing up a person or situation accurately | as in everything, rather than just one or two details about them, etc. |
| | | | | | | | | 39. having insight | as to why people act the way they do, etc. |
| | | | | | | | | 40. acting on gut reactions | as in making decisions, deciding to trust someone, etc. |
| ▓ | | | | | | | | 41. ability to visualize third-dimension | as in drawings, models, blue-prints, memory for faces, etc. |
| | | | | | | | | 42. other | |
| | | | | | | | | **G. Using Analytical Thinking or Logic** | |
| | | | | | | | | 43. researching, information gathering | as in finding out where a particular street is in a strange city |
| ▨ | | | | | | | | 44. analyzing, dissecting | as with the ingredients in a recipe, material, etc. |
| | | | | | | | | 45. organizing, classifying | as with laundry, etc. |
| ▓ | | | | | | | | 46. problem solving | as with figuring out how to get to a place, etc. |
| | | | | | | | | 47. separating important from unimportant | as with complaints, or cleaning the attic, etc. |
| | | | | | | | | 48. diagnosing | as in cause-and-effect relations, tracing problems to their sources |
| | | | | | | | | 49. systematizing, putting things in order | as in laying out tools or utensils in the order you will be using them |

| Sample Halloween | 1 | 2 | 3 | 4 | 5 | 6 | 7 | Name of Skill | Example of a Situation Where That Skill Is Used |
|---|---|---|---|---|---|---|---|---|---|
| | | | | | | | | 50. comparing, perceiving similarities | as with different brands in the supermarket, etc. |
| | | | | | | | | 51. testing, screening | as with cooking, deciding what to wear, etc. |
| ▨ | | | | | | | | 52. reviewing, evaluating | as in looking at something you made, to see how you could have made it better, faster, etc. |
| | | | | | | | | 53. other | |
| | | | | | | | | **H. Using Originality or Creativity** | |
| ▨ | | | | | | | | 54. imaginative, imagining | as in figuring out new ways to do things, or making up stories, etc. |
| | | | | | | | | 55. inventing, creating | as with processes, products, figures, words, etc. |
| | | | | | | | | 56. designing, developing | as with new recipes, new gadgets |
| | | | | | | | | 57. improvising, experiments | as in camping, when you've left some of the equipment home, etc. |
| | | | | | | | | 58. adapting, improving | as with something that doesn't work quite right, etc. |
| | | | | | | | | 59. other | |
| | | | | | | | | **I. Using Helpfulness** | |
| | | | | | | | | 60. helping, being of service | as when someone is in need, etc. |
| | | | | | | | | 61. showing sensitivity to others' feelings | as in a heated discussion, argument |
| | | | | | | | | 62. listening | |
| | | | | | | | | 63. developing rapport | as with someone who is initially a stranger, etc. |
| | | | | | | | | 64. conveying warmth, caring | as with someone who is upset, ill |
| | | | | | | | | 65. understanding | as when someone tells how they feel, etc. |
| | | | | | | | | 66. drawing out people | as when someone is reluctant to talk, share |
| | | | | | | | | 67. offering support | as when someone is facing a difficulty alone, etc. |
| | | | | | | | | 68. demonstrating empathy | as in weeping with those who weep |
| | | | | | | | | 69. representing others' wishes accurately | as when one parent tells the other what a child of theirs wants, etc. |
| | | | | | | | | 70. motivating | as in getting people past hangups, and into action, etc. |
| | | | | | | | | 71. sharing credit, appreciation | as when working in teams, etc. |
| | | | | | | | | 72. raising others' self-esteem | as when you make someone feel better, less guilty, etc. |
| | | | | | | | | 73. healing, curing | as with physical, emotional, and spiritual ailments, etc. |
| | | | | | | | | 74. counseling, guiding | as when someone doesn't know what to do, etc. |
| | | | | | | | | 75. other | |

continued

*Self-Inventory (The Flower Exercise)*

| Sample Halloween | 1 | 2 | 3 | 4 | 5 | 6 | 7 | Name of Skill | Example of a Situation Where That Skill Is Used |
|---|---|---|---|---|---|---|---|---|---|
| | | | | | | | | **J. Using Artistic Abilities** | |
| | | | | | | | | 76. composing music | |
| | | | | | | | | 77. playing (a) musical instrument(s), singing | |
| | | | | | | | | 78. fashioning or shaping things, materials | as in handicrafts, sculpturing, etc. |
| | | | | | | | | 79. dealing creatively with symbols or images | as in stained glass, jewelry, etc. |
| ▨ | | | | | | | | 80. dealing creatively with spaces, shapes, or faces | as in photography, art, architectural design, etc. |
| | | | | | | | | 81. dealing creatively with colors | as in painting, decorating, making clothes, etc. |
| | | | | | | | | 82. conveying feelings and thoughts through body, face, and/or voice tone | as in acting, public speaking, teaching, dancing, etc. |
| | | | | | | | | 83. conveying feelings and thoughts through drawing, paintings, etc. | as in art, etc. |
| | | | | | | | | 84. using words on a very high level | as in poetry, playwriting, novels |
| | | | | | | | | 85. other | |
| | | | | | | | | **K. Using Leadership, Being Up-front** | |
| ▨ | | | | | | | | 86. beginning new tasks, ideas, projects | as in starting a group, initiating a clothing drive, etc. |
| | | | | | | | | 87. taking first move in relationships | as with stranger on bus, plane, train, etc. |
| | | | | | | | | 88. organizing a game at a picnic, etc. | as with a Scout troop, a team, |
| | | | | | | | | 89. leading, directing others | as with a field trip, cheerleading |
| | | | | | | | | 90. promoting change | as in a family, community, organization, etc. |
| ▨ | | | | | | | | 91. making decisions | as in places where decisions affect others, etc. |
| ▨ | | | | | | | | 92. taking risks | as in sticking up for someone in a fight, etc. |
| ▨ | | | | | | | | 93. getting up before a group, performing | as in demonstrating a product, lecturing, making people laugh, entertaining, public speaking |
| ▨ | | | | | | | | 94. selling, promoting, negotiating, persuading | as with a product, idea, materials, in a garage sale, argument, recruiting, changing someone's mind |
| | | | | | | | | 95. other | |
| | | | | | | | | **L. Using Follow-Through** | |
| | | | | | | | | 96. using what others have developed | as in working with a kit, etc. |
| ▨ | | | | | | | | 97. following through on plans, instructions | as in picking up children on schedule |
| | | | | | | | | 98. attending to details | as with embroidering a design on a shirt, etc. |
| | | | | | | | | 99. classifying, recording, filing, retrieving | as with data, materials, letters, ideas, information, etc. |
| | | | | | | | | 100. other | |

Voilà! You are done with Story #1. However, "one swallow doth not a summer make," so the fact that you used certain skills in this first story doesn't tell you much. What you are looking for is **patterns**—transferable skills that keep reappearing in story after story. They keep reappearing because they are your favorites (assuming you chose stories where you were *really* enjoying yourself).

### 3. Write Six Other Stories, and Analyze Them for Transferable Skills

Now, write Story #2, from any period in your life, analyze it using the keys, etc., etc. And keep this process up, until you have written, and analyzed, seven stories.

### 4. Patterns and Priorities

When you've finished this whole Inventory, for all seven of your accomplishments/achievements/jobs/roles or whatever, you want to look for PATTERNS and PRIORITIES.

"RUN, SPOT, RUN."

a) For Patterns, because it isn't a matter of whether you used a skill once only, but rather whether you used it again and again. "Once" proves nothing; "again and again" is very convincing.

b) For Priorities (that is, Which Skills Are Most Important to You?), because the job you eventually choose may not be able to use all of your skills. You need to know *what you are willing to trade off, and what you are not.* This requires that you know which skills, or family of skills, are most important to you.

### Double-Color, Prioritize

When you are done filling out the Transferable Skills Inventory, it will help you greatly in deciding Patterns and Priorities if you will go photo-copy the preceding four pages of the Skills Inventory and spread them all out on a table or on the floor. With these four grid pages side by side you now have a complete view of the boxes you checked, or colored in, as you analyzed your stories. Next, take a red pen or pencil, and read over each skill description where you colored in more than once. As you now read each of these skill descriptions, say to yourself: "Sure, I used this skill in the past. But do I STILL REALLY ENJOY using this skill today?" If your answer is "Yes," put a red circle around the number in front of that skill. (The numbers are not significant; they're just "placeholders.") Next, if, in that particular skill description there are multiple phrases, but one or two of these really grabs you, then underline just that phrase, in red. When you've run through all four pages of the skills grid, in this manner, look it all over, choose your top ten favorites from among all the circled ones, and copy these ten onto a separate sheet of blank paper. Then prioritize these ten, using the grid on the next page.

# PRIORITIZING GRID FOR 10 ITEMS OR LESS

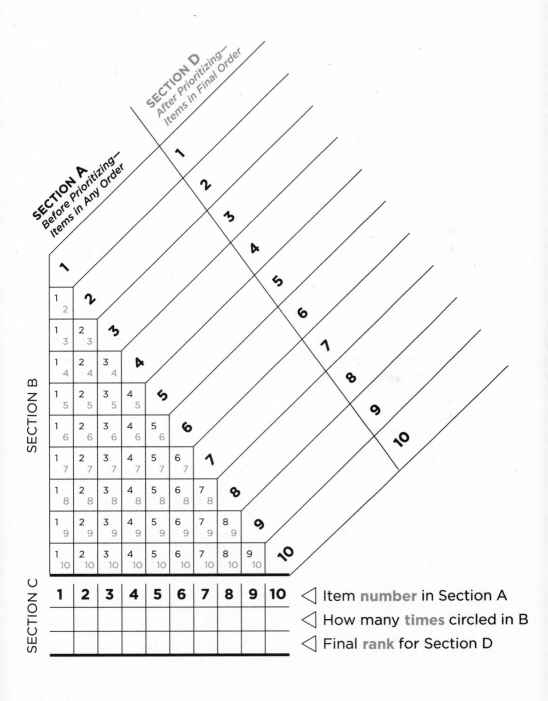

SECTION D
After Prioritizing—
Items in Final Order

SECTION A
Before Prioritizing—
Items in Any Order

SECTION B

SECTION C

◁ Item **number** in Section A
◁ How many **times** circled in B
◁ Final **rank** for Section D

*Self-Inventory (The Flower Exercise)*          247

Now, list the top six or ten, in order of priority, on the diagram below.

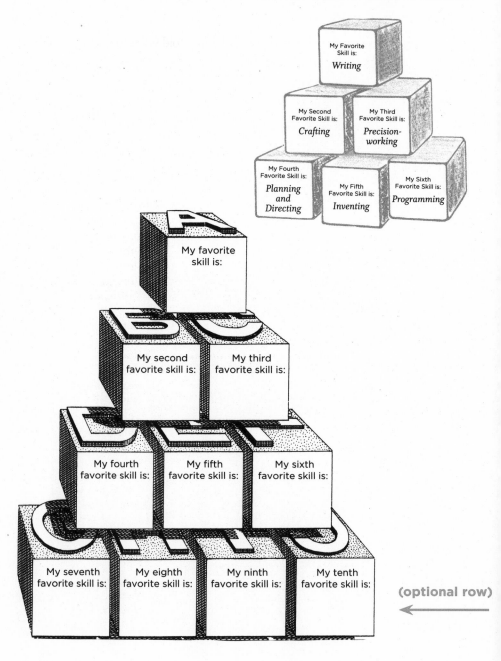

My Favorite Skill is:
*Writing*

My Second Favorite Skill is:
*Crafting*

My Third Favorite Skill is:
*Precision-working*

My Fourth Favorite Skill is:
*Planning and Directing*

My Fifth Favorite Skill is:
*Inventing*

My Sixth Favorite Skill is:
*Programming*

My favorite skill is:

My second favorite skill is:

My third favorite skill is:

My fourth favorite skill is:

My fifth favorite skill is:

My sixth favorite skill is:

My seventh favorite skill is:

My eighth favorite skill is:

My ninth favorite skill is:

My tenth favorite skill is:

**(optional row)**

## 5. "Flesh Out" Your Favorite Transferable Skills with Your Traits

We discussed traits earlier (pages 235–36). In general, traits describe:

How you deal with time, and promptness.

How you deal with people and emotions.

How you deal with authority, and being told what to do at your job.

How you deal with supervision, and being told how to do your job.

How you deal with impulse vs. self-discipline, within yourself.

How you deal with initiative vs. response, within yourself.

How you deal with crises or problems.

### A CHECKLIST OF MY STRONGEST TRAITS

## I am very . . .

- ❑ Accurate
- ❑ Achievement-oriented
- ❑ Adaptable
- ❑ Adept
- ❑ Adept at having fun
- ❑ Adventuresome
- ❑ Alert
- ❑ Appreciative
- ❑ Assertive
- ❑ Astute
- ❑ Authoritative
- ❑ Calm
- ❑ Cautious
- ❑ Charismatic
- ❑ Competent
- ❑ Consistent
- ❑ Contagious in my enthusiasm
- ❑ Cooperative
- ❑ Courageous
- ❑ Creative
- ❑ Decisive
- ❑ Deliberate
- ❑ Dependable/have dependability
- ❑ Diligent
- ❑ Diplomatic

- ❑ Discreet
- ❑ Driving
- ❑ Dynamic
- ❑ Extremely economical
- ❑ Effective
- ❑ Energetic
- ❑ Enthusiastic
- ❑ Exceptional
- ❑ Exhaustive
- ❑ Experienced
- ❑ Expert
- ❑ Firm
- ❑ Flexible
- ❑ Humanly oriented
- ❑ Impulsive
- ❑ Independent
- ❑ Innovative
- ❑ Knowledgeable
- ❑ Loyal
- ❑ Methodical
- ❑ Objective
- ❑ Open-minded
- ❑ Outgoing
- ❑ Outstanding
- ❑ Patient
- ❑ Penetrating
- ❑ Perceptive
- ❑ Persevering

- ❑ Persistent
- ❑ Pioneering
- ❑ Practical
- ❑ Professional
- ❑ Protective
- ❑ Punctual
- ❑ Quick/work quickly
- ❑ Rational
- ❑ Realistic
- ❑ Reliable
- ❑ Resourceful
- ❑ Responsible
- ❑ Responsive
- ❑ Safeguarding
- ❑ Self-motivated
- ❑ Self-reliant
- ❑ Sensitive
- ❑ Sophisticated, very sophisticated
- ❑ Strong
- ❑ Supportive
- ❑ Tactful
- ❑ Thorough
- ❑ Unique
- ❑ Unusual
- ❑ Versatile
- ❑ Vigorous

You need to flesh out your skill-description for each of your six or more favorite skills so that you are able to describe each of your talents or skills with more than just a one-word verb or gerund, like organizing.

Let's take organizing as our example. You tell us proudly: "I'm good at organizing." That's a fine start at defining your skills, but unfortunately it doesn't yet tell us much. Organizing WHAT? People, as at a party? Nuts and bolts, as on a workbench? Or lots of information, as on a computer? These are three entirely different skills. The one word *organizing* doesn't tell us which one is yours.

So, please flesh out each of your favorite transferable skills with an object—some kind of Data/Information, or some kind of People, or some kind of Thing, and then add an adverb or adjective, too.

Why adjectives? Well, "I'm good at organizing information painstakingly and logically" and "I'm good at organizing information in a flash, by intuition," are two entirely different skills. The difference between them is spelled out not in the verb, nor in the object, but in the adjectival or adverbial phrase there at the end. So, expand each definition of your six or more favorite skills, in the fashion I have just described.

> When you are face-to-face with a person-who-has-the-power-to-hire-you, you want to be able to explain what makes you different from nineteen other people who can basically do the same thing that you can do. It is often the adjective or adverb that will save your life, during that explanation.

## A Picture Is Worth a Thousand Words

When you have your top favorite skills, and *fleshed them out*, it is time to put them on the central petal of the Flower Diagram. Copy this diagram (from here or pages 194–95) on a larger piece of paper (or cardboard) if you need to.

# THE FLOWER
## "THAT ONE PIECE OF PAPER"

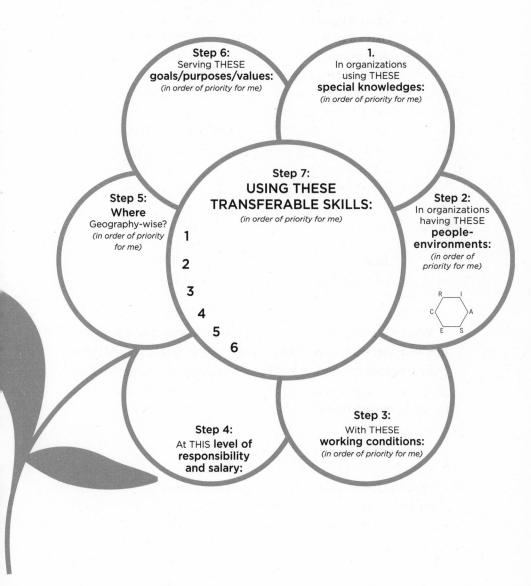

**Step 6:**
Serving THESE
**goals/purposes/values:**
*(in order of priority for me)*

**1.**
In organizations
using THESE
**special knowledges:**
*(in order of priority for me)*

**Step 5:**
**Where**
Geography-wise?
*(in order of priority for me)*

**Step 7:**
# USING THESE
# TRANSFERABLE SKILLS:
*(in order of priority for me)*

1

2

3

4

5

6

**Step 2:**
In organizations
having THESE
**people-
environments:**
*(in order of priority for me)*

R | I
C | A
E | S

**Step 4:**
At THIS **level of
responsibility
and salary:**

**Step 3:**
With THESE
**working conditions:**
*(in order of priority for me)*

## Informational Interviewing, Step 1:
## GIVING YOUR FLOWER A NAME

Well you're done with The Flower. Now what?

Put that sheet on a wall, or on the door of your refrigerator. And there you have it: a simple picture (as it were) of You.

And now what should happen? Many of you will look at your completed Flower Diagram, and you won't have *a clue* as to what job or career it points to. If that's *you*, take a piece of paper, with pen or pencil, or go to your computer, and keyboard in hand, make some notes:

1. First, look at your Flower Diagram, and from the center petal choose your three to five most *favorite* skills.

2. Then, look at your Flower Diagram and write down your three favorite special knowledges (interests, or favorite fields, or Fields of Fascination—whatever you want to call them).

3. Now, take both these notes, and show them to at least five friends, family members, or professionals whom you know. Yes, we're back to our old friend, Informational Interviewing—interviewing people solely to get information (see chapter 7).

4. Jot down *everything* these five people suggest or recommend to you.

5. After you have finished talking to them, you want to go home and look at all these notes. Anything helpful or valuable here? If not, if none of it looks valuable, then set it aside, and go talk to five more of your friends, acquaintances, or people you know in the business world or nonprofit sector. Repeat, as necessary.

6. When you finally have some worthwhile suggestions, sit down, look over their combined suggestions, and ask yourself some questions.

---

As you will recall, skills usually point toward a job-title or job-level, while interests or special knowledges usually point toward a career field. So, you want to ask them, in the case of your skills, *What job-title or jobs do these skills suggest to you?*

---

Then ask them, in the case of your favorite special knowledges, *What career fields do these suggest to you?*

- First, you want to look at what these friends suggested about your skills: *what job or jobs came to their minds?* It will help you to know that most jobs can be classified under nineteen headings or families, as below. Which of these nineteen do your friends' suggestions predominantly point to? Which of these nineteen grabs you?

## JOB FAMILIES

1. Executive, Administrative, and Managerial Occupations
2. Engineers, Surveyors, and Architects
3. Natural Scientists and Mathematicians
4. Social Scientists, Social Workers, Religious Workers, and Lawyers
5. Teachers, Counselors, Librarians, and Archivists
6. Health Diagnosing and Treating Practitioners
7. Registered Nurses, Pharmacists, Dieticians, Therapists, and Physician Assistants
8. Health Technologists and Technicians
9. Technologists and Technicians in Other Fields: Computer Specialists, Programmers, Information Technicians, Information Specialists, etc.
10. Writers, Artists, Digital Artists, and Entertainers
11. Marketing and Sales Occupations
12. Administrative Support Occupations, including Clerical
13. Service Occupations
14. Agricultural, Forestry, and Fishing Occupations
15. Mechanics and Repairers
16. Construction and Extractive Occupations
17. Production Occupations
18. Transportation and Material-Moving Occupations
19. Handlers, Equipment Cleaners, Helpers, and Laborers

- Next, you want to look at what your friends suggested about your interests or special knowledges: *what fields or careers came to their minds?* It will help you to know that most of the job families above can be classified under four broad headings: *Agriculture, Manufacturing, Information Industries, and Service Industries.* Which of these four do your friends' suggestions predominantly *point to?* Which of these four grabs you?
- The next question you want to ask yourself is: job-titles and career-fields can be broken down further, according to whether you like to work primarily with *people* or primarily with *information/data* or primarily with *things.*

Let's take the field of agriculture as an example. Within this field, you could be driving tractors or other farm machinery—and thus work primarily with *things;* or you could be gathering statistics about crop growth for some state agency—and thus work primarily with *information/data;* or you could be teaching agriculture in a college classroom—and thus work primarily with *people* and *ideas.* Almost all fields as well as career families offer you these three choices, though *of course* many jobs combine two of the three in some intricate way.

Still, you do want to tell yourself what your *preference* is, and what you *primarily* want to work with. Otherwise, your job-hunt or career-change is going to leave you very frustrated at the end. In this matter, it is often your favorite skill that will give you the clue. If it *doesn't*, then go back and look at the whole Skills petal, on your Flower Diagram. What do you think? Are your favorite skills weighted more toward working with *people*, or toward working with *information/data*, or toward working with *things?*

And, no matter what that *petal* suggests, which of the three do you absolutely prefer, in your heart of hearts?

Just remember what you are trying to do here, in finding a name for your flower. What you call it—"name of Flower," "name of a field based on your favorite subjects," "the name of your new career," or whatever—doesn't matter. You are trying to find the names of careers or jobs that would give you a chance to use your skills in the most effective way.

Just make sure that you get the names of at least *two* careers, or jobs, that you think you could be happy doing. Never, ever, put all your eggs in one basket. The secret of surviving out there in the jungle is *having alternatives.*

Be careful. Be thorough. Be persistent. This is your life you're working on, and your future. Make it glorious. Whatever it takes, find out the name of your ideal career, your ideal occupation, your ideal job—*or jobs.*

## Informational Interviewing, Step 2:
## FINDING WHAT KINDS OF ORGANIZATIONS
## HAVE SUCH JOBS

Before you think of individual places where you might like to work, it is necessary to stop and think of all the *kinds* of places where one might get hired.

Let's take an example. Suppose in your new career you want to be a teacher. You must then ask yourself: *what kinds of places hire teachers?* You might answer, *"just schools"*—and finding that schools in your geographical area have no openings, you might say, *"Well, there are no jobs for people in this career."*

But wait a minute! There are countless other *kinds* of organizations and agencies out there, besides schools, that employ *teachers.* For example, corporate training and educational departments, workshop sponsors, foundations, private research firms, educational consultants, teachers' associations, professional and trade societies, military bases, state and local councils on higher education, fire and police training academies, and so on and so forth.

*"Kinds* of places" also means places with different *hiring options,* besides full-time, such as:

- places that would employ you part-time (maybe you'll end up deciding to hold down two or even three part-time jobs, which altogether would add up to one full-time job, in order to give yourself more variety);
- places that take temporary workers, on assignment for one project at a time;
- places that take consultants, one project at a time;
- places that operate primarily with volunteers, etc.;
- places that are nonprofit;

- places that are for-profit;
- and, don't forget, places that you yourself could start up, should you decide to be your own boss (see chapter 10).

During this interviewing for information, you will not only talk to people who have a broad overview of the career or Flower Name that you have come up with. You will also want to talk, eventually, to actual workers in those kinds of organizations, who can tell you in more detail (than the overview-people can) exactly what the tasks are in the organizations you are intrigued by.

## Informational Interviewing, Step 3:
## FINDING THE NAMES OF PARTICULAR PLACES

As you interview workers about their jobs or careers, they will probably innocently mention actual names of organizations that have such jobs—plus what's good or bad about the place. This is important information for you. Jot it all down. Keep notes *as though it were part of your religion.*

But you will want to supplement what they have told you, by seeking out other people you can make the following little speech to: "I'm interested in this kind of organization, because I want to do this kind of job; do you know of particular places I might investigate, and if so, where are they located?" Use personal interviews, use LinkedIn, use the Yellow pages, use search engines, to try to find the answer(s) to that question.

Now when this name-gathering is all done, what do you have? Well, either you'll have *too few names* of places to work, or you'll end up with *too much information*—too many names of places that hire people in the career that interests you. There are ways of dealing with either of these eventualities. We'll take this last scenario, first.

### Cutting Down the Territory

To avoid ending up with the names of too many places, you will want to cut down the territory, so you are left with *a manageable number* of "targets" to research and visit.[7]

---

7. If you resist this idea of *cutting down the territory*—if you feel you could be happy anywhere just as long as you were using your favorite skills—then you'll have to go visit them all. Good luck! We'll see you in about forty-three years.

Let's take an example. Suppose you discover that the career that interests you the most is *welding.* You want to be a welder. Well, that's a beginning. You've cut the 23 million U.S. job-markets down to:

- I want to work in a place that hires welders.

But the territory is still too large. There might be thousands of places in the country, that use welders. You can't go visit them all. So, you've got to cut down the territory, further. Suppose that on your Geography petal you said that you really want to live and work in the San Jose area of California. That's helpful: that cuts down the territory further. Now your goal is:

- I want to work in a place that hires welders, within the San Jose area.

But, the territory is still too large. There could be 100, 200, 300 organizations that fit that description. So you look at your Flower Diagram for further help, and you notice that under *working conditions* you said you wanted to work for an organization with fifty or fewer employees. Good, now your goal is:

- I want to work in a place that hires welders, within the San Jose area, that has fifty or fewer employees.

This territory may still be too large. So you look again at your Flower Diagram for further guidance, and you see that you said you wanted to work for an organization that works with, or produces, wheels. So now your statement of what you're looking for, becomes:

- I want to work in a place that hires welders, within the San Jose area, has fifty or fewer employees, and makes wheels.

Using your Flower Diagram, you can thus keep cutting down the territory, until the *"targets"* of your job-hunt are no more than ten places. That's a manageable number of places for you to *start with.* You can always expand the list later, if none of these ten turns out to be promising or interesting.

5,708,000 POSSIBLE TARGETS

57,000 POSSIBLE TARGETS

5,700 POSSIBLE TARGETS

1,000 POSSIBLE TARGETS

500 POSSIBLE TARGETS

300 POSSIBLE TARGETS (EMPLOYERS)

60 POSSIBLE TARGETS

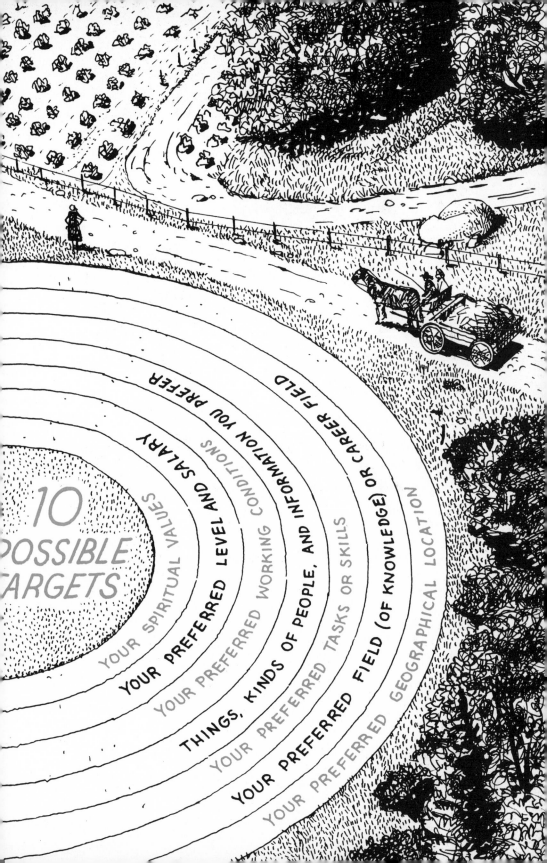

### Expanding the Territory

Sometimes your problem will be just the opposite. We come here to the second possibility: if your Informational Interviewing doesn't turn up enough names of places where you could get hired in your new career, then you're going to have to expand your list. You're going to have to consult some directories.

Your salvation is going to be, first of all, the Yellow Pages of your local phone book. Look under every heading that is of any interest to you. Also, see if the local chamber of commerce publishes a business directory; often it will list not only small companies but also local divisions of larger companies, with names of department heads; sometimes they will even include the North American Industry Classification System (NAICS) codes, should you care. If you are diligent here, you won't lack for names, believe me—unless it's a very small town you live in, in which case you'll need to cast your net a little wider, to include other towns, villages, or cities that are within commuting distance.

## Informational Interviewing, Step 4:
## TALKING TO WORKERS, "TRYING ON" JOBS

During Informational Interviewing, you want to talk to people who are actually doing the work you think you'd love to do. Why? In effect, you are mentally *trying on jobs* to see if they fit you.

It is exactly analogous to your going to a clothing store and trying on different suits (or dresses) that you see in their window or on their racks. Why try them on? Well, the suits or dresses that look *terrific* in the window don't always look so hot when you see them on *you*. The clothes don't hang quite right, etc.

Likewise, careers that *sound* terrific in books or in your imagination don't always look so great when you see them up close and personal.

What you're ultimately trying to find is a career that looks terrific inside and out—in the window, *and* also on you. Here are some questions that will help *with workers who are actually doing the career you think you might like to do*:

- How did you get into this work?
- What do you like the most about it?
- What do you like the least about it?
- And, where else could I find people who do this kind of work? (*You should always ask them for more than one name, here, so that if you run into a dead end at any point, you can easily go visit the other names they suggested.*)

If it becomes apparent to you, during the course of any of these Informational Interviews, that this career, occupation, or job you were exploring definitely *doesn't* fit you, then the last question (above) gets turned into a different kind of inquiry:

- Do you have any ideas as to who else I could talk to, about my skills and special knowledges or interests—so I can find out how they all might fit together, in one job or career?

Then go visit the people they suggest.

If they can't think of *anyone*, ask them if they know who *might* know.

### "THEY SAY I HAVE TO GO BACK TO SCHOOL, BUT I HAVEN'T THE TIME OR THE MONEY"

Next step: having found the names of jobs or careers that interest you, having mentally *tried them on* to see if they fit, you next want to find out how much training, etc., it takes, to get into that field or career. You ask the same people you have been talking to, previously.

More times than not, you will hear *bad news*. They will tell you something like: "In order to be hired for this job, you have to have a master's degree and ten years' experience at it."

If you have the time, and the money, fine! But what if you don't? Then you search for *exceptions:*

"*Yes, but do you know of anyone in this field who got into it without that master's degree, and ten years' experience?*

*And where might I find him or her?*

*And if you don't know of any such person, who might know?*"

Throughout Informational Interviewing, don't assume anything ("But I just assumed that . . ."). Question *all* assumptions, no matter how many people tell you that "this is just the way things are."

Keep in mind that there are people *out there* who will tell you something that absolutely *isn't* so, with every conviction in their being—because they *think* it's true. Sincerity they have, 100 percent. Accuracy is something else again. You will need to check and cross-check any information that people tell you or that you read in books (even this one).

No matter how many people tell you that such-and-so are the rules about getting into a particular occupation, and there are no exceptions— believe me there *are* exceptions, to almost *every* rule, except where a profession has rigid entrance examinations, as in, say, medicine or law.

Rules are rules. But what you are counting on is that somewhere in this country, somewhere in this vast world, *somebody* found a way to get into this career you dream of, without going through all the hoops that everyone else is telling you are *absolutely essential*.

You want to find out who these people are, and go talk to them, to find out *how they did it*.

Okay, but suppose you are determined to go into a career that takes *years* to prepare for, and you can't find *anyone* who took a shortcut? What then?

Every professional speciality has one or more *shadow* professions, which require much less training. For example, instead of becoming a doctor, you can go into paramedical work; instead of becoming a lawyer, you can go into paralegal work, instead of becoming a licensed career counselor, you can become a career coach.

## HAVE A "PLAN B"

Sooner or later, as you interview one person after another, you'll begin to get some definite ideas about a career that is of interest to you. It uses your favorite skills. It employs your favorite special knowledges or fields of interest. You've interviewed people *actually doing that work*, and it all sounds fine. This part of your Informational Interviewing is over.

As I said earlier, just make sure that you get the names of at least *two* careers, or jobs, that you think you could be happy doing. Never, ever, put all your eggs in one basket. I'll say it again—the secret of surviving out there in the jungle is *having alternatives*.

Eventually, you will get the names of careers that attract you, and after that, you will find the names of particular organizations that employ "people who can do *that*." Do you rush right over? No. You research those places, first.

## Researching Places Before You Approach Them

Why should you research places, before you approach them for a hiring-interview? Well, first of all, you want to know something about the organization from the inside: what kind of work they do there. And what their needs or problems or challenges are. And what kind of goals they are trying to achieve, what obstacles they are running into, and how your skills and knowledges can possibly help them. *(When you do at last go in for a hiring-interview, you want above all else to be able to show them that you have something they need.)*

Second, you want to find out if you would enjoy working there. You want to take the measure of those organizations. Everybody takes the measure of an organization, but the problem with most job-hunters or career-changers is it's *after* they are hired there.

In the U.S., for example, a survey of the federal/state employment service once found that 57 percent of those who found a job through that service were not working at that job just thirty days later, and this was *because* they used the first ten or twenty days *on the job* to screen out that job.

You, by doing this research ahead of time, are choosing a better path, by far. Essentially, you are *screening out* careers, jobs, places *before* you commit to them. How intelligent!

So, try to think of every way in the world that you can find out more about those organizations (*plural, not singular*) that interest you, *before you go to see if you can get hired there.* There are several ways you can do this research ahead of time.

- **What's on the Internet.** Many job-hunters or career-changers think that every organization, company, or nonprofit, has its own website, these days. Not true. Maybe they do, and maybe they don't. It often has to do with the size of the place, its access to a good Web designer, its desperation for customers, etc. Easy way to find out: if you have access to the Internet, type the name of the place into your favorite search engine (*Google, Yahoo, or whatever*) and see what it turns up. Try more than one search engine. Some-times one knows things the others don't.

- What's in Print. The organization itself may have stuff in print, or on its website, about its business, purpose, etc. The CEO or head of the organization may have given talks. The organization may have copies of those talks. In addition, there may be brochures, annual reports, etc., that the organization has put out, about itself. How do you get ahold of these? The person who answers the phone there, when you call, will know, or know who to refer you to. Also, if it's a decent-size organization that you are interested in, public libraries may have files on the organization—newspaper clippings, articles, etc. You never know; and it never hurts to ask your friendly neighborhood research librarian.

- Friends and Neighbors. Ask *everyone* you know, if they know any-one who works at the places that interest you. And, if they do, ask them if they could arrange for you and that person to get together, for lunch, coffee, or tea. At that time, tell them why the place interests you, and indicate you'd like to know more about it. (*It helps if your mutual friend is sitting there with the two of you, so the purpose of this little chat won't be misconstrued.*) This is the vastly preferred way to find out about a place. However, obviously you need a couple of additional alternatives up your sleeve, in case you run into a dead end here.

- People at the Organizations in Question, or at Similar Organi-zations. You can also go directly to organizations and ask ques-tions about the place, but here I must caution you about several *dangers*.

First, make sure you're not asking them questions that are in print somewhere, which you could easily have read for yourself instead of bothering *them*. This irritates people.

Second, make sure that you approach the people at that organi-zation *whose business it is to give out information*—receptionists, public relations people, "the personnel office," "the human rela-tions department," etc.—*before* you ever approach people higher up in that organization.

Third, make sure that you approach *subordinates* rather than the top person in the place, if the subordinates would know the answer to your questions. Bothering the boss there with some simple questions that someone else could have answered is committing *job-hunting suicide.*

Fourth, make sure you're not using this approach simply as a sneaky way to get in to see the boss, and make a pitch for them to hire you. You said this was just information gathering. Keep it at that.

• Temporary Agencies. Many job-hunters and career-changers have found that a useful way to explore organizations is to go and work at a temporary agency. To find these, put into Google the name of your town or city and (on the same search line) the words "Temp Agencies" or "Employment Agencies." Employers turn to such agencies in order to find: a) job-hunters who can work part-time for a limited number of days; and b) job-hunters who can work full-time for a limited number of days. The advantage to you of temporary work is that if there is an agency that loans out people with your particular skills and expertise, you get a chance to be sent to a number of different employers over a period of several weeks, and see each one from the inside. Maybe the temp agency won't send you to exactly the place you hoped for, but sometimes you can develop contacts in the place you love, even while you're temporarily working somewhere else—if both organizations are in the same field.

Some of you may balk at the idea of enrolling with a temporary agency, because you remember the old days when such agencies were solely for clerical workers and secretarial help. But the field has seen an explosion of services in the last decade, and there are temporary agencies these days (*at least in the larger cities*) for many occupations. In your city you may find temporary agencies for: accountants, industrial workers, assemblers, drivers, mechanics, construction people, engineering people, software engineers, programmers, computer technicians, production workers, management/executives, nannies (for young and old), health care/dental/medical people, legal specialists, lawyers, insurance specialists, sales/marketing people, underwriting professionals, financial services, and the like, as well as for the old categories: data processing, secretarial, and office services. See your local phone book, under "Temporary Agencies."

- **Volunteer Work.** Another useful way to research a place before you ever ask them to hire you there, is to volunteer your services at the place that interests you. Of course, some places will turn your offer down, cold. But others will be interested. If they are, it will be relatively easy for you to talk them into letting you work there for a while, because you offer your services *without pay,* and for a brief, limited, agreed-upon, period of time. In other words, from their point of view, if you turn out to be a *pain,* they won't have to endure you for long.

In this fashion, you get a chance to learn about organizations from the inside. Not so coincidentally, if you do decide you would really like to work there, and permanently, they've had a chance to see you in action, and when you are about to end your volunteer time there, *may* want to hire you permanently. I say *may.* Don't be mad if they simply say, "Thanks very much for helping us out. Goodbye." (That's what *usually* happens.) Even so, you've learned a lot, and this will stand you in good stead, in the future—as you approach other organizations.

## Send a Thank-You Note

After *anyone* has done you a favor, during this Informational Interviewing phase of your job-hunt, you must *be sure* to send them a thank-you note by the very next day, at the latest. Such a note goes to *anyone* who helps you, or who talks with you. That means friends, people at the organization in question, temporary agency people, secretaries, receptionists, librarians, workers, or whomever.

Ask them, at the time you are face-to-face with them, for their business card (if they have one), or ask them to write out their name and work address, on a piece of paper, for you. You *don't* want to misspell their name. It is difficult to figure out how to spell people's names, these days, simply from the sound of it. What sounds like "Laura" may actually be "Lara." What sounds like "Smith" may actually be "Smythe," and so on. Get that name and address, *but get it right,* please. And let me reiterate: thank-you notes must be prompt. E-mail the thank-you note that same night, or the very next day at the latest.

Follow it with a lovely printed copy, nicely formatted, and sent through the mail. (Most employers these days prefer a printed letter to a handwritten one, unless your handwriting is beautiful.)

Your thank-you note can be just two or three sentences. Something like: *"I wanted to thank you for talking with me yesterday. It was very helpful to me. I much appreciated your taking the time out of your busy schedule to do this. Best wishes to you,"* and then your signature. *Do* sign it, particularly if the thank-you note is printed. Printed letters sent through the mail without any signature seem to be multiplying like rabbits in the world of work, these days; the absence of a written signature is usually perceived as making your letter *tremendously* impersonal. You don't want to leave that impression.

## What If I Get Offered a Job Along the Way, While I'm Just Gathering Information?

You probably won't. Let me remind you that during this information gathering, you are *not* talking primarily to *employers*. You're talking to *workers*.

Nonetheless, an occasional employer *may* stray across your path during your Informational Interviewing. And that employer *may* be so impressed with the carefulness you're showing, in going about your career-change and job-search, that they want to hire you, on the spot. So, it's *possible* that you'd get offered a job while you're still doing your information gathering. Not *likely*, but *possible*. And if that happens, what should you say?

Well, if you're desperate, you will of course say *yes*. I remember one wintertime when I had just gone through the knee of my last pair of pants, we were burning old pieces of furniture in our fireplace to stay warm, the legs on our bed had just broken, and we were eating spaghetti until it was coming out our ears. In such a situation, *of course* you say yes.

But if you're not *desperate*, if you have time to be more careful, then you respond to the job-offer in a way that will buy you some time. You tell them what you're doing: that the average job-hunter tries to screen a job *after* they take it. But you are doing what you are *sure* this employer would do if they were in your shoes: you are examining careers, fields, industries, jobs, organizations *before* you decide where you would do your best and most effective work.

And you tell them that since your Informational Interviewing isn't finished yet, it would be premature for you to accept their job offer, until you're *sure* that this is the place where you could be most effective, and do your best work.

Then, you add: "Of course, I'm tickled pink that you would want me to be working here. And when I've finished my personal survey, I'll be glad to get back to you about this, as my preliminary impression is that this is the kind of place I'd like to work in, and the kind of people I'd like to work for, and the kind of people I'd like to work with."

In other words, *if you're not desperate yet,* you don't walk immediately through any opened doors, but neither do you allow them to be shut.

## CONCLUSION

And *don't* say to yourself: "Well, I see what it is that I would die to be able to do, but I *know* there is no job in the world like that, that *I* would be able to get." Dear friend, you don't know any such thing. You haven't done your research yet. Of course, it is always possible that when you've completed all that research, and conducted your search, you still may not be able to find *all* that you want—down to the last detail. But you'd be surprised at how much of your dream you may be able to find.

Sometimes it will be found in *stages.* One retired man I know, who had been a senior executive with a publishing company, found himself bored to death in retirement, after he turned sixty-five. He contacted a business acquaintance, who said apologetically, "We just don't have anything open that matches or requires your abilities; right now all we need is someone in our mail room." The sixty-five-year-old executive said, "I'll take that job!" He did, and over the ensuing years steadily advanced once again, to just the job he wanted: as a senior executive in that organization, where he utilized all his prized skills, for some time. He retired as senior executive for the second time, at the age of eighty-five. Like him, you may choose to go by stages.

What you need to keep in mind is how important passion is, to your dream, and to your job-hunt:

Well, there you have it: WHAT, WHERE, and HOW. You're done with chapter 13. You're done with this inventory of yourself. Now you have alternative ways of describing who you are, and what job(s) matches you. You have the survival skill so needed in today's crazy world. Congratulations.

# THE FIVE PARTS OF
# JOB-HUNTING AS
# A SURVIVAL SKILL:

# V.
# EACH ONE
# TEACH ONE

*A hundred years from now, it will not matter
what kind of car I drove, what kind of house
I lived in, how much money I had in the bank . . .
but the world may be a better place because
I made a difference in the life of a child.*

DR. FOREST E. WITCRAFT (1894–1967)

*Or an adult.*

# Chapter 14. Teaching Survival Job-Hunting to Others

A woman who had mastered the principles in this book had a husband who was a lawyer. It was increasingly apparent that he needed to find a new job, but he would not read this book. Being a compassionate and clever wife, she hit upon a strategy. Each night, at supper, she would read him one of the chapters here; or summarize the basic ideas, for him. This gave him enough knowledge that he was able to quit his job and find one that gave him true pleasure and enjoyment. *Each one teach one.*

A man living here in the U.S. had a brother in Pakistan. The American had mastered the principles in this book, and he knew that his brother was in somewhat desperate straits, and needed this knowledge. But the book at that time was not to be found in Pakistan. So he called his brother there, once a week, and summarized for him another chapter in this book. This gave the brother enough knowledge that he was able to change jobs successfully, and find new joy in his life. *Each one teach one.*

What has thus happened occasionally for many years, must be made a regular procedure now that job-hunting has become, increasingly, a survival skill.

As each one of us becomes knowledgeable about these principles, we must make it our discipline to teach this knowledge to others, if we are to avoid what has been increasingly called around the world "a lost generation": those without jobs and with no hope of finding jobs, because their job-hunting skills are only elementary.

There simply aren't enough formal trainers to teach this stuff in time. Each of us must become an instructor and trainer. If we know, we must share. Our motto has got to be: *each one teach one.*

Frank Laubach is the man who popularized this idea. Working in the Philippines in 1929, he was disturbed by the illiteracy he saw all around him. So he came up with the idea that each literate person had a responsibility to teach someone who was illiterate, how to read. He used life skills materials and Bible texts to teach literacy. And he became famous for the worldwide movement that built up around his principle: *Each one teach one.*

Today, illiteracy is still a problem worldwide. But so is a person's ability to survive, and find meaningful work. So his principle is just as urgent in this arena as it was in the matter of illiteracy.

If we accept this responsibility, what is it we should teach? Well, I think there are about 47 principal ideas that we should share with others:

1. The job-market is always churning.
2. Millions of people are unemployed even in the best of times; millions of people find work even in the worst of times.
3. The solution to unemployment cannot wait for government programs. You are in charge of your job-hunt; no one else will find a job for you.
4. Job-hunting is a repetitive experience in the world of today. You must master the job-hunt once and for all: you must aim for empowering yourself, not just look for "services" that rescue you just this one time.
5. Job-hunting has become a survival skill.
6. Every job is temporary. By their very nature, jobs are mortal; they get born, grow, prosper, decline, die. Jobs and job-titles are endlessly being born, and then dying.
7. All job-hunting methods are mortal, at least in their outward form: you must be continually changing how you hunt for work. What got you here, won't get you there; job-hunting has completely changed in the twenty-first century.
8. All of us basically job-hunt the way we live our life: depending on step-by-step well-thought-out plans, or on just intuition, or on just blind luck. If your job-hunt is not working, and you're depending on just luck, move up to intuition; if intuition isn't working for you, move up to step-by-step planning.

9. Even when you feel utterly powerless, you must work on what is within your control, even if it's only 2 percent.

10. You must be prepared for your job-hunt to take a long time.

11. You must be energy-conserving in your job-hunt, which means familiarizing yourself with the latest information about what job-hunting methods will repay you for the time invested, and what methods won't.

12. The business world is like a foreign country: if you visit it, you must learn its language, and how employers think.

13. You must learn that employers hunt for employees in exactly the opposite way that job-hunters search for employers.

14. You must rethink who you are; this involves doing some home-work and research—on yourself, not on the job-market (initially) or "hot jobs."

15. You are not your job-title; you are "a person who. . . ." You are a person who has *these* priorities, *these* enthusiasms, *these* gifts, *these* knowledges, and *this* experience.

16. It's hard to plan for finding meaningful *work* if you haven't first thought out what would be (or is) for you a meaningful *life*.

17. In the realities of today's market, you will probably have to settle initially for part of your dream; so make sure that dream is large to begin with. You can keep working closer and closer to it in future months and years.

18. Your self-inventory must be a search for what you did right, not for what you did wrong.

19. Your self-inventory must be a search for what you enjoy doing, not for what is most marketable. If you like doing something a lot, it's probably because you're good at it. The reverse does not follow. We are all good at many things that we have no appetite for doing, anymore, if ever.

20. There are three key elements to a self-inventory: your answers to three questions, WHAT, WHERE, and HOW. WHAT skills do you most enjoy using; WHERE do you most want to use those skills; and HOW do you find the person who has the power to hire you for such a job.

21. It helps to search for answers to these questions with two other people. Every one of us is blind to our own excellencies, initially.

22. Your uniqueness does not consist in one outstanding skill that you have, but in how you combine the skills you have (a necklace is worth more than a single pearl).

23. Your uniqueness does not consist in any one subject that you know, but in how you combine two or three different fields that you know.

24. Your uniqueness does not consist in what you do, but in the "invention" or "inventiveness" that you bring to what you do, that thereby makes you different from nineteen other people with the same background.

25. Down the road, if you continually strike out, in your job-hunt, you must rethink your job-hunt as a possible career-change; use your self-inventory as the tool for identifying *what*.

26. In job-hunting, don't wait until a place has declared it has a vacancy; explore any company that interests you, whether it has a vacancy or not.

27. Approach smaller companies rather than larger ones, if you consider you have any so-called handicap or barrier to getting hired, such as your age, etc. (Try companies in the field that interests you which have 50 or fewer employees; then, if nothing turns up, 100 or fewer employees.)

28. Gather as much information about a job, a company, a field as you can, before you ever go in for an interview (this is called Informational Interviewing).

29. If going to talk with people terrifies you, prepare for Informational Interviewing by first just doing a "practice field survey"— identifying a curiosity or enthusiasm you have, totally unrelated to any job you are thinking about, and then going to talk with someone who shares that enthusiasm. Do this repeatedly until you get over your fears.

30. The key to talking with anyone, is to find a mutual enthusiasm or passion. Example: a movie fan has no trouble talking to a movie fan. Fear disappears in the face of enthusiasm.

31. Generally speaking, the major purpose of a written or digital resume, if you use one, is not to "sell yourself," but simply to secure an invitation to come in for a talk.

32. Do not depend solely on your resume to get you into a place for an employment interview; use "bridge-people" (formerly called "contacts")—those who know you and also know them; find bridge-people through such sites as LinkedIn.

33. Keep in mind that once an employer is considering you, Google is your new resume; you can no longer control what an employer can know about you (as in the old days of just "resumes"); but you can and should "clean up" your "Google resume" a little (or a lot). See the Internet for instructions on how to do this (the rules keep changing; stay up-to-date, especially with Facebook).

34. The major purpose of your first interview with an employer is to get yourself invited back for a second interview.

35. An employment interview is more like "a first date" than it is like "buying a used car." Each of you, job-hunter and employer, must decide if you want to try "going steady." It's as much up to you as it is up to them. Your interview is still part of your research.

36. In the employment interview, talk 50 percent of the time, let the employer talk 50 percent of the time.

37. In the employment interview, never speak badly about a former employer; they may get the idea that that's how you will talk about them.

38. In the employment interview, answer each of the employer's questions no shorter than 20 seconds, no longer than 2 minutes, at a time.

39. At the end of an interview, if you have decided you really would like to work there, *ask for the job*. How? "Considering all that we've talked about, can you offer me this job?"

40. In the employment interview, do not discuss salary until the end of the interview, after the employer has definitely said, *We want you*. And remember, the first one to mention a figure generally loses in the negotiation. Here's a way for you to respond to an employer who asks what salary you are expecting: "Well

you created this job, so I'd be interested to know what salary range you had in mind."

41. If they say *the job is yours, you'll start on Monday*, do *not* give notice (if you are currently employed) until you have a firm written job offer in hand from the new place; a verbal *"you're hired"* on Friday can turn into a *"sorry, we discovered we just don't have the budget for it"* on Monday. This happens more often than you would think. Get the offer in writing.

42. When you start your new job, exceed their expectations: come in early, stay late, put their priorities before yours.

43. At your new place, keep a log of your accomplishments, done by yourself alone, or in a group or task force. Write in this log once a week (weekends are a good time). You can summarize its key points at the end of the year, when you want to ask for a raise.

44. If you just can't find a job, look around for what your community needs. Observe keenly. It's not what you see; it's what you notice that determines everything.

45. If you've decided you don't want to work for someone else, but want to start your own business, first interview others who have gone before you, in the same line of work, and learn what "land mines" they tripped over, and what skills were required, for them to succeed. Then review your own skills to see if there are any missing, that you will have to go out and hire.

46. If you want to make a radical career change (new job-title, new field) there is a way of doing this that enables you always to claim you have lots of experience: change *in two steps* in the next three years or so, first changing just the job-title, but staying in same field; then changing the field down the road—or vice versa (change just the field, but keep the same job-title as before, then change the job-title down the road). *E.g. accountant in television to consultant in renewable energy.*

47. Remember, every job is temporary. Including the one you just got or created. Start planning your next job-hunt the first day you are in this new job. Job-hunting is a repetitive activity in today's world.

# CONCLUSION

It is a great victory if you learn how to survive in today's hard times; it's an even greater victory if you help someone else survive and find meaningful work.

"I WANT TO EXPERIENCE A WARM CLIMATE, FLY THROUGH THE AIR, SEE SOME COLOR, EAT A PEACH — I WANT TO LIVE!"

# THE PINK PAGES

## INTRODUCTION TO FINDING YOUR MISSION IN LIFE

There are those who think that belief in God is just some fairy tale that mankind (or humankind) invented, to comfort themselves against the darkness. Naturally, therefore, they think that anyone who says they believe in God is demonstrably feebleminded, or a pathetic child who has never grown up intellectually.

Given this view, they are horrified to find a section on faith or religion in a job-hunting book. They have written to me, and said so.

Well, here it is, anyway.

That's because the percent of the world's population that says they don't believe in God is less than 3 percent (it varies from country to country: here in the U.S. the figure is 9 percent, while in Canada that figure is 19–30 percent)[1] Still, that leaves us with an overwhelming percentage of the U.S. population (91 percent) believing in God. And my ten million readers are a pretty typical cross-section of this country.

So, leaving out a section that 91 percent of my readers might be interested in, and helped by, in order to please 9 percent of my readers, seems to me insane.

But you are welcome to skip this section, if you wish. It's not mandatory reading; that's why it is an Appendix to this book.

As I started writing this section, I toyed at first with the idea of following what might be described as an "all-paths approach" to religion: trying to stay as general and nonspecific as I could. But, after much thought, I decided not to try that. This, because I have read many other writers who tried, and I felt the approach failed miserably. An "all-paths" approach to religion ends up being a "no-paths" approach, just as a woman or man who tries to please everyone ends up pleasing no one. It is the old story of the "universal" vs. the "particular."

Those of us who do career counseling could predict, ahead of time, that trying to stay universal is not likely to be helpful, in writing about faith. We know well from our own field that truly helpful career counseling depends upon defining the **particularity** or uniqueness of each person we try to help. No employer wants to know what you have in common with everyone else. He or she wants to know what makes you unique and individual. As I have argued throughout this book, the inventory of your uniqueness or *particularity* is crucial if you are ever to find meaningful work.

This particularity invades *everything* a person does; it is not suddenly "jettisonable" when he or she turns to matters of faith. Therefore, when I or anyone else writes about faith I believe we **must** write out of our own particularity—which *starts,* in my case, with the fact that I write, and think, and breathe as a Christian—as

---

1. See "Demographics of Atheism" in Wikipedia. Also see the Pew Research Center findings, at http://tinyurl.com/3kk78zu.

you might expect from the fact that I was an ordained Episcopalian minister for many years. Understandably, then, this chapter speaks from a Christian perspective. I want you to be aware of that, at the outset.

Balanced against this is the fact that I have always been acutely sensitive to the fact that this is a pluralistic society in which we live, and that I in particular owe a great deal to my readers who have religious convictions quite different from my own. It has turned out that the people who work or have worked here in my office with me, over the years, have been predominantly of other faiths. Furthermore, *Parachute*'s more than ten million readers have not only included Christians of every variety and persuasion, Christian Scientists, Jews, Hindus, Buddhists, and adherents of Islam, but also believers in "new age" religions, secularists, humanists, agnostics, atheists, and many others. I have therefore tried to be very courteous toward the feelings of all my readers, *while at the same time* counting on them to translate my Christian thought-forms into their own. This ability to thus translate is the indispensable *sine qua non* of anyone who wants to communicate helpfully with others in this pluralistic society of ours.

In the Judeo-Christian tradition from which I come, one of the indignant Biblical questions was, "Has God forgotten to be gracious?" The answer was a clear "No." I think it is important *for all of us* also to seek the same goal. I have therefore labored to make this chapter gracious as well as thought-provoking.

R.N.B.

"WHAT DO YOU MEAN 'DON'T EXPECT MIRACLES'? WHY SHOULDN'T I EXPECT MIRACLES??"

# Appendix A. Finding Your Mission in Life

## TURNING POINT

For many of us, the job-hunt offers a chance to make some fundamental changes in our whole life. It marks a turning point in how we live our life.

It gives us a chance to ponder and reflect, to extend our mental horizons, to go deeper into the subsoil of our soul.

It gives us a chance to wrestle with the question, "Why am I here on Earth?" We don't want to feel that we are just another grain of sand lying on the beach called humanity, unnumbered and lost in the billions of other human beings.

We want to do more than plod through life, going to work, coming home from work. We want to find that special joy, "that no one can take from us," which comes from having a sense of Mission in our life.

We want to feel we were put here on Earth for some special purpose, to do some unique work that only we can accomplish.

We want to know what our Mission is.

### The Meaning of the Word "Mission"

When used with respect to our life and work *Mission* has always been a religious concept, from beginning to end. It is defined by *Webster's* as "a continuing task or responsibility that one is destined or fitted to do or specially called upon to undertake," and historically has had two major synonyms: *Calling* and *Vocation*. These, of course, are the same word in two different languages, English and Latin. Both imply God.

To be given a Vocation or Calling implies *Someone who* calls. To have a Destiny implies *Someone who determined the destination for us*. Thus, the concept of Mission lands us inevitably in the lap of God, before we have hardly begun.

I emphasize this, because there is an increasing trend in our culture to try to speak about religious subjects without reference to God. This is true of "spirituality," "soul," and "Mission," in particular. More and more books talk about Mission as though it were simply "a purpose you choose for your own life, by identifying your enthusiasms."

This attempt to obliterate all reference to God from the originally religious concept of Mission, is particularly ironic because the proposed substitute word—enthusiasms—is derived from two Greek words, "en theos," and means "God in us."

In the midst of this increasingly secular culture, we find an oasis that—along with athletics—is very hospitable toward belief in God. That oasis is *job-hunting*. Most of the leaders who have evolved creative job-hunting ideas were—from the beginning—people who believed firmly in God, and said so: Sidney Fine, Bernard Haldane, and John Crystal (all of whom have departed this life), plus Arthur and Marie Kirn, Arthur Miller, Tom and Ellie Jackson, Ralph Matson, and of course myself.

I mentioned at the beginning of this Appendix that 91 percent of us in the U.S. believe in God. According to the Gallup Organization, 90 percent of us pray, 88 percent of us believe God loves us, and 33 percent of us report that we have had a life-changing religious experience.

However, it is not clear that we have made much connection between our belief in God and our work. Often our spiritual beliefs and our attitude toward our work live in separate mental ghettos, within our mind.

A dialogue between these two *is* opened up inside our head, and heart, when we are out of work. Unemployment, particularly in this brutal economy, gives us a chance to contemplate why we are here on Earth, and what our Calling, Vocation, or Mission is, uniquely, for each of us.

Unemployment becomes *life transition*, when we can't find a job doing the same work we've always done. Since we have to rethink one thing, many of us elect to rethink *everything*.

Something awakens within us. Call it *yearning*. Call it *hope*. We come to realize the dream we dreamed has never died. And we go back to get it. We decide to resume our search . . . for the life we know within our heart that we were meant to live.

Now we have a chance to marry our work and our religious beliefs, to talk about Calling, and Vocation, and Mission in life—to think out why we are here, and what plans God has for us.

That's why a period of unemployment can absolutely change our life.

## The Secret of Finding Your Mission in Life: Taking It in Stages

> I will explain the steps toward finding your Mission in life that I have learned in all my years on Earth. Just remember two things. First, I speak from a lifelong Christian perspective, and trust you to translate this into your own thought-forms.
>
> Second, I know that these steps are not the only Way. Many people have discovered their Mission by taking other paths. And you may, too. But hopefully what I have to say may shed some light upon whatever path you take.

I have learned that if you want to figure out what your Mission in life is, it will likely take some time. It is not a *problem* to be solved in a day and a night. It is a *learning process* that has steps to it, much like the process by which we all learned to eat. As a baby, we did not tackle adult food right off. As we all recall, there were three stages: first there had to be the mother's milk or bottle, then strained baby foods, and finally—after teeth and time—the stuff that grown-ups chew. Three stages—and the two earlier stages were not to be disparaged. It was all Eating, just different forms of Eating—appropriate to our development at the time. But each stage had to be mastered, in turn, before the next could be approached.

There are usually three stages also to learning what your Mission in life is, and the two earlier stages are likewise not to be disparaged. It is all "Mission"—just different forms of Mission, appropriate to your development at the time. But each stage has to be mastered, in turn, before the next can be approached.

Of course, there is a sense in which you never master any of these stages, but are always growing in understanding and mastery of them, throughout your whole life here on Earth.

As it has been impressed on me by observing many people over the years (admittedly through *Christian spectacles*), it appears that the three parts to your Mission here on Earth can be defined generally as follows:

1. *Your first Mission here on Earth* is one that you share with the rest of the human race, but it is no less your individual Mission for the fact that it is shared: and it is, **to seek to stand hour by hour in the conscious presence of God, the One from whom your Mission is derived.** *The Missioner before the Mission,* is the rule. In religious language, your Mission here is: *to know God, and enjoy Him forever, and to see His hand in all His works.*

2. Second, once you have begun doing that in an earnest way, *your second Mission here on Earth* is also one that you share with the rest of the human race, but it is no less your individual mission for the fact that it is shared: and that is, **to do what you can, moment by moment, day by day, step by step, to make this world a better place, following the leading and guidance of God's Spirit within you and around you.**

3. Third, once you have begun doing that in a serious way, *your third Mission here on Earth* is one that is uniquely yours, and that is:

   a) **to exercise the Talent that you particularly came to Earth to use—your greatest gift, which you most delight to use,**

   b) **in the place(s) or setting(s) that God has caused to appeal to you the most,**

   c) **and for those purposes that God most needs to have done in the world.**

When fleshed out, and spelled out, I think you will find that there you have the definition of your Mission in life. Or, to put it another way, these are the three Missions that you have in life.

## The Two Rhythms of the Dance of Mission: Unlearning, Learning, Unlearning, Learning

The distinctive characteristic of these three stages is that in each we are forced to *let go* of some fundamental assumptions that our culture has taught us, about the nature of Mission. In other words, throughout this quest and at each stage we find ourselves engaged not merely in a process of *Learning*. We are also engaged in a process of *Unlearning*. Thus, we can restate the above three Learnings, in terms of what we also need to *un*learn at each stage:

- We need in the first stage to *un*learn the idea that our Mission is primarily to keep busy *doing* something (here on Earth), and learn instead that our Mission is first of all to keep busy *being* something (here on Earth). In Christian language (and others as well), we might say that we were sent here to learn how *to be* sons of God, and daughters of God, before anything else. "*Our Father, who art in heaven . . .*"

- In the second stage, "Being" issues into "Doing." At this stage, we need to *un*learn the idea that everything about our Mission must be *unique* to us, and learn instead that some parts of our Mission here on Earth are *shared* by all human beings: e.g., we were all sent here to bring more gratitude, more kindness, more forgiveness, and more love, into the world. We share this Mission because the task is too large to be accomplished by just one individual.

- We need in the third stage to *un*learn the idea that the part of our Mission that is truly unique, and most truly ours, is something Our Creator just *orders* us to do, without any agreement from our spirit, mind, and heart. (On the other hand, neither is it something that each of us chooses and then merely asks God to bless.) We need to learn that God so honors our free will, that He has ordained that our unique Mission be something that we have some part in choosing.

- In this third stage we need also to *un*learn the idea that our unique Mission must consist of some achievement for all the world to see—and learn instead that as the stone does not always know what ripples it has caused in the pond whose surface it impacts, so neither we nor those who watch our life will always know *what we have achieved* by our life and by our Mission. *It may be* that by the grace of God we helped bring about a profound change for the better in the lives of other souls around us, but it also may be that this takes place beyond our sight, or after we have gone on. And we may never know what we have accomplished, until we see Him face to face after this life is past.

- Most finally, we need to *un*learn the idea that what we have accomplished is our doing, and ours alone. It is God's Spirit breathing in us and through us that helps us do whatever we do, and so the singular first-person pronoun is never appropriate, but only the plural. Not "*I* accomplished this" but "*We* accomplished this, God and I, working together. . . ."

That should give you a general overview. But I would like to add some random comments on my part about each of these three Missions of ours here on Earth.

## SOME RANDOM COMMENTS ABOUT YOUR FIRST MISSION IN LIFE

Your first Mission here on Earth is one that you share with the rest of the human race, but it is no less your individual Mission for the fact that it is shared: and that is, **to seek to stand hour by hour in the conscious presence of God, the One from whom your Mission is derived.** The Missioner before the Mission, is the rule. In religious language, your Mission is: to know God, and enjoy Him forever, and to see His hand in all His works.

### Comment 1:
### How We Might Think of God

Each of us has to go about this primary Mission according to the tenets of our own particular religion. But I will speak what I know out of the context of my own particular faith, and you may perhaps translate and apply it to yours. I will speak as a Christian, who believes (passionately) that Christ is the Way and the Truth and the Life. But I also believe, with St. Peter, "that God shows no partiality, but in every nation any one who fears Him and does what is right is acceptable to Him" (Acts 10:34–35).

Now, Jesus claimed many unique things about Himself and His Mission; but He also spoke of Himself as the great prototype for us all. He called Himself "the Son of Man," and He said, "I assure you that the man who believes in me will do the same things that I have done, yes, and he will do even greater things than these. . . ." (John 14:12).

Emboldened by His identification of us with His Life and His Mission, we might want to remember how He spoke about His Life here on Earth. He put it in this context: **"I came from the Father and have come into the world; again, I am leaving the world and going to the Father"** (John 16:28).

If there is a sense in which this is, in even the faintest way, true also of our lives (and I shall say in a moment in what sense I think it is true), then instead of calling our great Creator "God" or "Father" right off, we might begin our approach to the subject of religion by referring to the One Who gave us our Mission and sent us to this planet not as "God" or "Father" but—*just to help our thinking*—as: **"The One From Whom We Came and The One To Whom We Shall Return,"** when this life is done.

If our life here on Earth is to be at all like Christ's, then this is a true way to think about the One Who gave us our Mission. We are not some kind of eternal, preexistent *being*. We are **creatures**, who once did not exist, and then came into Being, and continue to have our Being, only at the will of our great Creator. But as creatures we are both body and soul; although we know our body was created in our mother's womb, our soul's origin is a great mystery. Where it came from, at what moment the Lord created it, is something we cannot know. It is not unreasonable to suppose, however, that the great God created our *soul* before it entered our body, and in that sense we did indeed stand before God before we were born; and He is indeed **"The One From Whom We Came and The One To Whom We Shall Return."**

Therefore, before we go searching for "what work was I sent here to do?" we need to establish—or in a truer sense *reestablish*—contact with **"The One From Whom We Came and The One To Whom We Shall Return."** Without this reaching out of the creature to the great Creator, without this reaching out of *the creature with a Mission* to *the One Who Gave Us That Mission*, the question *what is my Mission in life?* is void and null. The *what* is rooted in the *Who*; absent the Personal, one cannot meaningfully discuss The Thing. It is like the adult who cries,

*Appendix A*

"I want to get married," without giving any consideration to *who* it is they want to marry.

## Comment 2:
## How We Might Think of Religion or Faith

In light of this larger view of our creatureliness, we can see that *religion* or *faith* is not a question of whether or not we choose to (*as it is so commonly put*) "have a relationship with God." Looking at our life in a larger context than just our life here on Earth, it becomes apparent that some sort of relationship with God is a given for us, about which we have absolutely no choice. God and we **were** and **are** related, during the time of our soul's existence before our birth and in the time of our soul's continued existence after our death. The only choice we have is what to do about **The Time In Between**, i.e., what we want the nature of our relationship with God to be during our time here on Earth and how that will affect the *nature* of the relationship, then, after death.

One of the corollaries of all this is that by the very act of being born into a human body, it is inevitable that we undergo a kind of *amnesia*— an amnesia that typically embraces not only our nine months in the womb, our baby years, and almost one-third of each day (sleeping), but more important any memory of our origin or our destiny. We wander on Earth as an amnesia victim. To seek after Faith, therefore, is to seek to climb back out of that amnesia. Religion or Faith is **the hard reclaiming of knowledge we once knew as a certainty.**

## Comment 3:
## The First Obstacle to Executing This Mission

This first Mission of ours here on Earth is not the easiest of Missions, simply because it is the first. Indeed, in many ways, it is the most difficult. All we can see is that our life here on Earth is a very physical life. We eat, we drink, we sleep, we long to be held, and to hold. We inherit a physical body, with very physical appetites, we walk on the physical earth, and we acquire physical possessions. It is the most alluring of temptations, *in our amnesia*, to come up with just a *Physical* interpretation of this life: to think that the Universe is merely interested in the survival of species. Given this interpretation, the story of our individual life could be simply told: we are born, grow up, procreate, and die.

But we are ever recalled to do what we came here to do: that without rejecting the joy of the Physicalness of this life, such as the love of the blue sky and the green grass, we are to reach out beyond all this to **recall** and recover a *Spiritual* interpretation of our life. *Beyond* the physical and *within* the physicalness of this life, to detect a Spirit and a Person from beyond this Earth who is with us and in us—the very real and loving and awesome Presence of the great Creator from whom we came—and the One to whom we once again shall go.

## Comment 4:
## The Second Obstacle to Executing This Mission

It is one of the conditions of our earthly amnesia and our creatureliness that, sadly enough, some very *human* and very *rebellious* part of us *likes* the idea of living in a world where we can be our own god—and therefore loves the purely Physical interpretation of life, and finds it *anguish* to relinquish it. Traditional Christian vocabulary calls this "**sin**" and has a lot to say about the difficulty it poses for this first part of our Mission. All who live a thoughtful life know that it is true: our greatest enemy in carrying out this first Mission of ours is indeed *our own* heart and our own rebellion.

## Comment 5:
## Further Thoughts about What Makes Us
## Special and Unique

As I said earlier, many of us come to this issue of our Mission in life, because we want to feel that we are unique. And what we mean by that, is that we hope to discover some "specialness" intrinsic to us, which is our birthright, and which no one can take from us. What we, however, discover from a thorough exploration of this topic, is that we are indeed special—but only because God thinks us so. Our specialness and uniqueness reside in Him, and His love, rather than in anything intrinsic to our own *being*. The proper appreciation of this distinction causes our feet to carry us in the end not to the City called Pride, but to the Temple called Gratitude.

> What is religion? Religion is the service of God out of grateful love for what God has done for us. The Christian religion, more particularly, is the service of God out of grateful love for what God has done for us in Christ.
>
> PHILLIPS BROOKS, author of *O Little Town of Bethlehem*

## Comment 6:
## The Unconscious Doing of the Work We Came to Do

You may have *already* wrestled with this first part of your Mission here on Earth. You may not have called it that. You may have called it simply "learning to believe in God." But if you ask what your Mission is in life, this one was and is the precondition of all else that you came here to do. Absent this Mission, it is folly to talk about the rest. So, if you have been seeking faith, or seeking to strengthen your faith, you have— willy-nilly—already been about *the doing of the Mission you were given.* Born into **This Time In Between**, you have found His hand again, and reclasped it. You are therefore ready to go on with His Spirit to tackle together what you came here to do—the other parts of your Mission.

# SOME RANDOM COMMENTS ABOUT YOUR SECOND MISSION IN LIFE

Your second Mission here on Earth is also one that you share with the rest of the human race, but it is no less your individual Mission for the fact that it is shared: and that is, **to do what you can moment by moment, day by day, step by step, to make this world a better place—following the leading and guidance of God's Spirit within you and around you.**

## Comment 1:
## The Uncomfortableness of One Step at a Time

Imagine yourself out walking in your neighborhood one night, and suddenly you find yourself surrounded by such a dense fog, that you have lost your bearings and cannot find your way. Suddenly, a friend appears out of the fog, and asks you to put your hand in theirs, and they will lead you home. And you, not being able to tell where you are going, trustingly follow them, even though you can only see one step at a time. Eventually you arrive safely home, filled with gratitude. But as you reflect upon the experience the next day, you realize how unsettling it was to have to keep walking when you could see only one step at a time, even though you had guidance you knew you could trust.

Now I have asked you to imagine all of this, because this is the essence of the second Mission to which *you* are called—and *I* am called—in this life. It is all very different than we had imagined. When the question, "*What is your Mission in life?*" is first broached, and we have put our hand in God's, as it were, we imagine that we will be taken up to *some mountaintop*, from which we can see far into the distance. And that we will hear a voice in our ear, saying, "Look, look, see that distant city? That is the goal of your Mission; that is where everything is leading, every step of your way."

But instead of the mountaintop, we find ourselves in *the valley*—wandering often in a fog. And the voice in our ear says something quite different from what we thought we would hear. It says, **"Your Mission is to take one step at a time, even when you don't yet see where it all is leading, or what the Grand Plan is, or what your overall Mission in life is. Trust Me; I will lead you."**

## Comment 2:
## The Nature of This Step-by-Step Mission

As I said, in every situation you find yourself, you have been sent here to do whatever you can—moment by moment—that will bring more gratitude, more kindness, more forgiveness, more honesty, and more love into this world.

There are dozens of such moments every day. Moments when you stand—as it were—at a spiritual crossroads, with two ways lying before you. Such moments are typically called "**moments of decision.**" It does not matter what the frame or content of each particular decision is. It all devolves, in the end, into just two roads before you, *every time*. **The one** will lead to *less* gratitude, *less* kindness, *less* forgiveness, *less* honesty, or *less* love in the world. **The other** will lead to *more* gratitude, *more* kindness, *more* forgiveness, *more* honesty, or *more* love in the world. Your Mission, each moment, is to seek to choose the latter spiritual road, rather than the former, *every time*.

## Comment 3:
## Some Examples of This Step-by-Step Mission

I will give a few examples, so that the nature of this part of your Mission may be unmistakably clear.

You are out on the freeway, in your car. Someone has gotten into the wrong lane, to the right of *your* lane, and needs to move over into the lane you are in. You *see* their need to cut in, ahead of you. **Decision time.** In your mind's eye you see two spiritual roads lying before you: the one leading to less kindness in the world (you speed up, to shut this driver out, and don't let them move over), the other leading to more kindness in the world (you let the driver cut in). **Since you know this is part of your Mission, part of the reason why you came to Earth, your calling is clear. You know which road to take, which decision to make.**

You are hard at work at your desk, when suddenly an interruption comes. The phone rings, or someone is at the door. They need something from you, a question of some of your time and attention. **Decision time.** In your mind's eye you see two spiritual roads lying before you: the one leading to less love in the world (you tell them you're just too busy to be bothered), the other leading to more love in the world (you put aside your work, decide that God may have sent this person to you, and say, "Yes, what can I do to help you?"). **Since you know this is part of your Mission, part of the reason why you came to Earth, your calling is clear. You know which road to take, which decision to make.**

Your mate does something that hurts your feelings. **Decision time.** In your mind's eye you see two spiritual roads lying before you: the one leading to less forgiveness in the world (you institute an icy silence between the two of you, and think of how you can punish them or otherwise get even), the other leading to more forgiveness in the world (you go over and take them in your arms, speak the truth about your hurt feelings, and assure them of your love). **Since you know this is part of your Mission, part of the reason why you came to Earth, your calling is clear. You know which road to take, which decision to make.**

You have not behaved at your most noble, recently. And now you are face to face with someone who asks you a question about what happened. **Decision time.** In your mind's eye you see two spiritual roads lying before you: the one leading to less honesty in the world (you lie about what happened, or what you were feeling, because you fear losing their respect or their love), the other leading to more honesty in the world (you tell the truth, together with how you feel about it, in retrospect). **Since you know this is part of your Mission, part of the reason why you came to Earth, your calling is clear. You know which road to take, which decision to make.**

## Comment 4:
## The Spectacle That Makes the Angels Laugh

It is necessary to explain this part of our Mission in some detail, because so many times you will see people wringing their hands, and saying, "*I want to know what my Mission in life is*," all the while they are cutting people off on the highway, refusing to give time to people, punishing their mate for having hurt their feelings, and lying about what they did. And it will seem to you that the angels must laugh to see this spectacle. *For these people wringing their hands*, their Mission was right there, on the freeway, in the interruption, in the hurt, and at the confrontation.

## Comment 5:
## The Valley Versus the Mountaintop

At some point in your life your Mission may involve some grand *mountaintop experience*, where you say to yourself, "This, this, is why I came into the world. I know it. I know it." *But until then*, your Mission is here in *the valley*, and the fog, and the little callings moment by moment, day by day. More to the point, it is likely you cannot ever get to your mountaintop Mission unless you have first exercised your stewardship faithfully in the valley.

It is an ancient principle, to which Jesus alluded often, that if you don't use the information the Universe has already given you, you cannot expect it will give you any more. If you aren't being faithful in small things, how can you expect to be given charge over larger things? (Luke 16:10–12, 19:11–24). If you aren't trying to bring more gratitude, kindness, forgiveness, honesty, and love into the world each day, you can hardly expect that you will be entrusted with the Mission to help bring peace into the world or anything else large and important. If we do not live out our day-by-day Mission in the valley, we cannot expect we are yet ready for a larger *mountaintop* Mission.

Comment 6:
The Importance of Not Thinking of
This Mission as "Just a Training Camp"

*The valley* is not just a kind of "training camp." There is in your imagination even now an invisible *spiritual* mountaintop to which you may go, if you wish to see where all this is leading. And what will you see there, in the imagination of your heart, but the goal toward which all this is pointed: **that Earth might be more like heaven. That human life might be more like God's.** That is the large achievement toward which all our day-by-day Missions *in the valley* are moving. This is a *large* order, but it is accomplished by faithful attention to the doing of our great Creator's **will** in little things as well as in large. It is much like the building of the pyramids in Egypt, which was accomplished by the dragging of a lot of individual pieces of stone by a lot of individual men.

The valley, the fog, the going step by step, is no mere training camp. The goal is real, however large. **"Thy Kingdom come, Thy will be done, on Earth, as it is in heaven."**

## SOME RANDOM COMMENTS ABOUT YOUR THIRD MISSION IN LIFE

Your third Mission here on Earth is one that is uniquely yours, and that is:

a) **to exercise the Talent that you particularly came to Earth to use—your greatest gift that you most delight to use,**

b) **in those place(s) or setting(s) that God has caused to appeal to you the most,**

c) **and for those purposes that God most needs to have done in the world.**

It is customary in trying to identify this part of our Mission, to advise that we should ask God, in prayer, to speak to us—and **tell us** plainly what our Mission is. We look for a voice in the air, a thought in our head, a dream in the night, a sign in the events of the day, to reveal this thing that is otherwise *(it is said)* completely hidden. Sometimes, from just such answered prayer, people do indeed discover what their Mission is, beyond all doubt and uncertainty.

But having to wait for the voice of God to reveal what our Mission is, is not the truest picture of our situation. St. Paul, in Romans, speaks of a law "written in our members"—and this phrase has a telling application to the question of **how** God reveals to each of us our unique Mission in life. Read again the definition of our third Mission (above) and you will see: the clear implication of the definition is that God has **already** revealed His will to us concerning our vocation and Mission, by causing it to be "**written in our members**." We are to begin deciphering our unique Mission by studying our talents and skills, and more particularly which ones (or one) we most rejoice to use.

God actually has written His will *twice* in our members: *first in the talents* that He lodged there, and second *in His guidance of our heart*, as to which Talent gives us the greatest pleasure from its exercise (**it is usually the one that, when we use it, causes us to lose all sense of time**).

Even as the anthropologist can examine ancient inscriptions, and divine from them the daily life of a long-lost people, so we by examining **our talents** and **our heart** can *more often than we dream* divine the Will of the Living God. For true it is, our Mission is not something He **will** reveal; it is something He **has already** revealed. It is not to be found written in the sky; it is to be found written in our members.

## Comment 2:
## Career Counseling: We Need You

Arguably, our first two Missions in life could be learned from religion alone—without any reference whatsoever to career counseling, the subject of this book. Why, then, should career counseling claim that this question about our Mission in life is its proper concern, *in any way?*

It is when we come to this third Mission, which hinges so crucially on the question of our Talents, skills, and gifts, that we see the answer. If you've read the body of this book, before turning to this section, then you know without my even saying it, how much the identification of Talents, gifts, or skills is the province of career counseling. Its expertise, indeed its *raison d'être*, lies precisely in the identification, classification, and (forgive me) "prioritization" of Talents, skills, and gifts. To put the matter quite simply, career counseling knows how to do this better than any other discipline—**including** traditional religion. This is not a defect of religion, but the fulfillment of something Jesus promised: "When the Spirit of truth comes, He will guide you into all truth" (John 16:12). Career counseling is part (we may hope) of that promised late-coming truth. It can therefore be of inestimable help to the pilgrim who is trying to figure out what their greatest, and most enjoyable, Talent is, as a step toward identifying their unique Mission in life.

If career counseling needs religion as its helpmate in the first two stages of identifying our Mission in life, then religion repays the compliment by clearly needing career counseling as **its** helpmate here in the third stage.

And this place where you are in your life right now—facing the job-hunt and all its anxiety—is the perfect time to seek the union within your own mind and heart of both career counseling (as in the pages of this book) and your faith in God.

## Comment 3:
## How Our Mission Got Chosen:
## A Scenario for the Romantic

It is a mystery that we cannot fathom, in this life at least, as to why one of us has this Talent, and the other one has that; why God chose to give one gift—and Mission—to one person, and a different gift—and Mission—to another. Since we do not know, and in some degree cannot know, we are certainly left free to speculate, and imagine.

We may imagine that before we came to Earth, our souls, *our Breath, our Light*, stood before the great Creator and volunteered for this Mission. And God and we, together, chose what that Mission would be and what particular gifts would be needed, which He then agreed to give us, after our birth. Thus, our Mission was not a command given pre-emptorily by an unloving Creator to a reluctant slave without a vote, but was a task jointly designed by us both, in which as fast as the great Creator said, "I wish" our hearts responded, **"Oh, yes."** As mentioned in an earlier comment, it may be helpful to think of the condition of our becoming human as that we became amnesiac about any consciousness our soul had before birth—and therefore amnesiac about the nature or manner in which our Mission was designed.

Our searching for our Mission now is therefore a searching to recover the memory of something we ourselves had a part in designing.

I am admittedly a hopeless romantic, so of course I like this picture. If you also are a hopeless romantic, you may like it, too. There's also the chance that it just may be true. We will not know until we see Him face to face.

## Comment 4:
## Mission as Intersection

There are all different kinds of voices calling you to all different kinds of work, and the problem is to find out which is the voice of God rather than that of society, say, or the superego, or self-interest. By and large a good rule for finding out is this: the kind of work God usually calls you to is the kind of work a) that you need most to do and b) the world most needs to have done. If you really get a kick out of your work, you've presumably met requirement a), but if your work is writing TV deodorant commercials, the chances are you've missed requirement b). On the other hand, if your work is being a doctor in a leper colony, you have probably met b), but if most of the time you're bored and depressed by it, the chances are you haven't only bypassed a) but probably aren't helping your patients much either. Neither the hair shirt nor the soft birth will do. **The place God calls you to is the place where your deep gladness and the world's deep hunger meet.**

FRED BUECHNER
*Wishful Thinking—A Theological ABC*

## Comment 5:
## Examples of Mission as Intersection

Your unique and individual Mission will most likely turn out to be a mission of Love, acted out in one or all of three arenas: either in the Kingdom of the Mind, whose goal is to bring more Truth into the world;

or in the Kingdom of the Heart, whose goal is to bring more Beauty into the world; or in the Kingdom of the Will, whose goal is to bring more Perfection into the world, through Service.

Here are some examples:

"My mission is, out of the rich reservoir of love that God seems to have given me, to nurture and show love to others—most particularly to those who are suffering from incurable diseases."

"My mission is to draw maps for people to show them how to get to God."

"My mission is to create the purest foods I can, to help people's bodies not get in the way of their spiritual growth."

"My mission is to make the finest harps I can so that people can hear the voice of God in the wind."

"My mission is to make people laugh, so that the travail of this earthly life doesn't seem quite so hard to them."

"My mission is to help people know the truth, in love, about what is happening out in the world, so that there will be more honesty in the world."

"My mission is to weep with those who weep, so that in my arms they may feel themselves in the arms of that Eternal Love that sent me and that created them."

"My mission is to create beautiful gardens, so that in the lilies of the field people may behold the Beauty of God and be reminded of the Beauty of Holiness."

## Comment 6:
## Life as Long as Your Mission Requires

Knowing that you came to Earth for a reason, and knowing what that Mission is, throws an entirely different light upon your life from now on. You are, generally speaking, delivered from any further fear about how long you have to live. You may settle it in your heart that you are here until God chooses to think that you have accomplished your Mission, or until God has a greater Mission for you in another Realm. You need to be a good steward of what He has given you, while you are here; but you do not need to be an anxious steward or stewardess.

You need to attend to your health, *but you do not need to constantly worry about it*. You need to meditate on your death, *but you do not need to be constantly preoccupied with it*. To paraphrase the glorious words of G. K. Chesterton: **"We now have a strong desire for living combined with a strange carelessness about dying. We desire life like water and yet are ready to drink death like wine."** We know that we are here to do what we came to do, and we need not worry about anything else.

## Comment 7:
## Using Internet Resources

There is a website that deals with news, etc., about all faiths, which you may want to look at: www.beliefnet.com.

Then there is a Jesuit site that leads you in a daily meditation for ten or more minutes (in more than twenty languages with a visual, but otherwise no sound or distraction): http://sacredspace.ie.

There is also a site that gives you a daily podcast of church bells, music, Scripture reading, and meditations or homily, with no visuals, but with sound, and an audio MP3 file that can be sent to your phone, computer, PDA, etc: www.pray-as-you-go.org.

There is a site dedicated to helping you keep a divine consciousness 24/7: by helping you link up to other people of faith, through prayer circles, sharing of personal stories of faith, etc., aimed especially, but not exclusively, toward young adults. Its ultimate message: you are not alone: www.24-7prayer.com/communities.

Lastly, there is a site dedicated to helping you find a spiritual counselor (or "spiritual director"), as well as retreat centers, in the Christian, Islamic, Buddhist, Jewish, or Interfaith faiths: www.sdiworld.org.

# FINAL COMMENT

## A Job-Hunt Done Well

If you approach your job-hunt as an opportunity to work on this issue as well as the issue of how you will keep body and soul together, then hopefully your job-hunt will end with your being able to say: "Life has deep meaning to me, now. I have discovered more than my ideal job; I have found my Mission, and the reason why I am here on Earth."

# Appendix B. A Guide to Dealing with Unemployment Depression

## UNEMPLOYMENT DEPRESSION

Unemployment can take a terrible toll upon the human spirit. In a recent study of over 6,000 job-hunters, interviewed every week for up to 24 weeks, it was discovered

> *"that many workers become discouraged the longer they are unemployed. In particular, the unemployed express feeling more sad the longer they are unemployed, and sadness rises more quickly with unemployment duration during episodes of job search. In addition, reported life satisfaction is lower for the same individual following days in which comparatively more time was devoted to job search. . . . These findings suggest that the psychological cost of job search rises the longer someone is unemployed. . . . One reason why job search assistance may have been found to consistently speed individuals' return to work in past studies is that it may help the unemployed to overcome feelings of anxiety and sadness that are associated with job search."*[1]

---

1. Alan B. Krueger and Andreas Mueller. "Job Search, Emotional Well-Being and Job Finding in a Period of Mass Unemployment: Evidence from High-Frequency Longitudinal Data." *Brookings Papers on Economic Activity,* March 8, 2011. Found on the Web at http://tinyurl.com/4olmpj9.

I know the truth of this from my own experience. I have been fired twice, in my life. I remember how it felt each time I got the doleful news. I walked out of the building dazed, as though I had just walked away from a train wreck, each time. The sun was shining brightly, not a cloud in the sky; and, since it was lunch hour, as it happened, the streets were always filled with laughing happy people, who had not a care in the world, it seemed.

I remember thinking, "The world has just caved—my world at least. How can all these people act as though nothing has happened?"

And I remember the feelings. The overwhelming feelings, that only intensified in the weeks after that. I would describe my state as *feeling sad, being in a funk, feeling despair, feeling hopeless, feeling like things "will always be this way,"* or *feeling depressed.*

Why, oh why, *I remember thinking at the time,* don't "career experts" ever talk about *feelings?* Unemployment was rocking my soul to its foundations. I needed to know what to do about my *feelings.*

I have since learned that my experience was not the least unusual. Many of us, if not most of us, when we are out of work for a long time would tend not just to say we feel *sad,* but that we feel *depressed*—in the layperson's sense of that word, never mind the clinical definition.

Ours is situational depression, or what we might loosely call *unemployment depression.* It arises as a reaction to a particular problem time in our lives. If the problem gets solved, which in this case means we find a job, the depression will lift.[2]

In the case of unemployment depression, our greatest desire is to get rid of these feelings *now.* Anyone who then comes along and tells us they have a quick and easy way to cure it, should be avoided like the

---

2. It thus distinguishes itself from the much more serious *clinical depression*, which often has a lifelong history, and which requires treatment, particularly when a person is entertaining endangering thoughts, such as suicide. In such a case, an individual should seek competent psychological or psychiatric help. (For immediate help, this minute, call 1-800-273-8255 or go online to www.suicidepreventionlifeline.org. There are counselors 24/7 at both places who deal with anyone, including the military or veterans, in trouble.)

Clinical depression is an emotional illness of uncertain origin and cure. If we are the victims of this kind of depression, it usually antedates our period of unemployment, and is something we have wrestled with for some time. Many brave souls have endured this "dark night of the soul" for years, with astounding courage—even when the medicines and treatments that usually hold depression completely, or mostly, at bay, simply aren't doing all they should be doing.

plague. But after talking to thousands of job-hunters, I do think there are some things we can do, to make the depression feel not so bad, not so overwhelming.

*Unemployment depression* isn't just a matter of feelings. It's more like a river, fed by four tributary streams: Physical, Mental, Emotional (of course), and Spiritual. And, luckily, there are 12 things we can do about these tributaries, when we're out of work.

## FOURTEEN PRACTICAL STEPS WE CAN TAKE TO DEAL WITH OUR DEPRESSION WHILE UNEMPLOYED

### The Physical

1. We can catch up on our sleep, even if it means we have to take naps during the day because our attempt to sleep at nighttime is, at the moment, a disaster. We tend to feel depressed if we are short on our sleep, or our body is otherwise run-down.

   There are two states that can be easily confused. First of all, the world never looks bright or happy to us when we are very short on sleep. Secondly, the world never looks bright or happy to us when we are feeling depressed. It is therefore easy to confuse the two feeling-states. Over the years, I have seen many job-hunters who thought they were really depressed over their situation, discover they were really depressed just because they were so tired. Or a bit of both. Anyway, sleep or nap, we often turn into happier, more upbeat people, just by catching up on our sleep. This can make us feel better—sometimes much better.

2. There are other things that we can do to keep ourselves more physically fit while unemployed. When I was myself unemployed I found it important to:
   - get regular exercise, involving a daily walk;
   - drink plenty of water each day (this seems silly, but I found out we tend to skip the water, and get dehydrated, when we're out of work);
   - eliminate sugar as much as possible from the diet;

- take supplementary vitamins daily (no matter how many doctors and nutritionists try to tell us that we already get enough from our daily food);
- eat balanced meals (not just pig out on junk food in front of the telly);
- and all that other stuff that our mothers always told us to do.

3. **We can do something about our physical space around us.** Specifically, we can look critically at our apartment, or home, and ask ourselves if that physical space suggests the occupant is an upbeat person. This is important because our surroundings often mirror how we feel about ourselves. If our physical environment looks like a disaster area, that in itself can make us depressed. Now that we are unemployed, we can vow we will live *simpler*—something that maybe we've always wanted to do. We can begin by taking care that each time we handle a thing, we take it all the way to its new destination; we don't just drop it on the counter, thinking that we will deal with it later. We can take care that when we take our clothes off at night, we don't just drop them on the floor, but hang them up or put them in a laundry-hamper. And that when we finish eating, we put the dishes where they are going to be washed, and put our food back in the refrigerator. And we can determine that when we do such things as get a screwdriver out, to fix a screw that's dropped out of something, that we take the screwdriver all the way back to the tool box or wherever its final destination is. And so on.

When we determine to always put our things away in a timely fashion, neatness will start to appear in our physical environment; this can help lift our spirits immensely, as our physical space mirrors an upbeat life.

4. **We can get outdoors daily and take a good walk.** Hiding in our cave will only make us feel more "down." Green trees, sunlight, mountains, flowers, people!, will do our heart good to see, each day.

## The Mental

5. **We can focus on other people** and *their* problems—not just our own. If our unemployment is dragging on and on, and we're starting to have a lot of time on our hands, we can find someplace in

town that is dealing with people worse off than we are, and go volunteer there. I'm talking food banks, hospitals, housing aid, anything dealing with kids, especially deprived kids, or kids with tremendous handicaps—that sort of thing. We can do a search on Google, put in the name of our town or city plus the name of the problem we want to help with, and see what turns up. If we determine to help someone else in need, while we're unemployed, we won't feel so *discarded* by society.

6. We can go on fun mini-adventures. Often there are portions of our surroundings that we have never explored, but a tourist would "hit" on the very first day they were there.

I lived in New York City for a long time; never once went up in the Empire State Building. I lived in San Francisco for years; never once went out to the Zoo. You get the point. If I lived in either of these cities today, and was unemployed with time on my hands, I would set out on mini-adventures, going to visit those places I'd never visited before. We can learn to give up minding that we lost the old world we were so accustomed to. We can turn our face toward the future. There are new worlds to conquer, after all.

7. We can expand our mental horizons by learning something new. There are a million free videos online, where we can learn just about anything. A sampler of them can be found in chapter 3. In addition to videos, there are also videocasts, webcasts, podcasts, and every other kind of cast. We can type the word "webcast," plus the subject in which we are interested, into our favorite browser like Google, then pick through what turns up. There are also, of course, books. For our Kindle or Nook or iPad, or from online bookstores like Amazon or B&N, there are lots of eBooks available.

We can go read up on subjects that have always interested us, but we've never had enough time to explore. While we're unemployed, we have the time. If we can't think of any subject, there's always *the human mind.* The mind, after all, is what is troubling us in our present situation. The more we understand it, the better we can heal. If you're looking for suggestions, I'd read anything by Martin Seligman. There's *Learned Optimism: How to Change Your Mind and Your Life,* which, as one reviewer commented, "vaulted me out of my funk." It has excellent chapters on dealing with depression. Or there's Seligman's most recent book, *Flourish: A Visionary New Understanding of Happiness and Well-being.* It came out in April 2011, and it is splendid. If you want to delve into improving your memory, there's Joshua Foer's *Moonwalking with Einstein: the Art and Science of Remembering Everything,* again, just published. And, last but not least, if you want to learn more about how the mind influences another mind, there is Robert B. Cialdini's *Influence: The Psychology of Persuasion.* Incidentally, all these authors have extensive videos on YouTube.

Another subject to explore is the world around us. I love this year's *The Unofficial U.S. Census: Things the Official U.S. Census Doesn't Tell You About America,* by Les Krantz and Chris Smith. My favorite factoid, because it's related to what I was talking about in hint #1 here: "More than one-third of Americans take naps." Yes!

8. We can expand our mental horizons by revisiting something old. If our town still has a public library, we can revisit beloved books. If we have a computer, we can revisit old websites we haven't looked at *forever.* We can renew our acquaintance with old friends. Phillips Brooks used to say there are two kinds of exploration: one is going out to explore new country; the other is to dig more deeply down into the country we already occupy. This is that latter kind.

## The Emotional

9. If we feel we're at the mercy of factors completely beyond our control, we can still study to see what is within our control, even if it's only 5 percent or even just 2 percent of the whole, and work on that. You can go back and read chapter 3, again, where I went into this in much greater detail.

10. We can talk, talk, talk with our loved ones, or a close friend, about all that is troubling us. It's amazing how giving voice to thoughts and feelings, particularly when we don't much care for those thoughts and those feelings, causes them to lose their power over us. So we should do it, because otherwise stuff bottled up inside us tends to fester and grow. We don't want that. We must just take care that we don't pick the town gossip to confide in, nor a friend or loved one who can't keep their mouth shut.

11. **We can pound a punching bag or even some pillows, to get some of the angry energy out of us.** I don't know why, but it's astonishing how many of the unemployed have told me this actually helps get rid of some of their anger. And this helps lift our depression as well. Sometimes depression and anger do seem almost to be two different sides of the same coin. If we don't have a gym in our life we can build one at home, simply by putting a pile of pillows on top of our bed, and then pounding the pillows repeatedly, as hard as we can—*without breaking anything in our hands, wrists, or arms.* This often really helps. We are strange creatures.

12. **We can make a list each day of the things that made us grateful, glad, or even happy.** There is a habit of mind that is deadly while we're out of work, and that is spending too much of our day, every day, brooding about what is wrong in our lives: What is wrong with people, what is wrong with our situation, what is wrong with anything and everything. We can, by this list, teach ourselves to focus on what precious people we still have in our lives, what possessions we still have, what precious gifts we still have, whether they be intelligence, health, or love.

    If we want to get over being depressed, it is crucial that we give up endless complaint, it is crucial that we come to forgiveness for any past wrongs done to us, it is crucial that we, as Baltasar Gracián put it, "Get used to the failings of our friends, family, and acquaintances. . . ."

    We are all human. We are all capable of turning our face toward the future, rather than toward the past.

## The Spiritual

*Some of us have faith, some of us do not. If you are one of those who do not, just skip this section. It is really addressed only to those who have faith.*

13. **We can revisit our picture of God and how He works in this world.** The world out there might imagine that if we have faith we will find that faith our steady rock while we are going through a period of unemployment.

However, that's not necessarily true. Sometimes faith can actually *cause* depression! This unexpected *curve* arises from our view of God, and whether or not that begins with both love and trust.

In the Christian church, for example, the Creed does not begin with "I believe there is a God. . . ." It begins with "I *believe in* God. . . ." We all understand the difference between *believing something about* a friend of ours, say that she is tall, or smart, versus *believing in* that friend. To *believe in* someone is to trust them, and to trust that they feel toward us as they say they feel.

Imagine, then, how depressed we can feel if we have always believed in God, but now that we are unemployed for a long spell, we feel He has somehow deserted us, in this crisis. So for some who had faith, their unemployment turns out to be a major spiritual crisis in their life. We cry out, "How could God have let this happen to me—if He truly loved me?" We get depressed.

What can we do about this? What is the remedy when our depression has—even in part—a spiritual origin? Well, this brings us to the fourteenth action we can take, to deal with *unemployment depression*:

14. We can, instead of abandoning our faith, put some energy into rethinking our faith on a higher level. Some 91 percent of us in the U.S. say we believe in God, but the question is, *What kind of God* do we believe in?

Half a century ago, a man wrote a book entitled, *Your God Is Too Small.* What unemployment or any crisis often reveals is how poor and small our concept of God is. It is small because it holds God responsible for everything that happens in the world.

Each of us has to figure this out for ourselves. But since people have asked me what I think, after eighty-five years on this Earth, my thoughts ramble along in this fashion: Jesus said the most important thing in the world, to God, was that we love Him. Robots can't love. He has to give us freedom so we can choose to love, or not. With that freedom, however, comes the possibility that we will make wrong choices, and thus introduce tragedy into the world. Look at the mess the world is in right now. God didn't do that!

Well, then, what does God do? To what larger conception of God might we press? Let's try this: imagine that you have, in your dining room, a fine wooden chair, which one day has its back broken off completely—I mean, into smithereens—by a guest in your home. You run down the street, to call a carpenter who lives nearby. He comes and examines the chair. He pronounces the back unrepairable. "But," he says, "I think I could make a fine wooden stool out of the remainder of the chair, for you." And so he spends much time, shaping, polishing and sanding it, and fashioning out of the former chair a fine stool, more resplendent than anything you have ever dreamed. He inlays it with precious metals, and soon it is the treasure of your house.

This is, of course, a parable. Let me underline a couple of key points in it. First of all, the carpenter did not break the chair. Your houseguest did that. But the carpenter came quickly, and with all his art and powers. He tried, first of all, to see if he could repair it. Finding it was too late for that, he determined to make of it something even finer than it had been before. And, he labored mightily, to that end.

A faith that thinks God is responsible for our unemployment, and He could have and should have prevented it, needs to grow up. It has too small a God. Faith may lift us out of depression, or put us into depression. Faith may be either healthy or unhealthy.

We can reach, while we are out of work, toward a larger conception of our God and of ourselves. For, "to *believe in* God" has the power to lift us out of depression, unless our God is too small.

The question today is not "do you believe in God" (91 percent in America say they do, and 55 percent of all Americans say they consider their belief in God to be "a very important part of their lives," while 90 percent of all Americans categorized their faith as "fairly important"—according to a series of Gallup polls, in which there has been little change since the late 1960s).

No, the real question today is: "Do your beliefs make you healthier or unhealthier?" Look at the chart on the next page.

| Healthy Religion | unhealthy religion |
|---|---|
| Is obsessed with gratitude | Is obsessed with guilt |
| Focuses on the presence of God in the world; sees holiness everywhere | Focuses on the presence of evil in the world; sees contamination everywhere |
| Sees all the world as "us" | Sees all the world as "us vs. them" |
| Is closely related to mental health with its emphasis on repentance (metanoia) or "Most of my ills are self-inflicted." | Is distantly related to mental illness (paranoia) or "Most of my ills stem from what others are doing 'out there.'" |
| Unconsciously exhibits humility | Unconsciously exhibits arrogance |
| Treasures the differences in others | Wants everyone to be like them |
| Has a high sense of "all the saints" worshiping God together | Has a high sense of "the individual alone with his or her God" |
| Believes in learning from others | Believes in confronting others |
| Renounces manipulation of others, and lets them have their own beliefs | Desires to manipulate others into accepting their every belief |
| Wants God's forgiveness toward those who have harmed them or follow other gods; forgives readily | Wants God's vengeance toward those who have harmed them or follow other gods; often has low, long-simmering anger, masked beneath a smile |
| Focuses on what one can give, out of faith; anxious to give others benefits | Focuses on what one gets out of faith; anxious to get for themselves the benefits |
| Faith is primarily a matter of actions; words are used only to interpret one's actions | Faith is primarily a matter of words used as tests or orthodoxy. Shibboleth and sibboleth. |
| Is well aware that their faith may have some unhealthiness to it | Doesn't even dream their faith may be unhealthy |

If unemployment pushes us to rethink our faith, we should find not only our depression lifting, but also our understanding of faith increasing. That is a great gift. Depression is oftentimes a messenger bringing gifts, if only we open our eyes to see it.

# Appendix C. A Guide to Choosing a Career Coach or Counselor

## IF YOU DECIDE YOU NEED ONE

All readers of this book divide into two families, or groups. The first group are those who find the book is all they need, particularly if they do the exercises in chapter 13 successfully, on their own.

The second group are those who find they need a little bit of extra help. Either they bog down in their effort to complete the whole book, or they start the exercises in chapter 13 and then get stuck, at some point. So they want some additional help.

Fortunately, there are a lot of people out there, anxious to help you with your job-hunt or career-change, in case this book isn't sufficient by itself. They go by various names: career coach, career counselor, career development specialist, you name it. They're willing to help you for a fee—because this is how they make their living. That fee will usually equal the fee charged by other types of counselors in town, say a good psychologist. That will range from about $40 an hour in rural areas, on up to . . . *you don't want to know.* The fee may be charged by the hour (recommended) or as one large lump sum up front (definitely not recommended). And most towns or cities of any size have free or almost-free help, too, even though it's likely to be in a group and not face-to-face with an individual counselor. For "free," or "almost free," see Susan Joyce's marvelous website (job-hunt.org, or as she likes to say, "job dash hunt dot org") for the section called *Networking and Job Search Support by State*, at http://tinyurl.com/7a9xbb.

Now, about those coaches or counselors who charge to help you. There are some simply excellent ones, out there. In fact, I wish I could say that *everyone* who hangs out a sign in this business could be completely recommended. But—alas! and alack!—they can't all be. This career-coaching or career-counseling field is largely unregulated. And even where there is some kind of certification, resulting in their being able to put a lot of degree-soundin' initials after their name, that doesn't really tell you much. It means a lot *to them* of course; in many cases, they purchased those initials with their blood, sweat, and tears. (*Although a few, sad to say, got the initials after their name by mail-order or after one long weekend of training. Tsk, tsk. But, oh well, no different I suppose from a lot of other professions. Some people are always looking for shortcuts.*)

I used to try to explain what all those initials meant. There is a veritable alphabet-soup of them, with new ones born every year. But no more; I've learned, from more than forty years of experience in this field, that 99.4 percent of all job-hunters and career-changers don't care a fig about these initials. All they want to know is: *do you know how to help me find a job?* Or, more specifically, *do you know how to help me find my dream job—one that matches the gifts, skills, and experience that I have, one that makes me excited to get up in the morning, and excited to go to bed at night, knowing I helped make this Earth a little better place to be in? If so, I'll hire you. If not, I'll fire you.*

## How to Lose Your Shirt (or Skirt)

So, *bye-bye initials!* Let us start, instead, with this basic truth:
*All coaches and counselors divide basically into three groups:*

a) *those who are honest, compassionate, and caring, and know what they're doing;*

b) *those who are honest but don't know what they're doing; and*

c) *those who are dishonest, and merely want your money—large amounts, in a lump sum, and up front. These are often so-called executive counseling firms—**some** executive counseling firms—rather than individual counselors.*

In other words, you've got compassionate, caring people in the same field with bums and crooks. Your job, if you want help and don't want to waste your money, is to learn how to distinguish the one from the other. It would help, of course, if someone could just give you a list of those who are firmly in the first category—honest and know what they're doing. But unfortunately, no one (including me) has such a list, or ever has had. You've got to do your own homework or research here, and your own interviewing, in your chosen geographical area. *And if you're too lazy to take the time and trouble to do this research, you will deserve what you get.* Why is it that *you* and only *you* can do this particular research? Well, let's say a friend tells you to go see so-and-so. He's a wonderful coach or counselor, but unhappily when you meet him he reminds you of your Uncle Harry, whom you detest. Bummer! But, no one except you knows that you've always disliked your Uncle Harry.

> That's why no one else can do this research for you—because the real question is not "Who is best?" but "Who is best for you?" Those last two words demand that it be you who "makes the call."

A special word, here, to those considering paying any firm that focuses on executives or people who make or would like to make a high salary. (This warning is regarding *firms*, not *individual* counselors.) If you are an executive you are considered a fair target for any scam the mind can imagine. New ones appear every year. I have consulted with the Federal Trade Commission in Washington, and States Attorneys General over the years, where they have described the scams to me in detail. I have collected news items, done individual interviews with those who got "taken," and I wish I could tell you about individual firms, but that's not my job. Do your own research. If you are considering signing up with any such firm, Google them first: you will come across timely research about *any* firm. Example: http://corcodilos.com/blog/3219/theladders-how-the-scam-works-2. If you are too lazy to do this research, and subsequently get "taken," let me share the words a Scotsman once said to me, when I got "taken": *"I'm sorry ya lost yer money, but ya dinna do your homework."*

Now, for all my other readers: your dilemma is between categories *a* and *b* above. How do you find an honest counselor *who knows what they're doing*, and can give you a little bit of help, if you bog down in using this book, most especially chapter 13.

The first bright idea that will occur to you might be something along the lines of "Well, I'll just see who Bolles recommends." Sorry, no such luck. I rarely if ever recommend anyone. Some of the coaches or counselors listed in the *Sampler* at the end of this appendix, try to claim that their very listing here constitutes a recommendation from me. Oh, come on! They're there because they asked to be. I ask a few questions, but I don't have time to do any thorough research on them. This *Sampler* is more akin to the Yellow Pages, than it is to *Consumer Reports*. Let me repeat this—as I have for forty years now—and repeat it very loudly:

The listing of a career counselor or coach in this book does NOT constitute an endorsement or recommendation by me. Never has meant that. Never will. (Any counselor or coach listed here who claims that it does—either in their ads, or brochures, or publicity—gets permanently removed from this Sampler the following year after I find out about it, and without warning.) This is not "a hall of fame"; it is just a *Sampler* of names of those **who have** asked **to be listed**, *and have answered some reasonable questions.*

Consider the listings as just a starting point for your search. You must check them out. You must do your own homework. You must do your own research.

## A Guide to Choosing a Good Career Coach

So, how do you go about this research toward the goal of finding a good career coach or counselor, if you decide you need more help than this book can give you? Well, you start by collecting three names of career coaches or counselors in your geographical area.

How do you find those names? Several ways:

First, you can get names from your friends: ask if any of them have ever used a career coach or counselor. And if so, did they like 'em? And if so, what is that coach's or counselor's name? And how do you get in touch with them, so you can ask them some questions before deciding whether you want to sign up with them, or not?

Second, you can get some names from the aforementioned Sampler in Appendix D (which begins on page 330). See if there are any career coaches or counselors who are near you. They may know how you can find still other names in your community.

Need more names? Try your telephone book's Yellow Pages, under such headings as: *Aptitude and Employment Testing, Career and Vocational Counseling, Personnel Consultants*, and (if you are a woman) *Women's Organizations and Services.*

Once you have three names, it's time to go do some comparison shopping. You want to talk with all three of them and decide which of the three (if any) you want to hook up with.

What will this initial interview cost you, with each coach or counselor? The answer to that is easy: when first setting up an appointment, *ask.* You do have the right to inquire ahead of time how much they are going to have to charge you for the exploratory interview.

Some—a few—will charge you nothing for the initial interview. One of the brightest counselors I know says this: *I don't like to charge for the first interview because I want to be free to tell them I can't help them, if for some reason we just don't hit it off.*

However, do not expect that most coaches or counselors can afford to give you this exploratory interview for nothing! If they did that, and got a lot of requests like yours, they would never make a living.

If this is not an individual counselor, but *a firm* trying to sell you a "pay-me-first" package *up front*, I guarantee they will give you the initial interview for free. They plan to use that "intake" interview (as they call it) to sell you a much more expensive program. They will even ask you to bring your spouse or partner along. (If they can't persuade one of you, maybe they can persuade the other.)

## The Questions to Ask

When you are face to face with the coach or counselor, you ask each of them the same questions, listed on the form below. (Keep a little pad, notebook, or PDA with you, so you can write down their answers.)

After visiting the three places you chose for your comparison shopping, you can go home, sit down, put your feet up, look over your notes that evening, and compare those places. A chart like this, drawn in your notebook, may help:

### MY SEARCH FOR A GOOD CAREER COUNSELOR

| Questions I Will Ask Them | Answer from counselor #1 | Answer from counselor #2 | Answer from counselor #3 |
|---|---|---|---|
| 1. What is your program? | | | |
| 2. Who will be counseling? And how long has this person been counseling? | | | |
| 3. What is your success rate? | | | |
| 4. What is the cost of your services? | | | |
| 5. Is there a contract up front? If so, may I see it please, and take it home with me? | | | |

You need to decide a) whether you want **none** of the three, or b) **one** of the three (and if so, which one).

Remember, you don't have to choose *any* of the three coaches, if you didn't really care for any of them. If that is the case, go choose three new names out of the Yellow Pages or wherever, dust off the notebook, and go out again. It may take a few more hours to find what you want.

But **the wallet, the purse, the job-hunt, and the life, you save will be your own.**

As you look over your notes, you will soon realize there is no definitive way for you to determine a career coach's intentions. It's something you'll have to *smell out*, as you go along. But here are some clues:

## Bad Vibes, on Up to Real Bad Vibes

If they give you the feeling that everything will be done for you, by them (*including interpretation of tests, and decision making about what this means you should do, or where you should do it*)—rather than asserting that you are going to have to do almost all the work, with their basically being your coach,

(Give them 15 bad points)

*You want to learn how to do this for yourself; you're going to be job-hunting again, you know. That's the nature of our world today. Job-hunting is a repetitive activity in human life.*

If you don't like the counselor, period!,

(Give them 150 bad points)

*I don't care what their expertise is, if you don't like them, you're going to have a rough time getting what you want. I guarantee it. Rapport is everything.*

If you ask how long this particular counselor has been doing this, and they get huffy or give a double-barreled answer, such as: "I've had eighteen years' experience in the business and career counseling world,"

(Give them 20 bad points)

*What that may mean is: seventeen and a half years as a fertilizer salesman, and one half year doing career counseling. Persist: "How long have you been with this firm, and how long have you been doing formal career coaching or counseling, as you are here?" You don't want someone who's brand new to advising job-hunters. They may call this "their practice," but what they mean is that they are practicing . . . on you.*

If they try to answer the question of their experience by pointing to their degrees or credentials,

(Give them 3 bad points)

*Degrees or credentials tell you they've passed certain tests of their qualifications, but often these tests bear more on their expertise at career assessment, than on their knowledge of creative job-hunting.*

If, when you ask about that firm's success rate, they say they have never had a client who failed to find a job, no matter what,

(Give them 500 bad points)

*They're lying. I have studied career counseling programs for more than forty years, have attended many, have studied records at state and federal offices, and have hardly ever seen a program that placed more than 86 percent of their clients, tops, in their best years. And it goes downhill from there. A prominent executive counseling firm was reported by the Attorney General's Office of New York State to have placed only 38 out of 550 clients (a 93 percent failure rate). On the other hand, if they make it clear that they have had a good success rate, but if you fail to work hard at the whole process, then there is no guarantee you are going to find a job, give them three stars.*

If any counselor shows you letters from ecstatically happy former clients, but when you ask to talk to some of those clients, you get stonewalled,

(Give them 200 bad points)

Here is a job-hunter's letter about his experience with an executive counseling firm he was considering:

> *"I asked to speak to a former client or clients. You would have thought I asked to speak to Elvis. The counselor stammered and stuttered and gave me a million excuses why I couldn't talk to some of these 'satisfied' former clients. None of the excuses sounded legitimate to me. We went back and forth for about thirty minutes. Finally, he excused himself and went to speak to his boss, the owner. The next thing I knew I was called into the owner's office for a more 'personal' sales pitch. We spoke for about forty-five minutes as he tried to convince me to use his service. When I told him I was not ready to sign up, he became angry and asked my counselor why I had been put before 'the committee' if I wasn't ready to commit? The counselor claimed I had given a verbal commitment at our last meeting. The owner then turned to me and said I seemed to have a problem making a decision and that he did not want to do business with me. I was shocked. They had turned the whole story around to make it look like it was my fault. I felt humiliated. In retrospect, the whole process felt like dealing with a used car salesman. They used pressure*

*tactics and intimidation to try to get what they wanted. As you
have probably gathered, more than anything else this experience
made me angry."*

If you are dealing with a career counseling *firm*, and you ask what is
the cost of their services, and they reply that it is a lump sum that must
all be paid "up front" before you start or shortly after you start, all at
once or in rapid installments,

(Give them 300 bad points)

*We're talking about firms here, not the average individual counselor or
coach. The basic problem with firms is that both "the good guys" and "the
crooks" do this. The good guys operate on the theory that if you give them a
large sum up front, you will then be really committed to the program. The
crooks operate on the theory that if you give them a large sum up front, they
don't have to give you anything back, except endless excuses and subterfuge,
after a certain date (quickly reached).*

*And the trouble is that there is absolutely no way for you to distinguish
crook from good guy, at first impression; they only reveal their true nature
after they've got all your money. And by that time, you have no legal way to
get it back, no matter what they verbally promised.*[1]

*Let me repeat: with firms that make you sign a contract and pay basically
up front, there is no way to distinguish the good guys from the crooks. The
only safe counseling is one with no contract, and you just pay for each hour,
as you use it.*

*I have tried for years to think of some way around this dilemma, to be fair
to the good guys, but there just is none. So if you decide to pay up front, be
sure it is money you can afford to lose.*

---

1. Sometimes the written contract—there is *always* a written contract, when you are dealing with the bad guys, and they will probably ask your partner to sign it, too—will claim
to provide for an almost complete refund, at any time, until you reach a cutoff date in the
program, which the contract specifies. Unfortunately, fraudulent firms bend over backward to be extra nice, extra available, and extra helpful to you, from the time you first
walk in, until that cutoff point is reached. Therefore, when the cutoff point for getting a
refund has passed, you let it pass because you are very satisfied with their past services,
and believe there will be many more weeks of the same. Only, there aren't. At fraudulent
firms, once the cutoff point is passed, the career counselor suddenly becomes virtually
impossible for you to get ahold of. Call after call will not be returned. You will say to yourself, "What happened?" Well, what happened, my friend, is that you paid up in full, they
have all the money they're ever going to get out of you, and now, they want to move on.

## If Money Is a Problem for You: Hourly Coaching

Most career coaches or counselors charge by the hour. You pay only for each hour as you use it, according to their set rate. Each time you keep an appointment, you pay them at the end of that hour for their help, according to that rate. Period. Finis. You never owe them any money (unless you made an appointment, and failed to keep it). You can stop seeing them at any time, if you feel you are not getting the help you wish. The fee will probably range from $40 an hour on up to $200 an hour or more. It varies *greatly*. Counselors in cities tend to charge more than counselors out in the countryside.

That fee is for *individual time* with the career coach or counselor. If you can't afford that fee, ask whether they also run groups. If they do, the fee will be much less. And, in one of those delightful ironies of life, since you get a chance to listen to problems that other job-hunters in your group are having, the group will often give you more help than an individual session with a counselor would have. Not always; but often. It's always ironic when *cheaper* and *more helpful* go hand in hand.

If the career counselor in question does offer groups, there should (again) never be a contract. The charge should be payable at the end of each session, and you should be able to drop out at any time, without further cost, if you decide you are not getting the help you want.

There are some career counselors who run free (or almost free) job-hunting workshops through local churches, synagogues, chambers of commerce, community colleges, adult education programs, and the like, as their community service, or *pro bono* work (as it is technically called). I have had reports of workshops from a number of places in the U.S. and Canada. They exist in other parts of the world as well. If money is a problem for you, in getting help with your job-hunt, ask around to see if workshops exist in your community. Your chamber of commerce will know, or your church or synagogue.

As I mentioned earlier, you can find an incredibly useful list of all the job support groups in the U.S. compiled by Susan Joyce, on her site Job-Hunt.org: http://tinyurl.com/7a9xbb.

The assumption, from the beginning, was that career counseling would always take place face to face. Both of you, counselor and job-hunter, together in the same room. Just like career counseling's close relatives: marriage counseling, or even AA.

Of course, a job-hunter might—on occasion—phone his or her counselor the day before an interview, to get some last-minute tips or to answer some questions that a prospective interviewer might ask, *tomorrow.*

What is different, today, is that in some cases, career counseling is being conducted exclusively over the phone from start to finish. Some counselors now report that they haven't laid eyes on over 90 percent of their clients, and wouldn't know them if they bumped into them on a street corner. I call this "distance-coaching" or "telephone-counseling."

With the invention of the Internet, with the invention of Internet *telephoning,* we are witnessing "the death of distance"—that is to say, the death of distance as an obstacle. The world, as the wonderful *New York Times* columnist Thomas Friedman has famously written, is in effect *flat.*

An increasing number of counselors or executive coaches are doing this *distance-counseling.*[2] I'll bet we see this increase, geometrically, now that Microsoft has bought Skype, and we are going to have video counseling at our disposal in many shapes and forms.

This increasing availability of "distance-counseling" is good news, and bad news.

Why good news? Well, in the old days you might be a job-hunter in some remote village, with a population of only eighty-five, back in the hills somewhere, or you might be living somewhere in France or in China, miles from any career counselor or coach, and so, be totally out of luck. Now, these days you can be anywhere in the world, but as long as you have the Internet on your desk, you can still connect with the best distance-counseling there is.

And the bad news?

---

2. Two famous "distance coaches" are Joel Garfinkle in Oakland, California, www.dreamjobcoaching.com; and Marshall Goldsmith of www.marshallgoldsmithlibrary .com, international coach to the executive elite, and author (with Mark Reiter) of the popular book, *What Got You Here Won't Get You There.*

Well, just because a counselor or coach does distance-counseling or phone-counseling, doesn't mean they are really good at doing it. Some are superb; but some are not. So, you're still going to have to research any *distance-counselor* very carefully.

It is altogether too easy for a counselor to get sloppy doing distance-counseling—for example, browsing the newspapers while you are telling some long personal story, etc., to which they are giving only the briefest attention. (Of course, the increasingly wider use of video calling programs such as Skype may cure that!) To avoid any kind of sloppiness, *you* and the counselor need discipline. Experienced distance-counselors, such as Joel Garfinkle,[3] insist on forms being used, both before and after each phone session. With his permission, I have adapted his forms, and print them here. *And, P.S., they are equally useful for normal, face-to-face counseling, as well.*

## CLIENT COACHING FORMS

### 1. Before You Start

Prior to beginning the counseling, it helps if your coach or counselor asks you to fill out the following kind of form, for you to give to him or her. They are written by the counselor, addressed to you, the potential counselee. (And if they don't ask for a form like this to be filled out, you might volunteer to give them such a form on your own.)

### Questions to Understand You Better

*(Copy this onto another sheet of paper, and leave lots of space on the form for your answer, after each question below.)*

1. **Why have you decided to work with me?**
2. **How can I have the most impact on your life in the next ninety days (three months)?**
3. **List three key goals you want to accomplish through our work together.**
4. **What stops you from achieving what you want in question #2 or #3 above?**

---

3. www.dreamjobcoaching.com/about

5. Project ahead one year: As you look back, and things went well, how did you benefit from our coaching relationship?

6. What are your expectations from our work together? How can we exceed these expectations?

7. What else is helpful for me to know about you?

8. Explain your background (use the same format as the examples below).

*Examples:*

1. After thirty years as a commercial insurance broker, I hit a wall last May, and decided to change careers . . .

2. After twelve successful years in the high-tech industry, I found myself unfulfilled in finding a satisfying career. Over the years, I read countless books on the topic of finding one's true purpose in career pursuits, but was still missing a sense of purpose and clarity on what I wanted to do . . .

3. After working for twenty years in the investment industry I decided to start my own company . . .

4. Etc.

## 2. Before Each Session, Preparation Form

*Please fill out this form #2 for each coaching session. It should be filled out and E-mailed to me twenty-four hours before the next coaching session to assist me in preparing for that session.*

*(Copy this onto another sheet of paper, and leave lots of space on the form for your answer, after each question below.)*

**Commitments that I made to myself on the last coaching session and what I accomplished since we had the coaching session:**

**The challenges and opportunities I am facing now:**

**The one action I can take that will most affect my current goals and provide the highest payoff:**

**My agenda for the coaching session is:**

## 3. After Each Session: Reflection Form

*Immediately after each coaching session E-mail me form #3.*

*(Copy this onto another sheet of paper, and leave lots of space on the form for your answer, after each question below.)*

**This week's commitment:**

**My greatest insights during this session were:**

**What you, my coach, said or asked during the session that impacted me most:**

**What I'd like you, as my coach, to do differently/more of/less of:**

**How I feel I am evolving from our work together:**

What happens in a counseling session is our responsibility, not just the counselor's or coach's.

The forms, above, are one way of our taking responsibility. Another, is that when you first contact prospective coaches for distance-counseling in particular, you have a right to ask them: (1) "What training have you completed, relevant to distance-counseling, such as telephone skills, and supervised counseling?" (2) "How will our distance-counseling be organized and scheduled?" and (3) "What will the two of us do if and when interruptions occur during a session, at either end?"

You must always remember: distance-counseling, attractive as it will be for many, as necessary as it will be for some, definitely has its limits.

To the caveman, the technology that enables all this to happen in this twenty-first century, would be jaw-droppingly awesome. But, good career counseling or coaching *is not just about technology.* What is really truly awesome, in the end, is simply our power to help each other on this Earth. And how much that power resides, not in techniques or technology—though these things are important—but in each of us just being a good human being. A *loving* human being.

## A SAMPLER

The following Appendix is exactly what its name implies: a Sampler. Were I to list all the career coaches and counselors there are in the U.S.

(never mind the world), we would end up with an encyclopedia. Some states, in fact, have encyclopedic lists of counselors and businesses, in various books or directories, and your local bookstore or library should have these, in their Job-Hunting Section, under such titles as "How to Get a Job in . . ." or "Job-Hunting in . . ." Now, let me repeat this:

> I did not choose the places listed in this Sampler; rather, they are listed at their own request, and I offer their information to you simply as suggestions of where you can begin your investigation—when you're trying to find decent help.[4]

Do keep in mind that many truly helpful places and coaches are *not* listed here. If you discover such a coach or place, which is very good at helping people *with Parachute* and creative job-hunting or career-change, do send us their pertinent information. We will ask them, as we do all the listings here, a few intelligent questions, and if they sound okay, we will add that place as a suggestion in next year's edition.

What kind of questions? This directory appears nowhere but in this book, so we may presume you are interested in this book's approach, and if you need a little help it is help with the process in this book. We

---

4. Yearly readers of this book will notice that we do remove people from this Sampler, without warning. First of all, there are accidents: we drop places we didn't mean to, but a typographical error was made, somehow (it happens). *Oops!* Counselor or coach: call this to our attention; we'll put you back in next year.

But accidents aside, we do deliberately remove the following: places that have moved, and don't bother to send us their new address. *Coaches and counselors: If you are listed here, we expect you to be a professional at communication. When you move, your first priority should be to let us know, immediately. As one exemplary counselor wrote: "You are the first person I am contacting on my updated letterhead . . . hot off the press just today!" So it should always be, if you want to continue to be listed here. A number of places get removed every year, precisely because of their sloppiness in keeping us up-to-date with their phone and other contact information.*

Other causes for removal: Places that have disconnected their telephone, or otherwise suggest that they have gone out of business. Places that our readers lodge complaints against with us, as being unhelpful or even obnoxious. The complaints may be falsified, but we can't take that chance. Places that change their personnel, and the new person has never even heard of *Parachute*, or "creative job-search techniques." College services that we discover (belatedly) serve only "Their Own." Counseling firms that employ salespeople as the initial "intake" person that a job-hunter meets. If you discover that any of the places listed in this Sampler fall into any of the above categories, you would be doing a great service to our other readers by dropping us a line and telling us so (10 Stirling Drive, Danville, CA 94526-2921).

tried being broader in the past—there are obviously excellent counselors out there who have never heard of this book—but it turned out that our readers wanted counselors and places that have some expertise *with Parachute*, and can help job-hunters or career-changers finish the job-hunt in this book.

So, if they've never even heard of *Parachute*, we don't list them anymore. But even among those who have, we can't automatically assume they're good at what they do, no matter how many questions we asked them. So we list them and leave the research to you.

You must do your own sharp questioning before you decide to go with anyone. If you don't take time to research two or three places, before choosing a counselor, you will deserve whatever you get (or, more to the point, don't get). So, please, do some research.

The listings that follow are alphabetical within each state, with counselors listed by their name in alphabetical order, according to their last name.

Some offer group career counseling, some offer testing, some offer access to job-banks, etc. Ask.

One final note: places and counselors listed here have said they counsel anyone. Ninety-nine percent of them can absolutely be trusted, in this. A few, however, may turn out to have restrictions unknown to us ("we counsel only women," or "we only deal with alumni," etc.). If that turns out to be the case, your time isn't wasted. They may be able to help you with a referral. So, ask them, "Who else in the area can you tell me about, who helps with job-searches, and are there any (among them) that you think are particularly effective?" (Also, write us and let us know they only counsel *some* people, so we can remove them from this Sampler next year.)

## Area Codes

If you call a phone number in the Sampler that is any distance geographically from you, and they tell you "this number cannot be completed as dialed," the most likely explanation is that the area code was changed—maybe some time ago. Throughout the U.S. now, area codes are subdividing constantly, sometimes more than once during a short time span. (We ask counselors listed here to notify us when the area code changes, but some do and some don't.) Anyway, call Information and check, or look up their phone number on the Web.

Of course, if you're calling a local counselor, you won't need the area code (unless you live in one of the metropolitan areas in the U.S. that requires ten-digit dialing).

*Throughout this Sampler, an asterisk before their name, in red, means they offer religious counseling as well as secular—that is, they're not afraid to have you talk about God, if you're looking for some help in finding your Mission in life through faith.*

# Appendix D. Sampler List of Coaches

## Alabama

**Chemsak, Maureen J.**, NCC, LPC, MCC
Counselor
Athens State University
300 N. Beaty St.
Athens, AL 35611
Phone: 256-233-8285 or 256-772-7900
E-mail: maureen.chemsak@athens.edu

**Vantage Associates Inc.**
2100-B Southbridge Pkwy., Ste. 240
Birmingham, AL 35209
Phone: 205-879-0501
Cell: 205-533-0429
Contact: Ellen Glasgow
E-mail: info@vantageassociates.com
www.vantageassodiates.com

## Alaska

**Career Transitions**
2600 Denali St., Ste. 430
Anchorage, AK 99503
Phone: 907-274-4500
Fax: 907-274-4510
Contact: Deeta Lonergan, President
E-mail: deeta@alaska.net
www.careertransitions.biz

## Arizona

**Boninger, Faith**, PhD
10965 E. Mary Katherine Dr.
Scottsdale, AZ 85259
Phone: 480-390-6736
E-mail: faithboninger@cox.net

*Career Discovery Services, LLC**
3145 E. Chandler Blvd., Ste. 110-212
Phoenix, AZ 85048
Phone: 480-706-1262
Contact: Sandy Somers, RN, MS, ACC
E-mail: careerdiscovery@msn.com
www.careerdiscoveryservices.com

**Passport to Purpose**
7744 East Knots Pass
Prescott Valley, AZ 86314
Phone: 928-775-4949
Contact: Cathy Severson, MS
E-mail: cathy@passporttopurpose.com
www.passporttopurpose.com
www.retirementlifematters.com.

**Renaissance Career Solutions**
PO Box 30118
Phoenix, AZ 85046-0118
Phone: 602-867-4202
Contact: Betty Boza, MA, LCC
E-mail: bboza@cox.net
http://bboza-ivil.tripod.com

## California

**Bauer, Lauralyn Larsen**
Career Counselor & Coach
Napa, CA 94558
Phone: 707-363-7775
E-mail: lauralynbauer@hotmail.com

**Berrett & Associates**
533 E. Mariners Cir.
Fresno, CA 93730
Phone: 559-284-3549
Contact: Dwayne Berrett, MA, RPCC
E-mail: dberrett@me.com
www.berrett-associates.com

**California Career Services**
6024 Wilshire Blvd.
Los Angeles, CA 90036
Phone: 323-933-2900
Phone: 1-800-63CAREER
Fax: 323-933-9929
Contact: Susan Wise Miller, MA
E-mail: susan@californiacareerservices.com
www.californiacareerservices.com

**Career Balance**
215 Witham Rd.
Encinitas, CA 92024
Phone: 760-436-3994
Fax: 760-632-9871
Contact: Virginia Byrd, MEd
Career and Work-Life Consultant
E-mail: virginia@careerbalance.net
www.careerbalance.net

**\*Career Choices**
Dublin, CA
Contact: Dana E. Ogden, MS Ed, CCDV
E-mail: dana@careerchoices.us
www.careerchoices.us

**Career Counseling and Assessment Associates**
9229 W. Sunset Blvd., Ste. 502
Los Angeles, CA 90069
Phone: 310-274-3423
Contact: Dianne Y. Sundby, PhD
Director and Psychologist
E-mail: DYSD99@aol.com
www.dscounseling.com

**Career and Personal Development Institute**
582 Market St., Ste. 410
San Francisco, CA 94104
Phone: 415-982-2636
Contact: Bob Chope
www.cpdicareercounseling.com

**Career Possibilities**
3009 Lantana Ave.
Fullerton, CA 92835-1945
Phone: 714-990-6014
Contact: Cheryl A. Heil, MEd, JCTC, CPCM
E-mail: keytosuccess1@sbcglobal.net

**Center for Career Growth and Development**
453 Alberto Way, Ste. 257D
Los Gatos, CA 95032
Phone: 408-354-7150
Contact: Steven E. Beasley
E-mail: stevenbeasley@verizon.net

**Center for Creativity and Work**
2024 Vine St. #2D
Berkeley, CA 94709
Phone: 510-526-1600
Contact: Allie Roth, Career Coach
E-mail: allie@allieroth.com
www.allieroth.com

**\*Center for Life & Work Planning**
1133 Second St.
Encinitas, CA 92024
Phone/Fax: 760-943-0747
Contact: Mary C. McIsaac
Executive Director

**\*Cheney-Rice, Stephen**, MS
2113 Westboro Ave.
Alhambra, CA 91803-3720
Phone: 626-824-5244
E-mail: sccheneyrice@earthlink.net

**Christen, Carol**, Consultant
Career & Job Search Strategy
Co-author, *What Color Is Your Parachute? For Teens*
Atascadero, CA
Phone: 805-462-8795
E-mail: carol@carolchristen.com

**Collaborative Solutions**
3130 W. Fox Run Way
San Diego, CA 92111
Phone: 858-268-9340
Contact: Nancy Helgeson, MA, LMFT
E-mail: nhelgeson@san.rr.com
www.thebestcollaborativesolutions.com

**Dream Job Coaching**
6918 Thornhill Dr.
Oakland, CA 94611
Phone: 510-339-3201
E-mail: joel@dreamjobcoaching.com
www.dreamjobcoaching.com
www.garfinkleexecutivecoaching.com

## Experience Unlimited Job Clubs

There are many Experience Unlimited clubs in California, found at the Employment Development Department (EDD) in the following locations: Anaheim, Canoga Park, Contra Costa, Corona, Fremont, Fresno, Irvine, Lancaster, Manteca, Oakland, Pasadena, San Francisco, San Rafael, Santa Cruz/Capitola, Simi Valley, Sunnyvale, Torrance, and West Covina. Contact the chapter nearest you through your local EDD office.

**\*Frangquist, Deborah Gavrin**, MS
Chosen Futures
1801 Bush St., Ste. 121
San Francisco, CA 94109
Phone: 415-346-6121
E-mail: Deborah@ChosenFutures.com
www.ChosenFutures.com

**· Fritsen, Jan**, MS, MFT
Career Counseling and Coaching
23421 South Pointe Dr., Ste. 230
Laguna Hills, CA 92653
Phone: 949-497-4869
E-mail: janfritsen@cox.net
www.janfritsen.com

**Geary & Associates, Inc.**
1100 Coddingtown Ctr., Ste. A
PO Box 3774
Santa Rosa, CA 95402
Phone: 707-525-8085
Fax: 707-528-8088
Contact: Jack Geary, MA
Edelweiss Geary, MEd, CRC
E-mail: esgeary@sbcglobal.net
www.gearyassociates.com

**Hilliard, Larkin**, MA
Counseling Psychology
250 Curtner Avenue, Apt. 3
Palo Alto, CA 94306
Phone: 805-680-3496
E-mail: larkinhilliard@yahoo.com
(English, French, German, and Russian)

**HRS**
4421 Alla Rd., #2
Marina del Rey, CA 90292
Phone: 310-577-0972
Contact: Nancy Mann, MBA
Career Coach
E-mail: nanmanhrs@aol.com

**\*Miller, Lizbeth**, MS
Nationally Certified Career Counselor
3425 S. Bascom Ave., Ste. 250
Campbell, CA 95008
and 306 Esmeralda Dr.
Santa Cruz, CA 95060
Phone: 408-486-6763
Fax: 408-369-4990
E-mail: lizmillercareers@yahoo.com
www.lizmillercareers.com

**Nemko, Marty**, PhD
Career and Education Strategist
5936 Chabolyn Terr.
Oakland, CA 94618
Phone: 510-655-2777
E-mail: mnemko@comcast.net
www.martynemko.com

**Piazzale, Steve**, PhD
Career/Life Coach
Mountain View, CA
Phone: 650-964-4366
E-mail: Steve@BayAreaCareerCoach.com
www.BayAreaCareerCoach.com

**Saraf, Dilip G.**
Career and Worklife Strategist
Career Transitions Unlimited
39159 Paseo Padre Pkwy., #221
Fremont, CA 94538
Phone: 510-791-7005
E-mail: dilip@7keys.org
www.7keys.org

**\*Schoenbeck, Mary Lynne**, MA, NCCC, MCC, Career/Retirement Counselor, Coach, Consultant
Schoenbeck & Associates
Los Altos, CA
Phone: 650-964-8370
E-mail: schoenbeck@mindspring.com

**Struntz and Associates**
Career & Job Search Consulting
Saint Helena, CA 94574
Phone: 707-963-0843
Contact: Wolfgang Struntz, MA
E-mail: Struntz@netwiz.net

**Transitions Counseling Center**
171 N. Van Ness Ave.
Fresno, CA 93701
Phone: 559-233-7250
Contact: Margot E. Tepperman, MA,
LCSW, ACC
E-mail: mtepperman@aol.com
www.transitionscoaching.com

*Visions into Form
Coaching
223 San Anselmo Ave., Ste. 6
San Anselmo, CA 94960
Phone: 415-488-4998
Contact: Audrey Seymour, MA, PCC, CPCC
E-mail: inquiry@visionsintoform.com
www.visionsintoform.com

**Wilson, Patti**
Career Company
PO Box 35633
Los Gatos, CA 95030
Phone: 408-354-1964
E-mail: patti@careercompany.com
www.pattiwilson.com

**Zitron Parham Career Counseling & Life Coaching**
4724 25th St., Ste. A
San Francisco, CA 94114
Phone: 415-648-7377
Contact: Nick Parham
Career & Life Coach
E-mail: npcoach@gmail.com
www.zitronparhamcareerservices.com

Colorado

**Arapahoe Community College**
Career Center
Career Planning Seminars
Job Postings
5900 S. Santa Fe Dr.
PO Box 9002
Littleton, CO 80160-9002
Phone: 303-797-5805
E-mail: careers@arapahoe.edu

**Gary Ringler & Associates**
1747 Washington St., #203
Denver, CO 80203
Phone: 303-863-0234
E-mail: garyringler@msn.com

**Helmstaedter, Sherry**, MS
Englewood, CO 80111-1122
Phone: 720-560-9601
E-mail: changegrow@aol.com

**Pivotal Choices, Inc.**
PO Box 1098
Durango, CO 81302
Phone: 970-385-9597
Contact: Mary Jane Ward, MEd, NCC, NCCC
E-mail: mjw@pivotalchoices.com
www.pivotalchoices.com

**Women's Resource Agency**
750 Citadel Dr. E., #3116
Colorado Springs, CO 80909
Phone: 719-471-3170
www.wrainc.org

Connecticut

**Accord Career Services, LLC**
Salmon Brook Corporate Park
500 Winding Brook Dr
Glastonbury, CT 06033
Phone: 860-674-9654 or 860-508-1026
Contact: Tod Gerardo, MS, Director
E-mail: tod@accordcareerservices.com
www.accordcareerservices.com

**Center for Professional Development**
University of Hartford
50 Elizabeth St.
Hartford, CT 06105
Phone: 860-768-5619
Contact: Eleta Jones, PhD, LPC
E-mail: ejones@hartford.edu
www.hartford.edu/cpd

**The Offerjost-Westcott Group**
263 Main St., Ste. 100
Old Saybrook, CT 06475
Phone: 860-388-6094
Contact: Russ Westcott
E-mail: russwest@snet.net

**Pannone, Bob**, MA
Career Specialist
62 Lane St.
Huntington, CT 06484
Phone: 203-513-2290
E-mail: upstartinc@yahoo.com

**Preis, Roger J.**
RPE Career Dynamics
Stamford, CT
E-mail: rjpreis@rpecareers.com
www.rpecareers.com

**Bronson, Kris**, PhD
1409 Foulk Rd., Ste. 204
Foulkstone Plaza
Wilmington, DE 19803
Phone: 302-477-0708, ext. 4
www.krisbronsonphd.com

**Roggenkamp, Robin**
Certified Career and Leadership Coach
Washington, DC area (NoVa)
Phone: 703-298-2964
E-mail: robin@myauthenticcareer.com
www.myauthenticcareer.com

**The Women's Center**
1025 Vermont Ave. NW, Ste. 310
Washington, DC 20005
Phone: 202-293-4580
www.thewomenscenter.org

**Career Choices Unlimited**
4465 Baymeadows Rd., Ste. 7
Jacksonville, FL 32217
Phone: 904-443-0059 or 904-262-9470
Contact: Marilyn A. Feldstein, MPA,
JCTC, MBTI, PHR
Career Coach and Professional Speaker
www.careerchoicesunlimited.com

**The Centre**
305 S. Hyde Park Ave.
Tampa, FL 33606
Phone: 813-251-8437
Fax: 813-251-1288
E-mail: infor@thecentre.org
Contact: Alice Thompson
Employment Services
www.thecentre.org

**Chabon-Berger, Toby**, MEd, NCC, NCCC
Career and Professional Development
Coach
4900 Boxwood Circle
Boynton Beach, FL 33436
Phone: 561-596-3656
E-mail: tberger@chabongroup.com
www.tobycareer.com

**The Clarity Group**
PO Box 110084
Lakewood Ranch, FL 34211
Phone: 941-388-8108
Contact: George H. Schofield, PhD
E-mail: george.schofield@clarity-group
.com
or george@georgeschofield.com
or george@newbrightlife.com
www.clarity-group.com
www.georgeschofield.com
www.newbrightlife.com

**Cohen, James.**, PhD
7177 Granville Avenue
Boynton Beach, FL 33437
Fax / Phone # 561-509-9150
E-mail: vocdoc56@yahoo.com

**Focus on the Future: Displaced Homemaker Program**
Santa Fe College
3000 NW 83rd St., I-40
Gainesville, FL 32606
Phone: 352-395-5047
Contacts: Nancy Griffin
or JoAnn Wilkes
E-mail: focusonthefuture@sfcollege.edu
www.sfcollege.edu/DisplacedHomemakers
(Classes are free.)

**Life Designs, Inc.**
19526 E. Lake Dr.
Miami, FL 33015
Phone: 305-829-9008
Contact: Dulce Muccio Weisenborn
E-mail: dmw@lifedesigns-inc.com
www.lifedesigns-inc.com

**TransitionWorks**
Delray Beach, FL
Phone: 301-233-4287
Contact: Nancy K. Schlossberg, EdD
Principal
E-mail: nancyks4@gmail.com
Contact: Stephanie Kay, MA, LCPC
Principal
E-mail: stephaniekay4@gmail.com
www.transitionworks.com
(They also have offices in Rockville,
Maryland, and Sarasota, Florida.)

**Ashkin, Janis**, MEd, MCC, NCC, NCCC
2365 Winthrope Way Dr.
Alpharetta, GA 30009
Phone: 678-319-0297
E-mail: jashkin@bellsouth.net

**Career Quest/Job Search Workshop**
St. Ann's Catholic Church
4905 Roswell Rd. NE
Marietta, GA 30062-6240
Contact: John Marotto
Phone: 770-552-6400 ext. 6104
E-mail: careerquest-sa@comcast.net
www.st-ann.org/career_quest.php
LinkedIn Group: Career Quest at St.
Ann's Church

**D & B Consulting, Inc.**
3355 Lenox Rd., Ste. 750
Atlanta, GA 30326
Phone: 404-504-7079
Contact: Deborah R. Brown, SPHR, MBA,
MSW, Career Consultant
E-mail: Debbie@DandBconsulting.com
www.dandbconsulting.com

**Satterfield, Mark**
720 Rio Grand Dr.
Alpharetta, GA 30022
Phone: 770-643-8566
E-mail: msatt@mindspring.com

**Waldorf, William H.**, MBA, LPC
Path Unfolding Career Development
5755 North Point Parkway., Ste. 39
Alpharetta, GA 30022
Phone: 678-822-5505
E-mail: wwaldorf@earthlink.net

**\*Career Coaching 4U**
9882 W. View Dr.
Boise, ID 83704
Phone: 208-323-2462
Contact: Michael W. Reed, MEd, MS
Counseling, LPC
E-mail: michael@careercoaching4u.com
www.careercoaching4u.com

**Alumni Career Center**
University of Illinois Alumni Association
200 S. Wacker Dr., First Floor
Chicago, IL 60606
Phone: 312-575-7830
E-mail: careers@uillinois.edu
Contact: Julie Hays Bartimus, Vice
President
Bernice Allegretti, Assistant Director
www.uiaa.org/careers

**Career Vision/The Ball Foundation**
800 Roosevelt Rd., E-200
Glen Ellyn, IL 60137
Phone: 800-469-8378
Contact: Peg Hendershot, Director;
Paula Kosin, MS, LCPC
E-mail: info@careervision.org
www.careervision.org

**Davis, Jean**, MA
Counseling Psychology, specializing in
adult career transitions
1405 Elmwood Ave.
Evanston, IL 60201
Phone: 847-492-1002
E-mail: jdavis@careertransitions.net
www.careertransitions.net

**Dolan Career & Rehabilitation
Consulting, Ltd.**
307 Henry St., Ste. 411
Alton, IL 62002
Phone: 618-474-5328
Fax: 618-462-3359
Contact: J. Stephen Dolan, MA, CRC
Career & Rehabilitation Consultant
E-mail: dolanrehab@att.net

**Grimard Wilson Consulting, Inc.**
333 W. Wacker Dr., Ste. 500
Chicago, IL 60606
and
1140 W. Lake St., Ste. 302
Oak Park, IL 60301
Phone: 312-925-5176
Contact: Diane Wilson, LCPC, BCN
E-mail: diane.g.wilson@gmail.com
www.grimardwilson.com

**Harper College Community Career
Services**
1200 W. Algonquin Rd., Rm. A-347
Palatine, IL 60067
Phone: 847-925-6293
Contact: Kathleen Canfield, Director
E-mail: careers@harpercollege.edu
www.harpercollege.edu

**Inspired Career Options**
PO Box 7174
Buffalo Grove, IL 60089
Phone: 847-808-9982
Contact: Deb Morton, Certified Executive
Career & Entrepreneur Coach
E-mail: deb@inspiredcareeroptions.com
www.inspiredcareeroptions.com

**Lansky Career Consultants**
500 N. Michigan Ave. #820
Chicago, IL 60611
Phone: 312-494-0022
Contact: Judi Lansky, MA, MBA
E-mail: lanskycareers@yahoo.com

**LeBrun, Peter**
Career/Leadership Coach
Executive Career Management
4333 N. Hazel St., Ste. 100
Chicago, IL 60613
Phone: 773-281-7274
E-mail: peterlebrun@aol.com

**Moraine Valley Community College**
Job Resource Center
9000 College Pkwy.
Palos Hills, IL 60465
Phone: 708-974-5737
www.morainevalley.edu/jrc

Iowa

**Sucher, Billie**, MS, CTMS,
CTSB, JCTC, CCM
Private Practice Career Transition
Consultant
7177 Hickman Rd., Ste. 10
Des Moines, IA 50322
Phone: 515-276-0061
E-mail: billie@billiesucher.com
www.billiesucher.com

**Zilber, Suzanne**, PhD
Licensed Psychologist
Catalyst Counseling
600 5th St., Ste. 302
Ames, IA 50010-6072
Phone: 515-232-5340
Fax: 515-232-2070
www.catalystcounseling.com

Kansas

**Keeping the People, Inc.**
12213 Westgate St.
Overland Park, KS 66213
Phone: 913-620-4645
Contact: Leigh Branham
E-mail: LB@keepingthepeople.com
www.keepingthepeople.com

Kentucky

**Career Span, Inc.**
620 Euclid Ave., Ste. 210
Lexington, KY 40502
Phone: 859-233-7726 (233-SPAN)
Contact: Carla Ockerman-Hunter, MA,
MCC, NCC
E-mail: careerspan@aol.com
www.careerspanUSA.com

Louisiana

**Career Center**
River Center Branch, EBR Parish Library
120 St. Louis St.
Baton Rouge, LA 70802
Phone: 225-381-8434
Fax: 225-389-8910
Contact: Anne Nowak, Program Director
E-mail: anowak@careercenterbr.com
www.careercenterbr.com

**D. Gallant Management Associates**
75 Pearl St., Ste. 211
Portland, ME 04101
Phone: 207-773-4800
Contact: Deborah L. Gallant, SPHR,
CBP, CCP
E-mail: dgma@dgallant.com
www.dgallant.com

**Heart at Work Career Counseling**
**& Second Half of Life Career Transitions**
25 Middle St.
Portland, ME 04101
Phone: 207-775-6400
Contact: Barbara Babkirk, Master Career
Counselor
E-mail: barb@barbarababkirk.com
www.barbarababkirk.com

**Women's Worth Career Counseling**
9 Village Ln.
Westbrook, ME 04092
Phone: 207-856-6666
Contact: Jacqueline Murphy
Career Counselor
E-mail: wethepeople@maine.rr.com

**Maryland**

**The Career Evaluation and Coaching**
**Center**
21 West Rd., Ste. 150
Baltimore, MD 21204
Phone: 410-825-0042
Fax: 410-825-0310
Contact: Ralph D. Raphael, PhD
E-mail: drraphael@ralphraphael.com
www.ralphraphael.com

**CTS Consulting, Inc.**
3126 Berkshire Rd.
Baltimore, MD 21214-3404
Phone: 410-444-5857
Contact: Michael Bryant
E-mail: mb3126@gmail.com
www.go2ctsonline.com

**Friedman, Lynn**, PhD
Psychologist, Psychoanalyst,
Work-Life Consultant
Johns Hopkins University
5480 Wisconsin Ave.
Chevy Chase, MD 20815
Phone: 301-656-9050
E-mail: drlynnfriedman@verizon.net
www.washington-dc-psychologist.com
www.drlynnfriedman.com

**Headley, Anne S.**, MA
6510 41st Ave.
University Park, MD 20782
Phone: 301-779-1917
E-mail: asheadley@verizon.net
www.anneheadley.com

**Horizons Unlimited, Inc.**
17501 McDade Ct.
Rockville, MD 20855
Phone: 301-258-9338
Contact: Marilyn Goldman,
LPC, NCCC, MCC
E-mail: horizons@career-counseling.com
www.career-counseling.com

**Positive Passages Life/Career Transition**
**Counseling and Coaching**
4702 Falstone Ave.
Chevy Chase, MD 20815
Phone: 301-580-5162
Contact: Jeanette Kreiser, EdD
E-mail: jskreiser@yahoo.com

**Prince George's Community College**
Career Services
301 Largo Rd.
Largo, MD 20774
Phone: 301-322-0109
E-mail: Career_Job@pgcc.edu
Contact: H.Randall Polle,
Manager of Career Services
Stephanie Pair, Senior Career Advisor
www.pgcc.edu

**TransitionWorks**
Rockville, MD
Phone: 301-233-4287
Contact: Nancy K. Schlossberg, EdD,
Principal; Stephanie Kay, MA, LCPC,
Principal
E-mail: skay4@verizon.net

**Berke & Price Associates**
Newtown Way #6
Chelmsford, MA 01824
Phone: 978-256-0482
Contact: Judit E. Price, MS, CDFI, IJCTC,
CCM, CPRW
Career Consultant, Certified Resume
Writer, and Brand Specialist
E-mail: jprice@careercampaign.com
www.careercampaign.com
www.careercampaign.com/blog
www.linkedin.com/in/juditprice

**The Boston Career Coach**
26 Shanley St.
Brighton, MA 02135
Phone: 617-254-0791
Contact: Tom Jackson
www.thebostoncareercoach.com

**Career in Progress**
2 Marie Ann Dr.
Westford, MA 01886
Phone: 617-925-5289
Fax: 781-407-0955
Contact: Heather Maietta, EdD, GCDF,
JCDC, CPRW
Career and Professional Development
Coach
E-mail: info@careerinprogress.com
www.careerinprogress.com

\***Career Management Consultants**
108 Grove St., Ste. 204
Worcester, MA 01605
Phone: 508-756-9998
Contact: Patricia Stepanski Plouffe
Founder/Consultant
E-mail: info@careermc.com

**Career Source**
186 Alewife Brook Pkwy., Ste. 310
Cambridge, MA 02138
Phone: 617-661-7867
www.yourcareersource.com

\***Center for Career Development
& Ministry**
30 Milton St., Ste. 107
Dedham, MA 02026
Phone: 781-329-2100
Fax: 781-407-0955
Contact: Stephen Ott, Director
E-mail: info@ccdmin.org
www.ccdmin.org

**Changes**
Career Counseling and Job-Hunt Training
2516 Massachusetts Ave.
Cambridge, MA 02140
Phone: 617-868-7775 or 617-868-0660
Contact: Carl J. Schneider
E-mail: carl@changescareerservices.com
www.changescareerservices.com

**Hadlock, Joanne**, EdD, NCCC
Career/Life Transitions
223 Sandy Pond Rd.
Lincoln, MA 01773
Phone: 781-259-3752
E-mail: joannehadlock@comcast.net
www.joannehadlock.us

**Jewish Vocational Service, Career Moves**
29 Winter St., 5th Floor
Boston, MA 02108
Phone: 617-399-3131
Contact: Judy Sacks, Director
www.career-moves.org

**Jewish Vocational Service, Career
Moves**
Career Counseling and Testing
333 Nahanton St.
Newton, MA 02159
Phone: 617-965-7940
Contact: Amy Mazur, Career Counselor
E-mail: amazur@jvs-boston.org;
www.career-moves.org

\***Liebhaber, Gail**, MEd
40 Cottage St.
Lexington, MA 02420
Phone: 781-861-9949
Contact: Gail Liebhaber, MEd
E-mail: gail@yourcareerdirection.com
www.yourcareerdirection.com

**Miller, Wynne W.**
Leadership Coaching
Brookline, MA 02446-4707
Phone: 617-232-4848
E-mail: wynne@win-coaching.com
www.win-coaching.com

**Szekely, Bill**
10 Doral Dr.
N. Chelmsford, MA 01863
Phone: 978-251-3693
Cell: 978-423-3196
E-mail: Bill@LifeWorkDiscovery.com
www.lifeworkdiscovery.com

## Michigan

**°Careers Through Faith**
3025 Boardwalk St.
Ann Arbor, MI 48108
Phone: 734-332-8800, ext. 228
Contact: Cathy Synko
E-mail: Cathy@CareersThroughFaith.org
www.CareersThroughFaith.org

**°Keystone Coaching & Consulting, LLC**
22 Cherry St.
Holland, MI 49423
Phone: 616-396-1517
Contact: Mark de Roo
E-mail: mderoo@keystonecoach.com
www.keystonecoach.com

**°LifeSteward/EaRN Employment & Resource Network**
PO Box 888891
Grand Rapids, MI 49588-8891
Phone: 616-813-4998
Contact: Ken Soper, MDiv, MA, MCC, NCCC
E-mail: kensoper@yahoo.com
www.kensoper.com
www.earn-network.org

**New Options Town & Country Counseling**
Specializing in careers & education
Ann Arbor, MI
Phone: 734-973-0003 or 734-973-8699
Contact: Phyllis Perry, MSW, MFA
E-mail: pepstar27@yahoo.com

**Synko Associates, LLC**
3025 Boardwalk, Ste. 120
Ann Arbor, MI 48108
Phone: 734-332-8800 ext. 212
E-mail: csynko@SynkoAssociates.com
www.SynkoAssociates.com

## Minnesota

**°North Central Ministry Development Center**
(an Interdenominational Church Career Development Center)
516 Mission House Ln.
New Brighton, MN 55112
Phone: 651-636-5120
Contact: Mark Sundby, MDiv, PhD, LP
Executive Director
E-mail: ncmdc@comcast.net
www.ncmdc.org

**Prototype Career Service**
626 Armstrong Ave.
St. Paul, MN 55102
Phone: 800-368-3197
Contact: Amy Lindgren
Job Search Strategist
E-mail: getajob@prototypecareerservice.com
www.prototypecareerservice.com

## Missouri

**Eigles, Lorrie**, PCC, MSED, LPC
Authentic Communication
Life and Career Coach
432 W. 62nd Terr.
Kansas City, MO 64113
E-mail: Lorrie@myauthenticlifecoaching.com
http://myauthenticlifecoaching.com

**The Job Doctor**
505 S. Ewing Ave.
St. Louis, MO 63103
Phone: 314-863-1166
Contact: M. Rose Jonas, PhD
E-mail: jobdoc@aol.com
www.jobdoctoronline.com

**MU Career Center**
Student Success Center
University of Missouri
Columbia, MO 65211
Phone: 573-882-6801
Fax: 573-882-5440
Contact: Craig Benson
E-mail: career@missouri.edu
http://career.missouri.edu

**Women's Center**
University of Missouri-Kansas City
5100 Rockhill Rd., 105 Haag Hall
Kansas City, MO 64110
Phone: 816-235-1638
Contact: Brenda Bethman, Director
E-mail: umkc-womens-center@unkc.edu
www.umkc.edu/womenc

Montana

**Career Transitions**
20900 E. Frontage Rd., B-Mezz
Belgrade, MT 59714
Phone: 406-388-6701
E-mail: ct@careertransitions.com
Contact: Darla Joyner, Executive Director
www.careertransitions.com

New Hampshire

**Individual Employment Services (I.E.S)**
1 New Hampshire Ave., Ste. 125
Portsmouth, NH 03801
Established 1984
Phone: 603-570-4850
or 800-734-JOBS (5627)
Fax: 603-766-1901
Contact: James Otis, Career Counselor/
Recruiter/Principal Anita Labell,
Certified Professional  Resume Writer/
Career Coach
E-mail: ies@iosnh.com

**Tucker, Janet**, MEd
Career Counselor
10 String Bridge
Exeter, NH 03833
Phone: 603-772-8693
E-mail: jbtucker@comcast.net

New Jersey

**\*CareerQuest**
2165 Morris Ave., Ste. 15
Union, NJ 07083
Phone: 908-686-8400
Fax: 908-686-8400 (on request)
Contact: Don Sutaria, MS, IE (Prof.)
Founder, President, and Life-Work Coach
E-mail: don@careerquestcentral.com
www.careerquestcentral.com

**Creating Life Options**
Mendham, NJ 07945
Phone: 201-874-3264 or 973-543-3458
Contact: Katie McGinty
E-mail: katie@creatinglifeoptions.com
www.creatinglifeoptions.com
www.linkedin.com/in/katiemcginty

**Grundfest, Sandra**, EdD
Certified Career Counselor, Licensed
Psychologist
601 Ewing St., C-1
Princeton, NJ 08540
Phone: 609-921-8401
and
35 Clyde Rd., Ste. 101
Somerset, NJ 08873
Phone: 732-873-1212

**Job Seekers of Montclair**
St. Luke's Episcopal Church
73 S. Fullerton Ave.
Montclair, NJ 07042
Phone: 973-783-3442
www.jobseekersofmontclair.org
(Meets Wednesdays, 7:30–9:15 p.m.,
free of charge)

**JobSeekers in Princeton**
Trinity Church
33 Mercer St.
Princeton, NJ 08540
Phone: 609-921-9427
Contact: Richard Ober
www.trinityprinceton.org
(Meets Tuesdays, 7:30–9:30 p.m.)

**Mercer County Community College**
Career Services
Student Center Room 229
1200 Old Trenton Rd.
West Windsor, NJ 08550
Phone: 609-570-3399
Fax: 609-570-3880
Contact: Gail C. La France
Career Counselor
www.mccc.edu/careerservices

*W. L. Nikel
459 Passaic Ave., Ste. 171
W. Caldwell, NJ 07006
Phone: 973-439-1850
Contact: William L. Nikel, MBA
E-mail: wnikel@verizon.net

New York

**Bernstein, Alan B.**, LCSW, PC
122 E 82nd St.
New York, NY 10028
Phone: 212-288-4881
www.guidetoyourcareer.com
www.yourretirementyourway.com

*CareerQuest
c/o TRS, Inc., Professional Ste.
44 E. 32nd St.
New York, NY 10016
Phone: 908-686-8400
Fax: 908-686-8400 (on request)
Contact: Don Sutaria, MS, IE (Prof.)
Founder, President, and Life-Work Coach
E-mail: don@careerquestcentral.com
www.careerquestcentral.com
www.careerquestcentral.blogspot.com

**Careers by Choice, Inc.**
205 E. Main St., Ste. 2–4
Huntington, NY 11743
Phone: 631-673-5432
Contact: Marjorie ("MJ") Feld
E-mail: mj@careersbychoice.com
www.careersbychoice.com

**Careers in Transition, LLC**
Professional Career Services
and Counseling
11 Computer Dr. W., #112
Albany, NY 12205
Phone: 518-366-8451
Contact: Dr. Thomas J. Denham, MCDP
Founder and Career Counselor
E-mail: careersintransition@yahoo.com
www.careersintransitionllc.com

**Center for Creativity and Work**
19 W. 34th St., Penthouse Floor
New York, NY 10001
Phone: 212-490-9158
Contact: Allie Roth, Career Coach
E-mail: allie@allieroth.com
www.allieroth.com

*Greene, Kera, MEd, DTM
Board Member of the
Career Counselors Consortium,
Adjunct Lecturer, New York University
(NYU)
Career Counselor/Workshop Leader/
Lecturer
200 E. 24th St., #1008
New York, NY 10001
Cell: 917-496-1804
E-mail: KeraGr@gmail.com
www.keragreencareers.com

*Judith Gerberg Associates
250 W. 57th St., Ste. 2315
New York, NY 10107
Phone: 212-315-2322
E-mail: judith@gerberg.com
www.gerberg.com

**Optima Careers**
575 Madison Ave., between 56th and
57th Streets, Tenth Floor
New York, NY 10019
Phone: 212-876-3488
Contact: Marianne Ruggiero, President
and Founder
E-mail: mcruggiero@optimacareers.com
www.optimacareers.com

**Orange County Community College**
Office of Career and Internship Services
115 South St.
Middletown, NY 10940
Phone: 845-341-4444
Contact: Petra Wege-Beers, Director
E-mail: pwtra.wegegeers@sunyorange.edu

**Personnel Sciences Center**
140 Briarcliff Rd.
Westbury, NY 11590
Phone: 516-338-5340
Fax: 516-338-5341
Contact: Jeffrey A. Goldberg, PhD
President, Licensed Psychologist
E-mail: jag_psc@juno.com
(Services also provided in Manhattan)

**The Prager-Bernstein Group**
122 E. 42nd St., Ste. 2815
New York, NY 10168
Phone: 212-697-0645
Contact: Leslie B. Prager, MA, CMP
Senior Partner/Career Counselor
E-mail: Leslie-PBG@msn.com
www.prager-bernsteingroup.com

**Career Focus Workshops**
8301 Brittains Field Rd.
Oak Ridge, NC 27310
Phone: 336-643-1419
Contact: Glenn Wise, President
E-mail: gwise001@triad.rr.com
http://careerfocusworkshops.com

**Crossroads Career Network**
PO Box 49664
Charlotte, NC 28277
www.CrossroadsCareer.org
(Nonprofit Christian network of member
churches equipped to help people find
jobs, careers, calling)

**Joyce Richman & Associates, Ltd.**
2911 Shady Lawn Dr.
Greensboro, NC 27408
Phone: 336-288-1799
E-mail: jerichman@aol.com
www.joycerichman.com
www.richmanresources.com

**Kochendofer, Sally**, PhD
2218 Lilac Ln.
Indian Land, SC 29707
Phone: 803-396-0979
E-mail: westiefriend@comporium.net

**\*The Life/Career Institute**
131 Chimney Rise Dr.
Cary, NC 27511
Phone: 919-469-5775
Contact: Mike Thomas, PhD
E-mail: mikethomas@nc.rr.com
www.LifeCareerInstitute.com

**Life Management Services, LC**
127 Chimney Rise Dr.
Cary, NC 27511
Phone: 919-481-4707
Contact: Marilyn and Hal Shook

**Cuyahoga County Public Library**
The Career Center
5225 Library Ln.
Maple Heights, OH 44137-1291
Phone: 216-475-2225
E-mail: beaston@cuyahogalibrary.org
www.cuyahogalibrary.org/careerexpert
.aspx

**\*Flood, Kay Reynolds**, MDiv
3600 Parkhill Cir. NW
Canton, OH 44718
Phone: 330-493-1448
E-mail: nana1725@aol.com

**New Career**
328 Race St.
Dover, OH 44622
Phone: 330-364-5557
Contact: Marshall J. Karp, MA, NCC,
LPC, Career Counselor
E-mail: marshallkarp@hotmail.com

**Career Development Partners, Inc.**
4137 S. Harvard Ave., Ste. A
Tulsa, OK 74135
Phone: 918-293-0500
Toll-free: 866-466-1162
Fax: 918-293-0503
E-mail: Nancy@cdpartnersinc.com
www.cdpartnersinc.com

**Careerful Counseling Services**
12555 SW First St.
Beaverton, OR 97005
Phone: 503-997-9506
Contact: Andrea King, MS, NCC, MCC
Career Counselor
E-mail: aking@careerful.com
www.careerful.com

**\*Exceptional Living Coach, LLC**
1230 Arthur St.
Eugene, OR 97402
Phone: 541-484-6785
Contact: Lisa R. Anderson, MA, NCC,
GCDF
E-mail: lisa@ExceptionalLivingCoach.com
www.ExceptionalLivingCoach.com
(English and Spanish)

## Pennsylvania

\*Bartholomew, Uda
"Your Very Own Hidden Job Markets!"
Workshops
PO Box 2112
Center City Philadelphia, PA 19103
Phone: 215-618-1572
Contact: Uda Bartholomew
Lead Facilitator
E-mail: VocTransVocLib@gmail.com

**Delaware Valley Family Business Center**
340 N. Main St.
Telford, PA 18969
Phone: 215-723-8413, ext. 204
Contact: Henry D. Landes, Consultant
E-mail: henry@dvfbc.com
www.dvfbc.com

**William D. Morgan and Associates**
Career Counseling & Coaching Services
63 Chestnut Road, Ste. 3
Paoli, PA 19301
Phone: 610-644-8182
E-mail: info@Counseling4Careers.com
www.Counseling4Careers.com

\*Hannafin, Christine, PhD
Personal and Career Counseling
Bala Farm
380 Jenissa Dr.
West Chester, PA 19382
Phone: 610-431-0588
E-mail: chrishannafin@aol.com
www.christinehannafin.com

Haynes, Lathe, PhD
401 Shady Ave., Ste. C107
Pittsburgh, PA 15206
Phone: 412-361-6336

Kessler, Jane E., MA
Licensed Psychologist
252 W. Swamp Rd., Ste. 56
Doylestown, PA 18901
Phone: 215-348-8212, ext. 1
Fax: 215-348-0329
E-mail: jane@kesslerandclark.com

## South Carolina

**Crystal-Barkley Corp.**
(formerly The John C. Crystal Center)
293 E. Bay St.
Charleston, SC 29401
Phone: 800-333-9003
Fax: 800-560-5333
Contact: Nella G. Barkley, President
E-mail: crystalbarkley@careerlife.com
www.careerlife.com
(John Crystal, the founder of the John
C. Crystal Center, died in 1988; Nella, his
business partner for many years, now
continues his work throughout the US
and in the UK and the Netherlands.)

**White Ridgely Associates, Success
Management**
26 River Bend Dr.
Okatie, SC 29909
Phone: 443-829-9014
Contact: Daisy Nelson White, PhD
E-mail: Daisy@whiteridgely.com
http://whiteridgely.com
www.careeraid.com

## Tennessee

\*Career Resources, Inc.
208 Elmington Ave.
Nashville, TN 37205
Phone: 615-957-0404
Contact: Jane C. Hardy, Career
Strategist/Founder
E-mail: JHardy@CareerResources.net
www.CareerResources.net

## Texas

**Career Action Associates PC**
8350 Meadow Rd., Ste. 272
Dallas, TX 75231
Contact: Joyce Shoop, M.S., LPC, CRC
Phone: 214-378-8350
E-mail: joyshoop@sbcglobal.net
Contact: Rebecca Hayes, MEd, CRC, LPC
Phone: 817-926-9941
E-mail: rhayescaa@aol.com

**NB Careers**
2436 Dimmitt Dr.
New Braunfels, TX 78130
Phone: 830-237-2735
Contact: Shell Mendelson, MS
E-mail: shell@nbcareersnow.com
www.passiontocareer.com

**New Life Institute**
PO Box 4487
Austin, TX 78765
Phone: 512-469-9447
Contact: Bob Breihan
E-mail: newlifetexas@sbcglobal.net
www.newlifetexas.org

**Quereau, Jeanne**, MA, LPC, CPC
9500 Jollyville Rd., #121
Austin, TX 78759
Phone: 512-342-9552
E-mail: jeanneq19@gmail.com

### Utah

**Lue, Keith**
PO Box 971482
Orem, UT 84097-1482
Phone: 801-885-1389
E-mail: keithlue@keydiscovery.com

### Vermont

**Career Networks, Inc.**
1372 Old Stage Rd.
Williston, VT 05495
Phone: 802-872-1533
Contact: Markey Read
E-mail: markey@careernetworksvt.com
www.careernetworksvt.com

**Preis, Roger J.**
RPE Career Dynamics
PO Box 115
Shelburne, VT 05482
Phone: 802-985-3775
E-mail: rjpreis@rpecareers.com
www.rpecareers.com

### Virginia

**The BrownMiller Group**
312 Granite Ave.
Richmond, VA 23226
Phone: 804-288-2157
Contact: Bonnie Miller
E-mail: brownmillergroup@gmail.com
www.BrownMiller.com

**McCarthy & Company**
Executive Coaching,
Career Transition Management
4201 S. 32nd Rd.
Arlington, VA 22206
Phone: 703-671-4300
Contact: Peter McCarthy, President
E-mail: mccarthy@careertran.com
www.careertran.com

**The Women's Center**
127 Park St. NE
Vienna, VA 22180
Phone: 703-281-2657
E-mail: twc@thewomenscenter.org
(Subject line should read, "Attention:
Lauren Kellar")
www.thewomenscenter.org

### Washington State

**Bridgeway Career Development**
1611 116th Avenue NE, Ste. 219
Bellevue, WA 98004
Phone: 877-250-2103
Contact: Carolyn Kessler, Maria Escobar-
Bordyn, Partners
E-mail: services@bridgewaycareer.com
www.bridgewaycareer.com

**Career Management Institute**
8404 27th St. W.
University Place, WA 98466
Phone: 253-565-8818
Contact: Ruthann Reim McCaffree, MA,
NCC, LMHC, CPC
E-mail: careermi@nwrain.com
www.CareerMI.com

**Centerpoint Institute for Life and Career
Renewal**
4000 NE 41st St., Bldg. D West, Ste. 2
Seattle, WA 98105-5428
Phone: 206-686-LIFE (5433)
www.centerpointseattle.org

### West Virginia

**Ticich, Frank E.**, MS, CRC, CVE
Career Consultant
153 Tartan Dr.
Follansbee, WV 26037
Phone: 304-748-1772
E-mail: frankticich@comcast.net

## Wisconsin

**\*Career Momentum, Inc.**
49 Kessel Court, Ste. 103,
Madison, WI 53711
Phone: 608-274-2430
Contact: Clara Hurd Nydam, MDiv, MCC,
SPHR
E-mail: Clara.Nydam@CareerMomentum.
com
www.CareerMomentum.com

**Guarneri Associates**
6670 Crystal Lake Rd.
Three Lakes, WI 54562
Phone: 715-546-4449 or 866-881-4055
Contact: Susan Guarneri, NCCC, MCC,
CERW, CPBS, COIMS
E-mail: Susan@AssessmentGoddess.com

## Wyoming

**University of Wyoming**
The Center for Advising and Career
Services
1000 E. University Ave., Dept. 3195
Laramie, WY 82071-3195
Phone: 307-766-2398
E-mail: uwcacs@uwyo.edu
www.uwyo.edu/cacs

## CANADA

### British Columbia

**CBD Network, Inc.**
201-2033 Gordon Dr.
Kelowna, BC V1Y 3J2
Phone: 250-717-1821
E-mail: info@cbdnetwork.com
www.cbdnetwork.com

**Curtis, Susan**, MEd, RCC, CEAP
Vancouver, BC
Phone: 604-228-9618
E-mail: susancurtis@telus.net

## Ontario

**\*Careers by Design**
Coaching and Counseling
80 Harrison Garden Blvd.
Toronto, ON, M2N 7E3
Phone: 416-519-8408
Contact: (Ms.) Shirin Khamisa, BA Hons.,
BEd, ICF-Certified Coach and Career
Counselor
E-mail: shirin@careersbydesign.ca
www.careersbydesign.ca

**\*CareersPlus Inc.**
55 Village Pl., Ste. 203
Mississaugua, ON L4Z 1V9
Phone: 905-272-8258
Contact: Douglas H. Schmidt
BA, MEd, EdD
E-mail: info@careersplusinc.com
www.careersplusinc.com

**Career Strategy Counselling**
2 Briar Hill Pl.
London, ON N5Y 1P7
Phone: 519-455-4609
Contact: Ruth Clarke, BA
E-mail: rclarke4609@rogers.com
www.careerstrategycounselling.com

**donnerwheeler**
1 Belvedere Ct., Ste. 1207
Brampton, ON L6V 4M6
Phone: 905-450-1086
Contact: Mary M. Wheeler, RN, MEd, PCC
E-mail: info@donnerwheeler.com
www.donnerwheeler.com

**Human Achievement Associates**
22 Cottonwood Crescent
London, ON N6G 2Y8
Phone: 519-657-3000 or 519-200-6301
Contact: Mr. Kerry A. Hill
E-mail: haa.no.1@rogers.com

**Puttock, Judith**, BBA, CHRP
Career Management Consultant
The Puttock Group
913 Southwind Ct.
Newmarket, ON
Phone: 905-717-1738
E-mail: j.puttock@rogers.com
www.puttockgroup.com

**YMCA Career Planning & Development**
2200 Yonge St.
Toronto, ON M4S 2B8
Phone: 416-928-3362
Contact: Mr. Franz Schmidt
E-mail: franz.schmidt@ymcagta.org
www.ymcagta.org/assessment services

**Agence Ometz**
Employment, Family, and Immigration
Services
5151 Côte Ste-Catherine, Ste. 300
Montreal, QC H3W 1M6
Phone: 514-342-0000
Fax: 514-342-2371
Contact: Howard Berger or Gail Small,
Co-Executive Directors
E-mail: info@ometz.ca
www.ometz.ca
(Uses both French and English versions
of *Parachute*. Utilise des versions
Francaises et Anglaises de *Parachute*.)

**La Passerelle Employment &
Career Transition Centre**
1255 Phillips Square, Ste. 903
Montreal, QC H3B 3G1
Contact: Léa Benegbi, Executive Director
Phone: 514-866-5982
E-mail: info@lapasserelle.ca
www.lapasserelle.ca

## OVERSEAS

Australia

**Career Action Centre**
5 Bronte Ave.
Burwood, Victoria 3125
Phone: 03 9808 5500
Cell: 0403 136 260
Contact: Jackie Rothberg
E-mail: jackie@careeractioncentre.com.au
www.careeractioncentre.com.au

**The Growth Connection**
32 Grove St.
Earlwood, NSW 2206
Phone: 61 2 9787 2748
Fax: 612 9787 3185
Cell: 0407 477 225
Contact: Imogen Wareing, Director
E-mail: iwareing@growconnect.com.au
www.linkedin.com/in/imogenwareing
www.growconnect.com.au

**Life by Design**
PO Box 50
Newport Beach, NSW 2106
Phone: 61 2 9979 4949
Contact: Ian Hutchinson
Lifestyle Strategist
E-mail: info@lifebydesign.com.au
www.lifebydesign.com.au

**Milligan, Narelle**
Career Consultant (regional NSW)
Phone: 2 6584 3271
Cell: 0411 236 124
E-mail: nmilligan2000@yahoo.com.au

**Taccori, John**, EdD
Career Counsellor
Blue Mountains, NSW 2777
Phone: 04 0093 8574
www.careersdoctor.net

France

**Chavigny, Catherine**
11 bis, rue Huyghens
75014 Paris
Phone: (33) 6 30 51 40 56
E-mail: catherine.chavigny@me.com

Germany

**Buddensieg, Marc**
Niemeyerstrasse 17a
30449 Hannover
Phone: 49 0 163 624 2639
Fax: 49 0 12120 277 627
E-mail: buddensieg@gmx.de
www.www.lwp-institut-hannover.de

**Hoff, Ruådiger**
Zum Karpfenteich 11,
25826 St. Peter-Ording
Phone: 49 0 163 63 94 680
E-mail: ruediger.hoff@gmx.de
www.life-work-planning.de

**Leitner, Madeleine**, Dipl. Psych.
Ohmstrasse 8
80802 Munchen
Phone: 089 33079444
Fax: 089 33079445
E-mail: ML@Karriere-Management.de
www.Karriere-Management.de

**Webb, John Carl**
Meinenkampstr 83a
48165 Munster-Hiltrup
Phone: +49 0 2501 92 16 96
E-mail: john@muenster.de
www.lifeworkplanning.de
(Universities offering Life/Work Planning
courses designed by John, and based on
*Parachute* are located in Berlin, Bochum,
Bremen, Freiburg, Hannover, Konstanz,
Leipzig, and Potsdam.)

Ireland

**Brian McIvor & Associates**
Newgrange Mall, Unit 4B
Slane, County Meath
Phone: 353 41 988 4035
E-mail: brianmcivor@gmail.com
www.brianmcivor.com
(Brian was on the staff at my international
Two-Week Workshop for five years.)

Israel

**Mendel, Lori**
PO Box 148
Caesarea, Israel 38900
Phone: 972 3 524 1068
Cell: 972 54 814 4442
E-mail: bizcom@bezeqint.net

**Transitions & Resources, Ltd.**
6 Tzipornit, Apt. 3
Modiin, Israel 71808
Phone: 08 926 6102
Cell: 050 5739496
U.S. phone line in Israel until 4 p.m. EST:
516-216-4457
Fax: 08 926 6103
Contact: Judy Feierstein, CEO
E-mail: info@maavarim.biz
www.maavarim.biz

The Netherlands

**Crystal-Barkley Corp.**
Service in The Netherlands
Phone: 800-333-9003
E-mail: crystalbarkley@careerlife.com
www.careerlife.com

**Pluym Career Consultants**
Career Executive & Expats Coaching
Services
Boshoekerweg 16
NL/8167 LS EPE/OENE
Contact: Johan Veeninga
Senior Consultant
E-mail: johan.veeninga@gmail.com or
info@careerconsultants.nl
www.careerconsultants.nl

New Zealand

**The Career Company**
191 Peachgrove Rd.,
PO Box 24 195
Hamilton 3253
Contact: Megan Smith
Phone: 64 7 853 9177
E-mail: info@thecareercompany.co.nz
www.thecareercompany.co.nz

**Career Lifestyle**
175 Queen St., Level 5
Auckland CBC
New Zealand
Contact: Paula Stenberg
www.cvstyle.co.nz

*CV.CO.NZ (NZ) Ltd.**
373 Masters Rd.
Auckland 2682
Toll-Free: 0800 282 669
Phone: 09 235 8484
Contact: Tom O'Neil
E-mail: tom@cv.co.nz
www.cv.co.nz

Poland

**JC Coaching Justyna Ciecwierz**
Tarniny 5a
05-515 Nowa Iwiczna
Cell: 48 600 327 163
Contact: Justyna Ciecwierz, ACCC
Career Coaching, Work/Life Planning
E-mail: justyna.ciecwierz@jc-coaching.pl
www.jc-coaching.pl

**Transformation Technologies**
122 Thomson Green
574986 Singapore
Phone: 65 98197858
Contact: Anthony Tan, Director
E-mail: anthonyt@singnet.com.sg

**Andrew Bramley Career Consultants**
12 Ridge Way
PO Box 1311
Proteaville, Durbanville 7550
Phone: 27 0 21 9755573
Fax: 27 0 88 0 21 9755573
Contact: Andrew Bramley
E-mail: info@andrewbramley.co.za
www.andrewbramley.co.za

**Byung Ju Cho**, PhD
Professor of Business and Career
Ajou University
Suwon
Phone: 82 31 219 2709
Fax: 82 2 594 6236
Cell: 82 10 9084 6236
E-mail: chobju@ajou.ac.kr
(Byung Ju Cho is the translator of the
Korean version of *Parachute*.)

**Analisi-Nic**
Via Augusta, 120
Principal 1
08006 Barcelona
Phone: 34 932119503
Fax: 34 932172128
Contact: José Arnó
E-mail: analisi@arrakis.es

**Baumgartner, Peter**
Hummelwaldstrasse 18a
8645 Rapperswil-Jona
Phone: 41 0 55 534 14 47
E-mail: lebensunternehmer@bluewin.ch

**KLB LifeDesigning**
Alpenblickstrasse 33
CH-8645 Jona-Kempraten
Phone: +41 0 55 211 09 77
Fax: +41 0 55 211 09 79
Contact: Peter Kessler, LifeDesigning
Coach
E-mail: p.kessler@bluewin.ch
www.LifeDesigning.ch

**Porot & Partenaire**
Rue de la Terrassière 8
1207 Genève-Suisse
Phone: 41 0 22 700 82 10
Fax: 41 0 22 700 82 14
Contact: Daniel Porot, Founder
E-mail: daniel@porot.com
www.porot.com
(Daniel is the premiere career expert in
Europe; for the twenty years that I did
two-week workshops each August,
Daniel was always co-leader with me
each summer.)

**Sauser, Hans-U.**
Beratung und Ausbildung
Im Bungert 2
CH-5430 Wettingen
Phone: 056 426 64 09
E-mail: husauser@gmx.ch

**Vollenweider, Peter A.**
Career and Transition Coaching,
Work/Life Planning, Consulting
Kaepfnerweg 20
CH-8810 Horgen/Zurich
Phone: 41 0 44 715 15 63
Cell: 41 0 78 626 11 58
Contact: Dr. Peter A. Vollenweider
E-mail: peter.vollenweider@gmail.com

**Can Do It Now**
Contact: Janie Wilson
UK: London, Surrey, and Sussex; France:
Languedoc
Phone: +44 (0)7968 027344
E-mail: janie@candoitnow.co.uk
or
Contact: Alix Nadelman
London, Cambridge, Hertfordshire, and
East Midlands
Phone: +44 (0)7977 930223
E-mail: alix@candoitnow.co.uk
www.candoitnow.co.uk
www.lepuget.com

**Career Dovetail**
4 E. Hill Court
Oxted, Surrey RH8 9AD
*and*
**Hub Working Centre**
5 Wormwood St.
London EC2M 1RW
Contact: Duncan Bolam, Dip. CG
Director, Career Coach, and Founder
E-mail: duncanbolam@careerdovetail.
co.uk or enquiries@careerdovetail.co.uk
www.careerdovetail.co.uk

**Crystal-Barkley Corp.**
Service in the United Kingdom
Phone: 800-333-9003
E-mail: crystalbarkley@careerlife.com
www.careerlife.com

**Hawkins, Dr. Peter**
Mt. Pleasant
Liverpool, L3 5TF
Phone: 0044 0 151 709-1760
Fax: 0044 0 151 709-1576
E-mail: p.Hawkins@gieu.co.uk

**John Lees Associates**
37 Tatton St.
Knutsford, Cheshire WA16 6AE
Phone: 01565 631625
Contact: John Lees
E-mail: johnlees@johnleescareers.com
www.johnleescareers.com

**Sherridan Hughes**
Career Management Expert
110 Pretoria Rd.
London SW16 6RN
Phone: 020 8769 5737
E-mail: sherridan@sherridanhughes.com
www.sherridan-hughes.co.uk

# About the Author

DICK BOLLES (often known by his more formal name, Richard Nelson Bolles) is widely acknowledged as the founder of the modern career development field, due to his writings for the past forty years. A member of Mensa and the Society for Human Resource Management, he has been the keynote speaker at hundreds of conferences, around the world. Bolles was trained in chemical engineering at Massachusetts Institute of Technology, and holds a bachelor's degree cum laude in physics from Harvard University, a master's in sacred theology from General Theological (Episcopal) Seminary in New York City, and three honorary doctorates. He lives in the San Francisco Bay Area with his beloved wife, Marci. Contact information:

Office/Home Phone: 925-837-3002 (leave message)
E-mail address: dickbolles40@gmail.com
Website: www.jobhuntersbible.com
Blog: http://jobhuntersbible.typepad.com
Facebook: http://tinyurl.com/4zwxws6
LinkedIn: http://tinyurl.com/24mtryz
Twitter: http://twitter.com/@ParachuteGuy
Five-day workshop information (held every three months in our home near San Francisco): fivedayworkshop@aol.com

# Index

Organizations
  kinds of, 255–56
  making list of, 256–57, 260
  researching, 116, 263–66
  websites of, 263–64
  *See also* Large organizations; Small
    organizations
Overseas jobs, 346–49

## P

Pancer, S. Mark, 178
Pardo, Emilio, 32
Parker, Yana, 82
Part-time work, 132–33, 152, 255
  *See also* Temp agencies/temporary
    work
Party Exercise, 207–9
Passion, importance of, 107, 269
Pay. *See* Salary
People
  favorite to work with, 206–10
  skills dealing with, 233
  as sources of job information, 260
  as sources of salary information,
    128–30, 148–50
  *See also* Bridge-people; Family;
    Friends
People-environments, jobs as, 206–10
Personality types, 235–36
Person-who-has-the-power-to-hire-you
  fears of, 117–19, 127–29
  interview with, 55, 250
  in large vs. small organizations, 55
  *See also* Employers
Philosophy of life, 29–30
  *See also* Mission in life
Physical environment, effects of, 306
Physical fitness, 305–6
PIE Method, 108–12
*The Pie Method for Career Success*
  (Porot), 108
Plaxo, 75
*Please Understand Me* (Keirsey and
  Bates), 235
Pleasure interviews. *See* Practice
  Interviews
Plunkett, Kent, 147
Porot, Daniel, 66, 108, 119, 132, 152, 348
Portfolios, approaching employers with,
  88–89
Practice Interviews, 108–12
Prayer websites, 302
Prejudice, 39–40, 45–46
Prioritizing Grid, 211, 212, 229, 247

Psychological Assessment Resources
  (PAR), 207
Pyramid of Life, 14

## R

Raises, 138
*Ready, Aim, You're Hired* (Hellman),
  124, 144
Reiter, Mark, 26, 323
References, in resumes, 86
Relationships
  guide to, 94
  repairing, 32
Religious beliefs
  career counseling and, 298–99, 329
  definition of, 293
  healthy vs. unhealthy, 312
  importance of, 291
  prevalence of, 282, 283, 285
  unemployment and, 309–12
  websites on, 302
  *See also* Mission in life; Spirituality
Research
  before hiring-interviews, 116
  on home businesses, 160–61, 165–69
  on the Internet, 127–28, 147–48,
    263–64
  on job-hunting, 58
  on organizations, 116, 263–66
  on salary, 126–31, 146–51
  on self-employment, 161–64, 165–69
Resource person vs. job beggar, 43
Resumes
  alternatives to, 88–89
  contents of, 86
  dangers of depending on, 87–88
  e-mailing, 85
  employers' vs. job-hunters' views of,
    87–88
  first impression from, 85–86
  format and style for, 82
  good example of, 82–84
  Google search as, 73–77, 277
  mailing out randomly, 60–62
  posting online, 60–62, 84–85
  purpose of, in one sentence, 86, 89, 277
  success rate for, 60–62
  targeting particular employers with,
    85–86
  tips for writing, 77–82
Retirement, 41, 152, 159
Reviews, false, 105
Rewards, favorite, 218
RIASEC system. *See* Holland Codes
Robinson, Michael T., 210

# UPDATE 2012

To: PARACHUTE
   10 Stirling Drive
   Danville, CA 94526-2921

I think that the information in the 2012 edition needs to be changed, in your next revision, regarding (or, the following resource should be added):

_____

_____

_____

_____

_____

I cannot find the following resource, listed on page _____:

_____

_____

_____

_____

_____

_____

Name _____

Address _____

_____

Please make a copy.
Submit this so as to reach us by February 1, 2012. Thank you.

# FOREIGN EDITIONS
## of *What Color Is Your Parachute?*

Recent Translations (available now)

Dutch (Nieuwezijds Publishers, 2011): *Welke Kleur Heeft Jouw Parachute?*

German (Campus Verlag, 2011): *Durchstarten zum Traumjob Das Bewerbungshandbuch*

Turkish (Optimist/BZD Yayin ve Iletisim Hizmetleri, 2011): *En iyi is Nasil Bulunur?*

Polish (Studio Emka, 2010): *Jakiego Koloru Jest Twoj Spadochron?*

Simplified Chinese (China CITIC Press, 2010): 這樣求職才能成功?

Portuguese (Actual Editora, 2010): *De que cor é o seu pára-quedas?*

Russian (Mann, Ivanov & Ferber Publishers, 2010): Какого цвета ваш парашют?

Indonesian (PT Gramedia Pustaka Utama, 2010)

Italian (Edizioni Sonda, 2008): *Ce L'hai il Paracadute?*

Complex Chinese (Faces Publications, 2006): 你的降落傘是什麼顏色?

Latvian (Zvaigane ABC Publishers, 2003)

Japanese (Shoeisha, 2002)

Bulgarian (Kibea Publishers, 1998)

# ADDITIONAL HELPFUL RESOURCES
## FROM THE AUTHOR: BOOKS

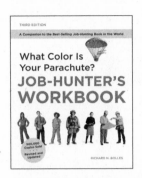

**The Job-Hunter's Survival Guide**
This little guide shows how to find hope and rewarding work—fast.
**$9.99 paper (Can $12.99)**
**ISBN 978-1-58008-026-2**

**What Color Is Your Parachute?**
**Job-Hunter's Workbook**
This handy workbook leads job-seekers through the process of determining exactly what sort of job or career they are most suited for, easily streamlining this potentially stressful and confusing task.
**$11.99 paper (Can $12.99)**
**ISBN 978-1-58008-009-5**

**The Career Counselor's Handbook,** Second Edition
(WITH HOWARD FIGLER)
A complete guide for practicing or aspiring career counselors.
**$19.95 paper (Can $24.95)**
**ISBN 978-1-58008-870-1**

**Job-Hunting Online,**
Sixth Edition, revised and expanded
(WITH MARK BOLLES)
This handy guide has quickly established itself as the ideal resource for anyone who's taking the logical step of job-hunting on the Internet.
**$12.99 paper (Can $14.99)**
**ISBN 978-1-58008-899-2**

## What Color Is Your Parachute? for Teens

(WITH CAROL CHRISTEN AND
JEAN M. BLOMQUIST)
Using *Parachute*'s central philosophy
and strategies, this new addition to
the *Parachute* library teaches high
school and college students to zero
in on their favorite skills and then
to apply that knowledge to finding
their perfect college major or job.
**$15.99 paper (Can $19.99)**
**ISBN 978-1-58008-141-2**

## What Color Is Your Parachute? for Retirement

(WITH JOHN E. NELSON)
Using *Parachute*'s central philosophy
and strategies, this new addition to
the *Parachute* library teaches those
approaching 50, or beyond, how to
prepare for the Fourth Movement of
their lives.
**$16.99 paper (Can $19.99)**
**ISBN 978-1-58008-205-1**

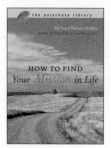

## How to Find Your Mission in Life

Originally created as an appendix to
*What Color Is Your Parachute?*, this
book was written to answer one of
the questions most often asked by
job-hunters.
**$7.99 paper (Can $10.99)**
**ISBN 978-1-58008-705-6**

**Available from Ten Speed Press wherever books are sold.**
**www.tenspeed.com**

# Five-Day Workshops in Dick Bolles's Home and Garden

**FOUR TIMES A YEAR**

Dick Bolles teaches in person, in his home near San Francisco, for five days.

The course runs from Saturday night through Thursday afternoon, 9 a.m. through 5:30 p.m. daily.

It is open to anyone: young adults, career counselors, the unemployed, ex-military, homemakers returning to the job-market, people in mid-career crisis, people facing retirement, and people needing to figure out a new career for themselves.

Past participants have come from the U.S., Canada, Mexico, Chile, the United Kingdom, Ireland, Belgium, the Netherlands, France, Switzerland, Germany, Spain, Italy, South Africa, New Zealand, Australia, South Korea, the Philippines, and other countries.

Workshops are restricted to the first twenty-one people who enroll. Meetings are held in the author's home, hosted by his beloved wife, Marci. Continental breakfast and lunch are served each day at the Workshop. Participants usually stay at a Best Western motel, a mile down the road.

Sessions consist of lectures by the author, interactive exercises, and working by oneself or in trios or in groups of six. Topics covered vary from workshop to workshop, depending on the participants' needs. No two workshops have identical curricula; hence, participants often return in later years.

For a schedule of dates, further information about the workshop, costs, and registration information, send an email to Marci at:

fivedayworkshop@aol.com

# *What Color Is Your Parachute?*
## The Online Course

The world's most popular job-hunting guide is now an online course!

- Proven techniques to uncover your passions, skills, and more.
- Exclusive insight, advice, and guidance from author Richard N. Bolles.
- A comprehensive report detailing your values, skills, passions, and more so you can design the life/work you want.

the job-hunting survival skills you most need in today's world.

For those who want guidance as to how to use this book. Enroll now!

Available November 15, 2011.

Powered by **CAPELLA**